INTERFACES

Series Editor: Barbara Green, O.P.

Jonah's Journeys

Barbara Green, O.P.

A Michael Glazier Book

LITURGICAL PRESS

Collegeville, Minnesota

www.litpress.org

A Michael Glazier Book published by the Liturgical Press

Cover design by Ann Blattner. Watercolor by Ethel Boyle.

| 1 | 2 | 3 | 4 | 5 | 6 | 7 | 8 |

Library of Congress Cataloging-in-Publication Data

Green, Barbara, O.P.
    Jonah's journeys / Barbara Green.
        p. cm. — (Interfaces)
    "A Michael Glazier book."
    Summary: "A reading of the Book of Jonah that interfaces biblical studies with biblical spirituality"—Provided by publisher.
    Includes bibliographical references and index.
    ISBN-13: 978-0-8146-5038-7 (pbk. : alk. paper)
    ISBN-10: 0-8146-5038-4 (pbk. : alk. paper)
    1. Bible. O.T. Jonah—Criticism, interpretation, etc. I. Title. II. Series: Interfaces (Collegeville, Minn.)

BS1605.52.G74   2005
224'.9206—dc22

                           2005004757

To Sandra Schneiders,
a friend of God, prophets, and whales,
in immense gratitude for all she has taught me and many others
about biblical spirituality.

CONTENTS

Acknowledgments	vii
Preface	ix
Introduction	xiii
CHAPTER ONE Finding a Flexible Framework for Interpretation	1
CHAPTER TWO The Long Reception of the Jonah Narrative	15
CHAPTER THREE Locating Biblical Jonah Historically	33
CHAPTER FOUR Ancient Analogical Readings	52
CHAPTER FIVE Literary Features	81
CHAPTER SIX Jonah's Journey in the Whale	107
CHAPTER SEVEN Jonah's Journeys: Fruitful Flailings	134
Provisional Conclusions	154
Bibliography	159
Index of Topics	165
Index of Bible Citation	168
Index of Authors	171

ACKNOWLEDGMENTS

I am indebted in many ways to many people for the insights gained while writing this book. Notable among them are Arthur Holder, who initiated my interest in this small book by asking me to write an article on Old Testament Spirituality for the *Blackwell Companion to Christian Spirituality;* the Wabash Center for Teaching and Learning, which funded a grant project on the prophet Jonah; various sets of Cistercians, great study companions; Carleen Mandolfo, friendly but critical reader; and Kris Veldheer and the Graduate Theological Union library staff, resourceful and generous.

PREFACE

The book you hold in your hand is one of fifteen volumes in an expanding set of volumes. This series, called INTERFACES, is a curriculum adventure, a creative opportunity in teaching and learning, presented at this moment in the long story of how the Bible has been studied, interpreted, and appropriated.

The INTERFACES project was prompted by a number of experiences that you, perhaps, share. When I first taught undergraduates, the college had just received a substantial grant from the National Endowment for the Humanities, and one of the recurring courses designed within the grant was called Great Figures in Pursuit of Excellence. Three courses would be taught, each centering on a figure from some academic discipline, with a common seminar section to provide occasion for some integration. Some triads were more successful than others, as you might imagine. But the opportunity to concentrate on a single individual—whether historical or literary—to team teach, to make links to another pair of figures, and to learn new things about other disciplines was stimulating and fun for all involved. A second experience that gave rise to this series came at the same time, connected as well with undergraduates. It was my frequent experience to have Roman Catholic students feel quite put out about taking "more" biblical studies, since, as they confidently affirmed, they had already been there many times and done it all. That was, of course, not true; as we well know, there is always more to learn. And often those who felt most informed were the least likely to take on new information when offered it.

A stimulus as primary as my experience with students was the familiarity of listening to friends and colleagues at professional meetings talking about the research that excites us most. I often wondered: Do her undergraduate students know about this? Or how does he bring these ideas—clearly so energizing to him—into the college classroom? Perhaps some of us have felt bored with classes that seem wholly unrelated to research, that rehash the same familiar material repeatedly. Hence the idea for this series of books to bring to the fore and combine some of our research interests with our teaching and learning. Accordingly, this series is not so much about creating texts *for* student audiences but rather about *sharing* our scholarly passions with them. Because these volumes are intended each as a piece of original scholarship, they are geared to be stimulating to both students and established scholars, perhaps resulting in some fruitful collaborative learning adventures.

The series also developed from a widely shared sense that all academic fields are expanding and exploding, and that to contemplate "covering" even a testament (let alone the whole Bible or Western monotheistic religions) needs to be abandoned in favor of something with greater depth and fresh focus. At the same time, the links between our fields are becoming increasingly obvious as well, and the possibilities for study that draw together academic realms that had once seemed separate is exciting. Finally, the spark of enthusiasm that almost always ignited when I mentioned to students and colleagues the idea of single figures in combination—interfacing—encouraged me that this was an idea worth trying.

And so with the leadership and help of Liturgical Press Academic Editor Linda Maloney, as well as with the encouragement and support of Editorial Director Mark Twomey, the series has begun to take shape.

Each volume in the INTERFACES series focuses clearly on a biblical character (or perhaps a pair of them). The characters from the first set of volumes are in some cases powerful—King Saul, Pontius Pilate—and familiar—John the Baptist, Jeremiah; in other cases they will strike you as minor and little-known—the Cannibal Mothers, Herodias. The second "litter" I added notables of various ranks and classes: Jezebel, queen of the Northern Israelite realm; James of Jerusalem, "brother of the Lord"; Simon the Pharisee, dinner host to Jesus; Legion, the Gerasene demoniac encountered so dramatically by Jesus. In this third set we find a similar contrast between apparently mighty and marginal characters: the prophet Jonah who speaks a few powerfully efficacious words, and ben Sira, sage in late second temple Judah; less powerful but perhaps an even greater reading challenge stand Jephthah's daughter and Ezekiel's wife. In any case, each of them has been chosen to open up a set of worlds for consideration. The named (or unnamed) character interfaces with his or her historical-cultural world and its many issues, with other characters from biblical literature; each character has drawn forth the creativity of the author, who has taken on the challenge of engaging many readers. The books are designed for college students (though we think they are suitable for seminary courses and for serious Bible study), planned to provide young adults with relevant information and at a level of critical sophistication that matches the rest of the undergraduate curriculum.

In fact, the expectation is that what students are learning of historiography, literary theory, and cultural anthropology in other classes will find an echo in these books, each of which is explicit about at least two relevant methodologies. To engage at least two significant methods with some thoroughness is challenging to do. Implicit in this task is the sense that it is not possible to do all methods with depth; when several volumes of the series are used together, a balance will emerge for readers. It is surely the case that biblical studies is in a methodology-conscious moment, and the INTERFACES series embraces it enthusiastically. Our hope is for students to continue to see the relationship between their best questions and their most valuable insights, between how they approach texts and what they find there. The volumes go well beyond familiar paraphrase of narratives to ask questions that are relevant in our era. At the same time, the series authors also have each dealt with the notion of the Bible as Scripture in a way condign for them. None of the books is preachy or hortatory, and yet the self-implicating aspects of working with the revelatory text are handled frankly. The assumption is, again, that college can be a good time for people to reexamine and rethink their beliefs and assumptions, and they need to do so in good company.

The INTERFACES volumes all challenge teachers to re-vision radically the scope of a course, to allow the many connections among characters to serve as its warp and weft. What would emerge fresh if a Deuteronomistic History class were organized around King Saul, Queen Jezebel, and the two women who petitioned their nameless monarch? How is Jesus' ministry thrown into fresh relief when structured by shared concerns implied by a demoniac, a Pharisee, James—a disciple, and John the Baptist—a mentor? And for those who must "do it all" in one semester, a study of Genesis' Joseph, Herodias, and Pontius Pilate might allow for a timely foray into postcolonialism. With whom would you now place the long-suffering but doughty wife of Ezekiel: with the able Jezebel, or with the apparently celibate Jonah? Or perhaps with Herodias? Would Jephthah's daughter organize an excellent course with the Cannibal Mothers, and perhaps as well with the Gerasene demoniac, as fresh and under-heard voices speak their words to the powerful? Would you effectively study monarchy by working with bluebloods Jezebel and Saul, as they contend with their opponents, whether those resemble John the Baptist or Pontius Pilate? Depending on the needs of your courses and students, these rich and diverse character studies will offer you many options.

The INTERFACES volumes are not substitutes for the Bible. In every case they are to be read with the text. Quoting has been kept to a minimum for that very reason. The series is accompanied by a straightforward companion, *From Earth's Creation to John's Revelation: The INTERFACES Biblical Storyline Companion,* which provides an overview of the whole storyline into which the characters under special study fit. The companion is available gratis for those using two or more of the INTERFACES volumes. Already readers of diverse proficiency and familiarity have registered satisfaction with this slim overview narrated by biblical Sophia.

The series' challenge—for publisher, writers, teachers, and students—is to combine the volumes creatively, to INTERFACE them well so that the vast potential of the biblical text continues to unfold for us all. These volumes offer a foretaste of other volumes currently on the drawing board. It has been a pleasure to work with the authors of these volumes as well as with the series consultants: Carleen Mandolfo for Hebrew Bible and Catherine Murphy for New Testament. It is the hope of all of us that you will find the series useful and stimulating for your own teaching and learning.

Barbara Green, O.P.
INTERFACES Series Editor
May 16, 2005
Berkeley, California

INTRODUCTION

This volume in the INTERFACES series aims to explore meaning, specifically with the Old Testament book of Jonah. But the concern runs deeper—with meaning from, in, and with Scripture in general. Provisionally, let us assume that meaning is rooted in relevant connection perceived between us and some other entity: here between our lives and a biblical narrative. *How does meaning work?* We may assume that we know—and of course we all have experience in negotiating meaning. But what we will do in these pages is explore in much greater detail what meaning is, how it works, how we can understand our moves and those of others as we make meaning. Already I have offered you a crucial question to ponder: *Do we make meaning? Find it? Is it given to us? Is meaning common or private, objective or subjective? Or is it best seen as some blend of those?* What you assume and think will affect how you proceed here, to no small extent, as will what you are willing to question.

The primary strategy we will use is questions. Again, we likely feel on solid ground with questions, asking and even answering them so long as we can remember. *But what do questions do? How do they work? What happens when we go the question route rather than the answer route?* For one thing, we step out of certitude when we ask a question. If we are prone to smugness, laziness, or a certain "shut-down-ness," we move differently when, instead of telling, we ask. When we ask questions we engage and exercise our imaginations, consider multiple and even alternative possibilities. But posing queries is not simply a wild ride. We must also, when questioning, consider the constraints or limits within which our questions work.

An example can help here. If you contemplate, with a certain openness, how you will spend this evening, you must at once calculate what circumstances pertain if certain things are to happen. Can you take an evening off and go out with your friends, perhaps to a concert? But to engage that option is to have to calculate several things: What is scheduled for tomorrow: An exam? A Saturday? How will you get to the event: In someone's car? Whose car? What is the likely availability of tickets at this late date? At what cost? Questioning is actually a highly disciplined use of our imagination. Questions—at least the sort we will be working with—have to have their bases and grounding exposed, which will provide us with a great exercise in logic as well as in imagination. We can acquire a good deal of information we may not already know, if we attend carefully to what we are doing. It may turn out that, once you have explored your options for the evening, it becomes clear that the only person with whom you might get a ride to the concert is not someone you wish to spend an evening with, though you were not conscious of that feeling before you began to ask your strategic questions. You have learned many things while tracking your questions, not least something about yourself: You thought you wanted to go to a concert, but now you have discovered—or perhaps just now decided—not with him! Questioning is a valuable strategy for both uncovering and constructing what we assume and value.

But are questions a suitable approach for reading this biblical book, or for reading the Bible in general? If you are uncertain here, I can only suggest that you test out the possibility for the duration of this book. It is my contention—along with many others currently writing on Scripture—that questions are crucial if we are to "do meaning" with Scripture. Answers have their place, to be sure. But a narrative like Jonah is highly amenable to the strategy of questions, as is biblical literature in general. That the Bible has functioned as Scripture for Christian and Jewish communities over many hundreds of years now, without adding new books or dropping old ones (generally speaking), implies a certain flexibility. If it were simply a book of answers we might well have ceased being interested in what was generated so long ago. We might judge that what the ancients thought, said, or wrote has little relevance to our modern selves. But such has not proved to be the case. If it has been your past experience that the Bible is associated mostly with answers, with dogmatic and even intolerant certitude, I can only ask you to try another route as we journey with Jonah. Questions often generate insight, and such will be the aim of this particular reading. It may not be incidental that the biblical book itself ends with a question, not its first to be posed.

I invite you to ask yourself: *What am I interested in learning from this book concerning biblical studies, even about my place in this universe?* To encounter your own best questions is the place to start. You may not feel quite ready to do that now. So part of our inquiry will be to see what many others have asked and thought, and to understand why their questions were urgent and may remain so, however much time may have passed since they reflected. We may even pose the "question question" to the book of Jonah: *What is its most basic question?* After I had been working on the Jonah story for some time, I decided that I would use it to generate a mystery. I am a great reader of mysteries, feel I understand the genre well, and have even dabbled in writing one before. But to my chagrin, as I opened a new notebook to begin my fun adventure in the Jonah mystery, I found I was not sure what the biblical book was about, hence what the mystery should center upon and develop. *What is most centrally happening in the Jonah story, and in response to what question?* Is it about being swallowed by a fish? Does it concern Jews and Gentiles most foundationally? Is it about Jonah's intransigence and un-cooperative spirit? I will not (yet) tell you what I concluded. But I could not start my project without making a decision, which in fact drove the whole architectonic of that book and this one!

Why Jonah, you may now be asking? The book of Jonah is short (forty-eight verses), and it seems clear. Its narrative is vivid, packed with adventure and issues, yet moving with suitable complexity: A prophet is commissioned to preach repentance to wicked Ninevites, but he flees, boarding a ship that on his account is whipped by a fierce storm; the crew, learning from him that he is avoiding God, reluctantly jettisons him (ch. 1). But God has appointed a large fish to rescue him, and from within its innards Jonah cries to God (ch. 2). Delivered, he proceeds to Nineveh and preaches a single sentence that produces conversion from all who hear; and God, responsive, calls off what had been threatened (ch. 3). The last chapter (4) is taken up by discussion between prophet and deity about what has transpired. The book is much commented upon in tradition; in fact, Jonah is popular in Judaism, Christianity, and Islam—a boast not so many writings can make! Jonah has been enacted in popular culture, including art and literature, and Jonah is engaged liturgically by Jews and Christians.

Another question you may have at this point is *who is undertaking this study?* Who is "we"? It is a good query, since the ones we journey with will make a big difference. You know who you are, of course—but once again, resist the complacency of your status quo. *What do you want as you start a new phase of biblical study?* Spend some time asking yourself what has changed with you since you last gave biblical texts deep attention, or perhaps any attention at all. Listen as your instructor and the others in your class disclose their personal information, however it may emerge. Be leery of writing off those whose views seem incompatible with your own. They may improve as you know them, and yourself, better.

The "narrating I" of this particular volume is a Roman Catholic Dominican Sister who has been teaching in college, seminary, and graduate school for more than twenty-five years while working with other kinds of study groups as well. My particular Bible interest is Old Testament narratives and the many ways in which they can work effectively in the lives of those searching for God, wishing the companionship of others doing the same. If I were to search the evidence for my most consistent "non-Bible" interests, I would conclude that the study of nonviolence and especially some of its most brilliant practitioners (Mahatma Gandhi and Martin Luther King, Jr., most famously but not exclusively) is a most consistent focus. So it is likely that we will spend some time on "othering," as the manner of intersecting with various allies is called. I have already told you as well that I love reading mysteries. All these points are relevant. That I am an Anglo North American, raised without consciousness of lacking basic material goods or professional status, may also signify. That I am female may prompt questions about feminist interpretation, especially if you have noted the paucity of females in the Jonah story. We will think about all these issues additionally as we engage other readers.

As we think some more about our common study—you as you have opened this book and engaged the world I have placed here for you—there are more questions to ponder. *How are we going to spend a whole book on so short a narrative?* The interface between biblical studies, with its various critical methodologies and interests, and biblical spirituality, which utilizes many of those strategies but specifically with the intent of engaging readers transformatively toward what is of ultimate value to us, is what engages me most centrally. That is, though we will surely learn a great deal about diverse matters, we will also be challenged to greater self-knowledge and prompted to deepen the awareness of our relationship with God and creatures. *How can, does, and even should our learning change us deeply?* We live and are studying in a moment when methodology is important, so we are challenged to know what we are doing when we work with texts. Another way to put that last point is to say we will proceed hermeneutically, with careful attention to the manner in which we derive or construct meaning. All the books in this INTERFACES series meet that basic challenge in their own way, and I hope you are using more than one of them in your course—perhaps the study of Jezebel and his opponent Elijah, with whom Jewish tradition closely connects Jonah—or John the Baptist, who shares their prophetic role![1] Additionally, we will investigate the insights of a variety of scholars who have studied and written about Jonah since the

---

[1] Catherine M. Murphy, *John the Baptist: Prophet of Purity for a New Age* (Collegeville: Liturgical Press, 2003), and Patricia Duizler-Walls, *Jezebel: Portraits of a Queen* (Collegeville: Liturgical Press, 2004).

early days of Christianity and Rabbinic Judaism. So there are many "we's" undertaking this particular journey with Jonah. *What have other interpreters asked, assumed, negotiated?* I have found, when working with this text in various settings and with various individuals and groups, that—perhaps counter to expectations—it has been great fun and highly useful to read the work of diverse interpreters. Our circle will widen. But central will be our own issues: *How can our study of diverse readings assist us with our questions?*

Since we are making questions central, and since we are about to take a necessary detour before opening our Jonah story, let me offer you for your own consideration some of the most provocative and persistent issues that our wider circle of Jonah readers have raised in the twenty-five hundred or so years that "we" have been reading. You will be gratified to find that some of them have occurred to you as well. Others may surprise you. It is my experience that some of these matters seem banal at first but acquire greater interest for us as we learn more. I have arranged them in story order, that is, according to the unfolding of the story in its four biblical chapters. When we track some of them later, we will rearrange them.

Jonah 1:
>   who is Jonah?
>   what is wrong in Nineveh?
>   why does the prophet flee his assignment?
>   with what dispositions?
>   how does he engage the ship?
>   when in the sequence of events does he go below-deck?
>   what motivates and prompts the sailors as the storm increases?
>   what are the various assumptions of characters about the storm?
>   what are their diverse constructions of the storm deity?
>   how important are the religious/ethnic tags of the participants?
>   what changes of heart does Jonah have from start to finish of ch. 1?

Jonah 2:
>   who is the fish and where is it from?
>   what are its relevant characteristics?
>   is it a threat or a deliverance?
>   how is the fish related to other (Bible) animals?
>   how does his utterance fit with the attendant circumstances?
>   what can be made of the three days spent in the fish?
>   what is God's demeanor throughout this event?
>   what is the experience Jonah has had: entering, being in, leaving the fish?
>   does he learn something important?
>   is his language sincere?
>   where does the fish journey take him?

Jonah 3:

might Jonah think the whole adventure was over once he emerges from
   the fish?

is Jonah's proclamation God-given, or is it his construction?

with what demeanor, or in what tone is the proclamation delivered?

does Jonah understand his own proclamation?

how do the Ninevites understand Jonah's proclamation?

is the proclamation a threat? a warning? a promise? a choice?

why do the Ninevites believe it?

how do they know what to do?

how do the Ninevites proceed without knowing quite what their options are?

why do these Ninevites repent/respond so readily?

are the Ninevites sincere?

what does God desire?

does God undergo a change of mind?

is the punishment simply deferred—so it still hangs over Nineveh's head?

does Jonah become a false prophet when God had a(n apparent) change
   of mind?

what does Jonah want?

Jonah 4:

why is Jonah angered?

what does Jonah know that makes him react so intensely?

is Jonah telling the truth about why he fled when he explains it?

what is the root of his reactions?

is Jonah praising or blaming God for the divine attributes named?

whose viewpoint is Jonah representing when he names such qualities?

when God questions Jonah about "doing well," what is implied?

is the implied answer yes or no?

is God making a statement or asking a question?

what is God's intent in querying/commenting?

what does Jonah await outside the city?

what does Jonah want?

is Jonah's delight in the plant excessive?

is the worm a shrunk dragon?

is Jonah's reaction about the plant's destruction excessive?

why does God appoint the wind?

when Jonah claims to be angry unto death, does it link to his earlier prayer?

what are the Ninevites doing while Jonah keeps watch?

does Jonah sleep through the destruction of the gourd-plant?

what is to be understood in the construction of God's final questions?

what exactly is the analogy God proposes?

how orienting is the story's end?

Do not be overwhelmed by the multiplicity of the questions, since we will only sort and make use of what will help us with our quests for meaning, complex as they may be. But even if we discard a question after first weighing it, we gain: We can learn usefully what questions we are not asking. In fact, when we do not feel prompted by issues that have in fact intrigued or worried others considerably, even that very point is food for thought!

How, finally, will we proceed? What is the plan of this book? There are several ways we might have moved forward, and I attempted several of them before settling on what you will find here. We will start with two rather theoretical tasks: first by inquiring into the process of interpretation, its dynamics and conclusions (Chapter 1), and second by reviewing as briefly as possible the major stages and accomplishments of interpretation in general, which will help us with readings of the book of Jonah (Chapter 2). We will then practice our own reading by considering four "architectonics" or ways of interpreting Jonah, each of which proposes its own coherence. That is, we will ask what happens if we assume explicitly that the book was designed for a particular fifth-century B.C.E. Jewish audience (Chapter 3). We will next follow the implications of reading Jonah allegorically and typologically as a Christ figure, as did ancient and medieval Christian interpreters (Chapter 4). We will then explore interpretive riches that become visible if we are focusing on Jonah as a literary masterpiece (Chapter 5). And we will investigate the possibilities that emerge if Jonah's story is seen as one of many that re-enact struggle with watery chaos, a very ancient interest that many readers still like (Chapter 6). Finally, I will offer my own best sense of how to read the story responsibly and well, imaginatively and sensitively, as most basically a struggle between Jonah and God (Chapter 7). We will conclude by revisiting the issues raised in this introductory reflection, on which you will have become experts! We will not so much close down or silence our questions as appreciate where they have taken us, how the best insights of many others have nourished us, and what journeys may lie ahead.

CHAPTER ONE

Finding a Flexible Framework for Interpretation

Now that we have established some sense of our journey's process—the construction of meaning—we can get underway. Given that our primary strategic tool is the question, that our challenge is to discover the significance of this story in the lives of those who have read it, and our more precise quest is to make meaning ourselves, we might begin with some of the questions listed at the end of the last chapter. But that is not where we will start. If it is important to know how meaning works, we need to spend some time establishing a framework for our questions. That is, having begun our journey by asking about the meaning of meaning, the dynamics of questions, their value for the biblical text, the suitability of strategic questions for our particular narrative, the identity of those with whom you are engaged, and the path of our study, we will lay out some initial matters that can organize our whole investigation. A framework for our questions will ensure that we do not waste them or fail to get from them what they offer.

A Flexible Framework: Its First Portion

Jonah does not come as a stand-alone short story, but as part of the Bible. So a huge question to probe before we work with our small narrative is: *What is the Bible, or what is Scripture?* Those are actually two questions, but we can deal with them for a time as one. You may need to scrutinize your assumptions here, whether you come from a religious tradition other than Judaism or Christianity, or if you are a Christian or Jew who has not studied the matter for some time. If you think the Bible is a book God spoke or wrote and sent forth, clothed in a special jacket that identified it as "The Holy Bible," then matters seem simple. But if it did not arrive in such a clear and authorized way we will need to find out where it did come from and how it got the distinctive covers we see in bookstores today! Let us contemplate the process by thinking in terms of events, recitals, and subsequent readings.

First we can think about the events the Bible narrates. So far as scholars can discover, those happened over a period of about one thousand years, from the turn of the first millennium B.C.E. (around 1000 or a bit later) until the close of the first century of the current era (100 C.E. or so). "Bible characters" and their narrated adventures, virtually all of which concern ways in which human beings and their communities struggle to make good sense of their lives and their relationships with God, fill its pages. Not only the events but also the recounting of them occurred in this privileged time, some no doubt oral and all eventually in written form. There has to have been much more involved than we can recover accurately or in much detail, but envision at least family stories told in kinship groups, tribal customs enunciated and preserved for village governance, songs sung and poetry recited at festivals and liturgies, proverbs repeated and enriched in various apt circumstances, lists preserved in royal archives and reviewed at clan gatherings, sagas told by victorious warriors and wise women, oracles spoken enigmatically by prophets, psalms keened by mourners—and of course much more.

So we may suppose that a story can start around a campfire—or on a battlefield, or in a bedroom—and be retold, recomposed for a special occasion, or shaped to suit a festival like Passover. A narrative or song may be commissioned to suit a major water-crossing event like the departure from Egypt and then reworked to sustain the return of the community from Babylon to Judah at the start of what historians call the Persian period. The story—or poem, proverb, hymn, or oracle—retains something of its basic or first identity but undergoes retrofitting as well, since it is asked to sustain the community in fresh circumstances. In this stage of the biblical process we are envisioning not so much initial events that are referenced as the efforts of later groups to "live into" their stories as they experience their own events; that is, by recounting older stories people find fresh meaning for their own adventures. The most profound of past experience needs to be kept usable. So this first long point suggests that it is successive communities of God's people that struggle—and rejoice—to tell the stories of how, specifically, they are God's people. God is not absent from either the events or the recitals, but neither are the human processes to be short-circuited or underestimated.

Now a second point: In this one-thousand-(or so)-year-process of "Bible-making," two watershed events occurred in the first century of the present era. The first was the life and death circumstances of the Jew, Jesus of Nazareth. The second was the destruction of the Jewish Temple in Jerusalem and its complex attendant culture, an event culminating in a war with

Rome that took place about 66–70. The result of those "moments" (and in fact of their blend) brought the biblical period to a close. The sudden end of the way of life centering around the Temple and the eventual proscription of Jews from the area around Jerusalem, as well as the challenges brought about by the claims of the followers of Jesus, meant that the Jewish way of life-with-God-in-community demanded rethinking. Once again, events happened and were reflected upon, and fresh meaning emerged around familiar recitals, new stories around older life-experience. Judaism reconstituted itself around its sacred documents—including its Tanakh or Bible, but not restricted to what was precipitating as canonical—and continued to interpret those intensively: in rabbinic materials, in the Mishnah, in the Talmuds, eventually in commentaries and in mystical literature. Christians—or those who would eventually bear that name—found the life and work of Jesus to be so signal that they, too, rethought all of God's past deeds, but in terms of the Christ-event. Stories about Jesus borrowed elements from earlier Hebrew materials and emerged afresh amidst the Christian communities; these were reflected upon and refitted in various new circumstances and became life-giving for those groups. Christians, like Jews, commented upon the biblical materials and generated other sorts of writings as well to meet the particular challenges of their own lives.

Again, the complexity of these processes, especially as they occurred over centuries and in diverse cultures and with many distinctive players, is more than we will ever know. But the main outlines are clear enough as each "Bible community" settled more or less its sense of which of its sacred books were Scripture and which were not. It was not enough for a book (or manuscript, scroll, or codex) to have "been there," even to have survived in the requisite language. The early post-biblical leaders had additional standards for deciding on their canonical books. Among them were the criteria of use: *What books were copied most, were most beloved, evidently most useful, most important for keeping—guarding and managing—the values of the communities? That is, which parts of the tradition seem to have worked most effectively to sustain their communities?*

As successive post-biblical generations of both Jews and Christians worked with the Scriptures—i.e., with the materials that had been declared "canonical" for them—they understood the biblical text deeply to be God's word, able to be interpreted in order to mediate the experience of being God's people. In some cases the Bible was considered almost dictated by God, in others simply to have been organized and uttered by God with every need in mind. To the Ancients, as we shall see in the next chapter, that the Bible was God's—composed of God-centered events and divinely-inspired utterances—was the main point and its most important feature.

That understanding affected the sorts of questions early readers brought to it and the various processes of interpretation they engaged it with. Ancient biblical events and persons were revered, though not usually well understood in historical contexts. The text was carefully tended, but it was also translated so as to be of use to new peoples. Meaning was found in many ways, as we shall examine shortly, but always with the end of love of God and neighbor focal. And this long era, called pre-critical to distinguish it from what would follow, kept the Bible central.

Starting around the fifteenth to sixteenth century or so and extending up to the present, educated interpreters of the Bible came to see things quite otherwise. Their change of mindset grew from events beginning around that time—new ways of looking, seeing, asking, investigating, judging—and changed biblical reading radically. If heretofore the Bible had seemed, roughly speaking, primarily a divine product that believers searched in many ways for wisdom in their lives, now it became, at least for the educated, an almost exclusively human product. Historical questions about its core events and its long period of growth became primary. The Bible was taken apart so that its genetic processes could be better understood. All who wished to see the Bible as God's word were challenged by the history, science, and politics of their day to maintain such sacral features of and uses for it. The modern critical era can be seen as almost a reverse image of the pre-critical: If many ancient Christian interpreters overstressed the divine communication available from Scripture and underestimated its human processes, many modern scholars became so consumed with the human cultural aspects of the Bible that they all but eliminated God's presence from it. The chasm grew between critical study and the Bible's spiritual identity, such that to our day many feel that critical study is the enemy of a genuine spiritual life nourished by the Bible. Our challenge now, made possible as the modern period strains toward something fresh, is to recognize both that we are reading a classic and that we must bring to it appropriate questions, insights, and interpretive processes.

Our first framework, then, asks us to be mindful of our present selves reading an ancient and privileged text: First, *what do we need to know about* **past events** *(from biblical times and since), about the processes of* **text formation** *(and preservation), and about the needs and* **interpretive moves** *of the Bible's many readers?* Additionally this "past/present" framework prompts us to inquire: *What do we need to understand about our present* **situatedness** *(the events that have given rise to our lives), about the multiple* **dynamics of the biblical narrative** *that we can explore (many of which are a result of modern language philosophy), and what is the impact on interpretation of the* **lives of actual readers**—*ourselves and our contemporaries?*

One of the points that I want to emerge clearly as a result of this discussion is that we can only usefully ask our own questions. That is, though others may have asked them as well, when we pick up what is of interest to us, we do it as our modern/postmodern selves, living in the actual worlds we inhabit. Our interests and questions may sound like those asked earlier, but they will differ substantially from earlier articulations. That we live in a world so different from the globe earlier readers trod guarantees that our questions will not be riding on the same worldview as did theirs. This point needs emphasis for a variety of reasons, as will become clear when we do our readings. Primary here, though, is the importance of recognizing the implications of our own participation in the process of interpretation. We are not doing it from any stance other than that which actually generates our lives as we live them.

A Flexible Framework: Its Second Portion

A second framework-sorting will earn the name "three worlds." *Do we need data about and from the past? Or do we need more information from the narrative itself? Might it be the case that our own experience is the prime source of our insight?* More specifically: *Is the biblical story of Jonah a narrative of a historical event, one that happened in the past and that we hope to investigate in its "happened-ness"?* The first world to query stands behind the text. *Or is it a work of art that does not refer directly to an actual event it seems derivative of, drawing rather from some other source?* The textual world is our second place to investigate. That it tells a story that may have happened as told does not restrict us to its facticity. Many crucial narratives far transcend their actual referents, while including them as well. You can no doubt think about an event that, though important, gains more value to you as you recall, relate, and relive it, especially as you share it with other people. The event itself acquires significance, for you and perhaps for others, in the retelling. This facet of interpretation leads us to the third world, that in front of the text, emerging as actual readers make sense of it.

Thus the questions rising from the "three worlds" framework take shape: *Is the story of Jonah important primarily because it happened, and we need to learn more about the event in order to appreciate it more? How is the articulation itself the place where we can find deep significance? Or is the narrative offering for our consideration some more existential experience about life, where our appreciation will depend on searching for significance in other realms beyond the factual? If your life has, to date, proceeded without major failure, disappointment, or frustration, do you think you will be well-positioned to understand the story of Jonah?* So in addition to a framework that works with the categories of past and present we need also to think about the world of which the text purportedly speaks, the world of the textual dynamics themselves, and the realm of experience from which texts can be understood by those who receive them.

Let's sidetrack to a "practice example" we may be able to work with more directly than is the case with biblical issues. During the U.S. Civil War (1861–1865), a battle occurred near Gettysburg, Pennsylvania; President Abraham Lincoln attended the dedication of that battleground into a cemetery and spoke at the event. We can ask some questions about that set of things to understand the anatomy of our questions better. The Gettysburg events are surely "historical" in that they occurred and we can study the past to learn about the war, the battle, the dedication ceremony, and the President's participation. We can also ask some historical questions about the talk the President gave: how he wrote it, what kinds of speeches were typical and popular in the mid-nineteenth century. And we could ask historical questions about the reception of the speech: what those who heard it thought, reactions of various persons who would have known about the talk at the time it was delivered. All those questions are fundamentally *historical,* sharing a particular moment in the past as a central focus; if we have no access to history we will lack a good deal of crucial information. Conversely, if we know how to do such research we can learn a lot.

But suppose we say that history is "not our thing"; we prefer language and literature. And what we wish to do is to study Lincoln's talk for its aesthetic appeal: its use of imagery, its sentence construction, its unusual diction, its shape. We might track the biblical language in the talk, either direct or allusive reference. We can take the speech apart and, again, learn a great deal simply from investigating the linguistic or *literary* features. Of course, there is nothing to stop us from doing both historical and literary procedures at the same time. We can learn about the historical event while studying the speech's beautiful language. And we might even ask some historical questions about the language: When the President refers to "fourscore and seven years," would his audience have understood readily what the number meant and been able to know what event he referred to? Would they have appreciated that in fact he had also alluded obliquely to a biblical passage from the book of Psalms? And we may ask whether such a speech as the "Gettysburg Address" would have appealed to people of the time, given the expectations and norms for speeches, or perhaps not?

Of course, once again we may choose to make a clean category and say that we do not care about history, nor much about language; our interest is primarily readerly or pragmatic: how the speech was received by various hearers and what it achieved. We might set up an experiment to ascertain from any number of our friends what they think of the cemetery dedication speech and why. If such were our quest, our interest would be in the realm of its *reception,* the reaction people have to the Gettysburg speech. But once again, suppose our interests cross: Suppose, discovering historically who had heard the President speak or had read the speech shortly after it was given, we ask about the reaction of various actual "first hearers." Did soldiers who had survived the battle like the President's talk? Did relatives of those who died there appreciate it—whether kin of Union soldiers now buried in the battleground-become-cemetery, or families of Confederate soldiers who perhaps wished the bodies of their dead to return for burial closer to home? Would Lincoln's political opponents have thought he spoke well or poorly? Once we investigated this set of possibilities—with their historical roots—we would learn, among other things, that the speech was *not* much appreciated, partly because it was so short! Many at the ceremony felt the President had not risen well to the occasion, had seemed and sounded unprepared–even if all did not know that he wrote the speech on the back of an envelope during his train ride to the dedication![1] If we were alert, we might marvel that a short speech would be disfavored, since it would be the case at least with me that, with speeches, short is beautiful! So it depends whose reception we are examining.

Recall our double framework: The "past/present" portion of it asks us to be mindful of what we do when we read a classic, to ask whether our interest is primarily the nineteenth-century event or our own current interest in one of its referents—perhaps the valorization of war. The "three worlds" portion of our framework prompts us to pay close attention to what several sorts of information and strategies we need in order to interpret adequately. To ask good questions about the "Gettysburg Address" we need to consider *historical factors, literary aspects,* and *issues of reception* (which do not quite correspond to our first frame's past/present categories); and while those can all be distinguished and pursued in isolation, we get a better fix on the event by asking questions of all those types. We do not have to know all about the Civil War to read and appraise the speech. We can take a shine to the talk or not, whether others liked long speeches or did not. We can analyze the contextual relevance of the speech without much metaphor theory. And while our views on the recent wars in the Middle East will surely color our appreciation of Lincoln's language, we will not presume to hold others to the same views we have ourselves. Insofar as we can do all of those

[1] All my information about the "Gettysburg Address" comes from Garry Wills, *Lincoln at Gettysburg: The Words that Remade America* (New York: Simon & Schuster, 1992) 19–40, 148–75.

things, we are ahead. But our questions cannot simply be a jumble; we need to keep them orderly. So as our "past/present" framework for interpretation reminds us to sort past from present concerns, this "three worlds" portion directs us to note whether we are dealing *primarily* with the world behind the narrative, the world it projects, or the one from which readers are making our/their existential meaning. But as we recognized that past and present are not cleanly separated, neither are these three biblical "worlds."

Using Our Frameworks

Back to Jonah: What kinds of questions shall we generate? Our "past/present" tool cues us in one way. Why are you reading it: To what extent for its past and to what degree for your own present? As you give this question your best attention, *why do you want to read the biblical book of Jonah?* In a course on Jonah I taught recently, I insisted that students clarify their most urgent "Jonah questions" before embarking on the papers they needed to write. So of the young Christian man who wanted to write about God's putative change of mind (ch. 4), I asked: Why is this question so vital for you? He owned his discomfort with the "slippery" assumptions about God voiced by some of his peers. To the Jewish woman who wanted to write "about Jewish interpretation," I pressed: Where of the many places rabbis have explored the story do you wish to investigate, and why? Her discovery was that it was the education of the prophet that she wished to probe and discuss, and even the implications of construing God as a textual character. They both could have written papers on Jonah 4 without clarifying their personal urgency. But the papers that emerged were substantially—and appropriately—colored by their awareness of what they really wanted to learn more about, be changed by. Note here that we are not doing some research and then trying to apply it to our own lives; we are letting our lives generate the agenda for our reading, so that insight accrues helpfully as we learn. Whatever you want—and it will be more than one thing, likely a package of desires—your expectations will contribute significantly to what you gain. So follow your questions, and allow for their growth and change.

And our "three worlds" tool helps us know how to proceed. Is our *primary* interest *historical:* questions about the event that is narrated, about its social matrix and pertinent conventions of the time in which it was told, about the expectations and reactions of those for whom it was generated? Or are we aiming *primarily* at elements of *language:* the book's own use of questions, the information withheld by the author, or the interlocking structure of the story? Or is our concern perhaps *primarily* about the audiences that *receive and read* the text over time, especially ourselves? We can do all of those, and in fact we will. But if we can see that we need to do a mix of things when we address questions to the text, it will help if we find a home base. My suggestion is that, whatever else we decide, *we are first ourselves reading, and we interpret from our present and actual lives.* Our various strategies, such as they emerge, all come from our individual interests, shaped as those have been fundamentally by communal influences. The one frame we can never leave is our own viewpoint, and our first challenge is to inventory our own expectations and viewpoints as closely as we can.

Let us sample a likely Jonah question from each of the book's chapters and see if we can classify them. Chapter 1 may lead us to ask: *Why did Jonah resist God's command that he go to Nineveh?* That seems to be a historical question, if we assume a kernel event. We can make a general study of ancient Near Eastern prophets, Israelites in particular, to get a sense of their typical demeanors. Did prophets normally refuse assignments? But our question is actually quite resistant to any precise historical inquiry we can do now. So we turn to the narrative's own proffered insight on the question of motivation. Jonah explains his flight, but only after enough things have happened that we may question his recollected explanation! Not unrelated, however, will be our own sense of being assigned onerous or dangerous tasks, our own desires to avoid what we dread. But I would say that the question of Jonah's motivation is more literary than historical, and surely susceptible of many readerly constructions.

A question from Jonah 2: *Can a man be swallowed by a large fish and emerge healthy three days later?* That seems on the face of it a question of fact, and indeed evidence from the past has been brought forward to demonstrate that it seems to have happened and been documented in relatively recent times. Scholars have also explored the possibilities that the large fish was some creature unknown to us today, similar to other huge animals that once roamed the planet. Certainly there is not much literary help—no detail about the type of fish or the digestive dynamics involved. We will see that, though Jonah will speak about his experience, he does not tell us the things we may wish to know about the interior of the fish, or whale, as it tends to be called now. That stories of struggles within and passages through turbulent waters abound in the ancient Near East is surely relevant. But I suspect the other place to anchor this question is as a matter of reception: Are we looking for a literal explanation, or do we decide that this detail is meant to be almost purely imaginative? Again, since this issue has, over time, been very prominent, we will not neglect it. But my sense is that we will not resolve it historically but perhaps literarily and surely existentially, as we slot it.

A likely question from the book's third chapter is: *What made the people of Nineveh so wholehearted in their change of heart, having heard simply a sentence of challenge from a visiting prophet?* Here we have a question susceptible of historical analysis in several aspects, since we can learn a lot about ancient Nineveh, discover the meaning of sackcloth and ashes, learn the role of fasting for entreating the deity in Hebrew culture. We may wonder how Assyrians would have understood the language of a Hebrew preacher, but it seems obvious that they not only understood but accepted his word as urgent to obey. However, as we seek to understand the simple sentence Jonah spoke (especially when we have done a bit more study!), we may factor some semantic complexity from it, as we seek to understand the possibilities of a Hebrew participle and to imagine how it sounded in various ears. In a story about re-routings and reversals, over-turnings and changes of mind, what does the sentence of 3:4 actually say? We—every "we" hearing it—will have to decide. So once again, our kinds of concerns cross borders historical, literary, readerly.

Finally, from the final chapter of Jonah we inquire: *What set of factors prompted God's dealings with the people of Nineveh, and what in the divine dealings was so irritating to Jonah?* We are unlikely to be able to uncover historical information to help us, though we will attend to the likely assumptions of the intended (or presumed) Jonah audience. The narrative itself begs us in many ways to probe the question, almost fakes us out to settle on a clear motive. But in the final analysis, the best source of our understanding of those matters will be our own experience and expectation of how God's people deal with God and God deals with people—no small topic that! Before proceeding, take a look at the chart on the next page and see if it makes basic sense to you. The framework we establish will substantially determine our study—how we journey with Jonah—so it is worth your time to know where you are!

Interpretive Frameworks: Final Considerations

Before we end this initial discussion there is need for me to say a bit more about what I plan for us to do as we work with this book as well as with the biblical narrative. When I introduced myself above, briefly, I gave you some information that might help you know me better so you can be critical in your use of the book I have written. But in addition to that information, I owe you a clearer statement of my purpose. Though I write for many reasons—it generates my best thinking, it demonstrates me as professionally productive, it stimulates my creativity, it brings me into contact with many people I would not otherwise engage—I have other specific purposes as well. I desire us to see what it is like to interpret a text in conversation with about twenty-five hundred years worth of others who have engaged it as well. *How are their interests like and unlike ours, and how*

The past of the narrative: world behind the text	The narrative itself: world within the text	The engaged reading: world before the text
Who, what, when was the prophet Jonah? What are the book's ANE antecedents? Who, what, when was Nineveh?	What is the book's genre, and what bearing does that have? What is the role of the story's many questions, notably at the end?	How does God deal with people: with prophets? pagans? innocents? "guiltys"? Does God have favorites?
When was the book written, for whom, and why? When is the book set, and what is pertinent from that setting? Did the story attract odd bits to itself—e.g., ch. 2? Did it lose bits—e.g., the ending?	How do motif words and tight structure signify? How does characterization work? Are there agreed-upon valences? What does "overturn/*hpk*" mean in this narrative?	Who/what are opponents, and how are they to be dealt with? What does God want, and how do we know? Do some know more than others? What do readers assume about the authoring of this text?
What does knowing the form of the "psalm" help us to know? What does the word "overthrow/*hpk*" mean in biblical Hebrew? Why is Jonah with the minor prophets rather than with DH?	How does the psalm match the story, or not? How is Jonah related intertextually to the rest of the Bible? Is the large fish helpful or dangerous? How is Jonah's "Nineveh experience" related to that of others in the Bible?	Why have Jewish scholars and Christian scholars tended to get rather different readings of the book? What does the book "do" about gender and violence issues? Why is it so popular and enactable?

YOU ARE HERE!
(YOU DEFINE WHERE "HERE" IS.)

might we find ourselves in unexpected agreement and disagreement with people whose lives are so very different from ours? How will we learn from their questions, not only about the story but about ourselves? These IN-TERFACES volumes are asked to name their methodologies, and here is my first: the hermeneutics (or interpretation dynamics) of reading with the long chain of interpreters from a diverse tradition.

And I have hinted at my second major strategy, which I can now name: biblical spirituality. All of the books in the INTERFACES series, this one included, participate in the large field of biblical studies. But additionally I will engage another dimension of that field. First, Christian spirituality is at once a more focused and a wider term than Christian biblical studies. Some biblical study falls outside Christian spirituality, and spirituality enfolds wider practice than Christian appropriation of the Bible. You may notice that we have now sidled back to our earlier question of *what is the Bible, what is Scripture?* To be clear on that topic is important. You need not accept my view of things, but you will do best to know what it is. When I use the term Christian spirituality I will do so with the help of two scholar-practitioners.

One is Sandra Schneiders, who suggests that spirituality is the experience of conscious involvement in the project of life-integration through self-transcendence toward the ultimate value one perceives, which for Christians is the triune God revealed in Jesus, approached via the paschal mystery and the church community and lived through the gift of the Holy Spirit.[2] She further parses Christian spirituality to include: first, a radical capacity for the human spirit to engage God's spirit; second, the experience of so doing that is mediated and expressed in a variety of ways; and third, a field of study of how humans have engaged God deeply, attentive to the interpretive processes by which an intentional spiritual life can grow and be made understandable. Her sense is that Scripture does several things: It mediates the foundational and normative access of the Christian to revelation; it not only supplies the positive data of the earliest Christian experience and its Jewish matrix, but also contributes its basic symbol system and the meta-story into which each individual and communal Christian story can be integrated and by which it is patterned, crucial for underlining the importance of the whole Bible for Christians.[3] Christian spirituality begins as Jesus—steeped in the already old and rich Jewish tradition of divine self-disclosure—interacted with those who responded to him, and that experience was converted into language and

---

[2] Sandra Schneiders, "Approaches to the Study of Christian Spirituality," in Arthur Holder, ed., *The Blackwell Companion to Christian Spirituality* (Oxford: Basil Blackwell, 2005) 15–33.

[3] Sandra M. Schneiders, "The Study of Christian Spirituality: Contours and Dynamics of a Discipline," *Journal of the Society for the Study of Christian Spirituality* 6 (1998) 1, 3.

shared with others. For our immediate purposes Christian spirituality begins as Jesus discusses Jonah with interlocutors, challenging all those he engages to make sense of the Jonah figure, as he himself does by referring to it. Schneiders notes additionally that all Christian spirituality is inherently biblical.[4] It is my hope and plan that the very process of interpreting this story will change our lives—yours as well as mine—as we proceed. The questions, the search for meaning, the processes of interpretation, the awareness of our steps are all oriented toward this goal. There will, or at least can, be other gains as well: information about the long tradition, new knowledge about the Bible, a deeper awareness of hermeneutical strategies. But my main goal is that study shape our lives in the profound way of which Schneiders speaks. *Do you have to go along with that goal?* No, you can resist it, which is part of my reason for telling you what I am about. But I hope you will consider the possibilities of such an engagement before deciding against it.

A second helper for our spirituality quest is contemplative art historian Wendy Beckett, whose more blunt and inductive discussion of how art mediates the sacred is useful in this discussion of Hebrew Bible texts that are not explicitly christocentric. What Beckett says about the process of experiencing spiritual art deeply provides practical insight into what can happen when we read the most profoundly revelatory narratives and prayers of the OT. We can call her process "getting perspective," for that is what she describes to us. Great art (including literature) involves a deep yearning for what is sensed but not yet present. It makes tangible for our engagement the most profound needs and desires of the human heart: love, death, joy, pain, all of which are for Christians places of the encounter of the human spirit with God's. We engage by bringing our deepest attention, our most alert gaze to what has been represented before us. We surrender to it with loving trust but very actively as well, striving to be as honest in our reactions as we can be, to know and articulate our response as well as we can do. The opposite of such honesty is anything false, ranging from a careless imposition of prescriptive categories to an easy surrender to our prejudices; "false" ranges from denying what we feel to making a defensive posture of our own ego. The gain, Beckett promises, is that we deepen our awareness of what most matters, which for her and many is to be with or belong to God as wholly as is possible: the process and endpoint of Christian spirituality. Great art—visual or textual—enables expanding limits that might otherwise confine us. It increases our integrity, makes us more "there" than we would otherwise have been. The more we respond, the more we become. In some way not wholly abstractable or explainable such art helps us to "get perspective,"

---

[4] Sandra Schneiders, "Biblical Spirituality," *Interpretation* 56 (2002) 134.

recognize ourselves with clarity, and reach more fully toward the community of God and other creatures in which we long to live. Great art is, in that deep sense, disclosive of God and renders us susceptible to God.[5]

So as we bring this first foundational chapter to a close, you have been invited to think about meaning in several senses. You have been challenged to utilize questions to sharpen your awareness. We have practiced asking some questions about the Jonah story and sought frameworks for their classification, the better to make use of them. One of our frameworks rises from the recognition that we are, in our present, dealing with a privileged text from the past; the second helps us factor the sorts of information we need from that narrative to appropriate it well. I have invited you to ask what you want from this particular moment of biblical study and have offered you— and challenged us all—to allow the transformative processes that can always be a part of serious reading to engage you, and I hope that insofar as your hopes are for a greater closeness to God and all God's projects, you will allow that to happen as well. We have talked, in an introductory way, about who is asking the questions: *Who are you? Whom are you reading with? Who am I, reading along with you in a somewhat privileged way? How will we proceed in this book, and why in that way? What are your purposes for reading? And what are mine? How linked are our projects?* I wish us to read in such a way as to allow the text to transform us in a profound way: *Does that seem necessary for you? How does such a process seem to work, at least in the view of those who consider it central?* You may not be able to answer all those questions to your own satisfaction, but I hope you have begun to let them work at you as you work at them. Our next step will be to consider ways in which other interpreters have grappled with these very questions, and to see if their insights are useful for us as well.

---

[5] Wendy Beckett, *The Gaze of Love: Meditations on Art and Spiritual Transformation* (New York: HarperCollins, 1993).

CHAPTER TWO

The Long Reception of the Jonah Narrative

Recall that our *ultimate quest* is the con struction of meaning with and from the book of Jonah. Our *strategy* is questions, employed to accomplish various purposes: to disclose information, diagnose assumptions, spur imagination. The *skill* we are honing is rich interpretation. And our *meta-goal* is to understand what we are doing, what works effectively, so we can transfer our knowledge or allow it to seep into other parts of our lives. The purpose of this chapter is to investigate how others have read Jonah, for some twenty-five hundred years. Our sample, necessarily brief and schematic, will "interview" nine readers from different eras.[1] Consider this chapter in terms of our *frameworks:* These readers, like ourselves, are reading an ancient text, convinced of its utter relevance in their lives. Until we get close to the end of this chapter, their interests will seem primarily literary, minimally historical; they are intent, sensitive readers of biblical text. But each is also very attentive to contemporary issues, and so without owning or even seeing it, all are reader-alert, even pragmatic! And *we* are reading *them*—while *they* read—to acquaint ourselves with the richly diverse tradition of Christian reading of Scripture so that we approach it more skillfully ourselves.

The Pre-Modern/Pre-Critical Period: Antiquity

Jesus of Nazareth

The writers of New Testament books make extensive use of the Hebrew Bible to speak of the events that cluster around Jesus, the Jew from

---

[1] For considerably more detail consult Barbara Green, "The Old Testament in Christian Spirituality," in Arthur Holder, ed., *The Blackwell Companion to Christian Spirituality* (Oxford: Basil Blackwell, 2005) 37–54; also R. H. Bowers, *The Legend of Jonah* (The Hague: Martinus Nijhoff, 1971); Yvonne K. Sherwood, *A Biblical Text and Its Afterlives: The Survival of Jonah in Western Culture* (Cambridge: Cambridge University Press, 2000).

Nazareth who becomes central for many Jews and Gentiles. Steeped in the Hebrew Bible language world, they sought to make sense of the young "Christian" community's experience of Jesus by reinterpreting God's projects with humans as related in the Jewish heritage. Jesus is quite typical of Jewish practice when he refers to the Jonah story while talking of God. Though it is wholly possible that these are actual utterances of the historical Jesus, we have them now embedded in the gospels of Matthew and Luke, where Jesus is a character. So however Jesus saw himself and spoke of it, we read the way in which Matthew and Luke saw him and drew him, articulating his identity and mission. They suggested at least two analogies between Jesus and Hebrew Bible Jonah.[2] By referring to the "sign of Jonah" without explaining it explicitly, the invitation extends to the characters with whom Jesus interacts to construe the saying situationally, existentially. Since they fall silent, the challenge comes to us. The interpretation works contextually in each gospel as we sense two possibilities: One set of biblical characters queries what they will learn about Jesus after his death and resurrection three days later, and another audience seems prompted to trust and heed an effective preacher. Note: Gospel evocations of the sign of Jonah and the story do not mean simply one thing, but invite negotiation that will take us to various places.[3]

Augustine of Hippo

Early Christian post-biblical interpretation, driven by various problems faced vis-à-vis relatedness with Judaism and the Roman Empire, continued to center primarily around understanding the person of Jesus. Readings done by the early Church Fathers tend to be classified as allegorical, typological, or intertextual, depending on the strategic moves made. Since we will examine all three of these influential reading modes in our Chapters 4 and 6, here we can simply note the original and integrative work of Augustine, eventually bishop of Hippo (354–430), who remains premier among biblical scholars. Mary Clark characterizes his diverse lifework and intensely dialogical writings as opposing four main groups: Manichees, who urged a gnostic, fundamentalist, and polarized sense of the divine with an odd distribution of materialist elements that came into

---

[2] Matt 12:38-42; 16:4; Luke 11:29-32. We can also make sense of a place like Mark 8:11-12, where Jesus mutters about those who "seek signs" without specifically naming Jonah-signs. We can look at the passage and see if, in fact, the "Jonah conversation" is actually going on without being named.

[3] For additional discussion of how the NT draws on the book of Jonah, see Chapter 6 below.

conflict with Augustine's sense of God's transcendence; Donatists, whose teachings about sacraments were opposed by Rome but dominant in Augustine's North African context; Pelagians, who taught an understanding of human freedom that Augustine's sense of the radical necessity of grace fiercely opposed; and various others who accused Christians of responsibility for (among other things) the fall of Rome.

Augustine's early classical education steeped him in rhetoric but omitted study of the Bible, a literature that did not appeal to him when he first encountered it. But once he became convinced of the value and necessity of Revelation he spent the last four decades of his life studying, commenting upon, and theorizing about Scripture. Lacking the modern sense of the Bible as a collection of books authored at various times and in various circumstances, Augustine saw it as a single vast puzzle comprising in minute detail the story of God's salvific deeds, a single coherent message within an intricate code. The challenge of interpreters was to bring to light the significance of the myriad patterns and tiny details. Scripture offers, most foundationally, a means to enjoyment of God for God's sake: Such is its purpose and end. The base challenge of the Scripture-based spirituality was, for Augustine, the re-formation of the Trinitarian image of God in us, given to us by grace and appropriated by us freely: friendship with God.

Augustine's assumptions, and in particular his Platonist formation and commitments, inclined him toward the allegorical modes of interpretation, although he was heavily invested in the historical literal level as well, spending years struggling to explicate the literal meaning of Genesis. But since his first experience with biblical study had been with the literalistic Manichees, Augustine was leery of consequences when the literal sense of Scripture was seized upon inappropriately or when the figurative was mistaken for the literal. He did not see the literal and the spiritual as inevitably opposed; the letter transports the reader to a deeper (or higher) realm. But Augustine pushed the allegorical method beyond what others had done and theorized more explicitly on what he understood of it. He grounded the necessity for allegorical reading on the choice of Adam and Eve (Genesis 3), since at that moment humanity became somehow alienated from ready access to God; signs were needed. For Augustine "the Fall" was a historical event and one that he recognized deeply within his own experience. He taught firmly that solid theology was prerequisite for interpretation as well as sound philology; and of course one must be deeply committed to love of God and neighbor. For him as for virtually all the Christian exegetes for some time, the Old Testament is clarified in the New.

Augustine did not write a commentary on Jonah, though across his works he cited a number of its passages for various reasons; we can gather those here, mostly without reference to the contexts where they appeared.[4] Augustine sees in Jonah's flight from and resistance to God a classic human move that he himself made in his youth: the choice to abandon our basic goal and to chase a shadow instead. Augustine refers to Jonah's experience with the fish in order to suggest that God is able to communicate with animals as well as with humans, to command water creatures as well as others, to utilize whales or worms.[5] Augustine makes a lovely reflective comment on Jonah within the whale in a piece on Psalm 130:1:

> "Out of the deep I have called unto Thee, O Lord: Lord, hear my voice" (ver. 1). Jonas cried from the deep; from the whale's belly. He was not only beneath the waves, but also in the entrails of the beast; nevertheless, those waves and that body prevented not his prayer from reaching God, and that beast's belly could not contain the voice of his prayer. It penetrated all things, it burst through all things, it reached the ears of God: if indeed we ought to say that, bursting through all things, it reached the ears of God, since the ears of God were in the heart of him who prayed.[6]

The repentance of the Ninevites prompts two comments from Augustine: First, that God provides opportunities for all kinds of people to repent, and second, that the Ninevites repented without total confidence that mercy was available to them. He picked up two points where he was able to speak of the importance of attending to the language and to textual variants. First, when discussing the number of days in Jonah's cry for repentance (whether the Ninevites were advised they had three or forty days) Augustine urges that the point is deeper than the literal number of days, and that both three and forty have reference to the life of Jesus, a more profound key to the passage. And when Augustine alludes in a letter to Jerome to the controversy stirred up by Jerome's non-traditional translation of the plant as an "ivy," after chiding Jerome for unnecessary perturbation of the faithful, Augustine advised the possibility of consulting Jews about such things.[7]

---

[4] Augustine's comments are scattered: see Philip Schaff, ed., *Nicene and Post-Nicene Fathers, 1st ser.,* Vol. 1: *The Confessions and Letters of Augustin* [sic], *with a Sketch of his Life and Work*; Vol. 2: *Augustin: City of God, Christian Doctrine*; Vol. 3: *Augustin: On the Holy Trinity, Doctrinal Treatises, Moral Treatises*; Vol. 8: *Expositions on the Book of Psalms* (Peabody, MA: Hendrickson, 1994).

[5] J. H. Taylor, Jr. (translation, annotation), *St. Augustine: The Literal Meaning of Genesis* (New York, NY, and Ramsey, NJ: Newman Press, 1982) 87.

[6] Schaff, *Nicene and Post-Nicene Fathers,* 8:613.

[7] For these comments see Schaff, *Nicene and Post-Nicene Fathers,* 1:58–59; 2:387; 3:303; 8:193.

John Cassian

Another vital life-form in the early church contributes insight into Scripture somewhat differently.[8] The Egyptian desert monastic tradition (traceable from the early fourth century) fed hungrily on the Bible, seeking to be transformed by Scripture into women and men of deep relatedness with God and seeing God's authoritative word as its daily food and drink. The Bible was not primarily an object but a dialogue partner, not simply a site of interpretation but a quest to embody what was read. The early monks sought to derive particular and present meaning from ancient texts. The words of Scripture were to be learned "by heart," ruminated upon— aloud—and engaged while living; hearing was key as well, and surely doing. The monks' quest to make Scripture into their own flesh and bone both showed its utter efficacy and also made it shareable in the lives of others, since those who had absorbed it well were able to speak its richness to others. Constituted substantially by the constant murmuring the psalms in prayer, the desert quest for holiness was not characterized by novel modes of interpretation so much as by intensive appropriation in the desert terrain, which brought to the fore the sort of issues that a busy urban life can occlude. The early monks struggled with issues of anger, learned how to curb or reorder their desires, and trained daily in compassion—all amid extreme physical and social conditions of the *solitudo vastissima* which was harsh and dangerous, where choices were stark and illusions lethal. The desert tradition, valuing silence and using words sparingly, stressed the need to discern what words were appropriate for, fitted well into, just what situation. The biblical words were thus reset in fresh narratives, issuing from wise and experienced teachers. Meaning was not speculative but deeply experiential. Words were to be heard, savored, done.

John Cassian (360–430), traveling from Dacia to Bethlehem via Egypt, Constantinople, Rome, and Antioch, has left for our scrutiny two typically dialogical and word-reverencing works: the *Institutes* and the *Conferences* (which remained popular long after his day).[9] These genres called for Cassian and his typically silent friend and companion to seek

---

[8] Another exemplar of early monasticism, Brendan the Navigator, will be investigated below in Chapter 6.

[9] Columba Stewart, *Cassian the Monk* (New York and Oxford: Oxford University Press, 1998). See also Bernard McGinn and Patricia Ferris McGinn, *Early Christian Mystics: The Divine Vision of the Spiritual Masters* (New York: Crossroad, 2003) 59–75. For primary documents see Boniface Ramsey, trans. and annotations, *John Cassian: The Conferences* (New York and Mahwah: Paulist, 1997) and *John Cassian: The Institutes* (New York and Mahwah: Paulist, 2000).

wisdom from and listen attentively to their elders on topics classic in the ascetical life, with the conviction that careful attention to wise words is transformative. Hence the challenge was to the holiness of the interpreter, not to the obscurity of the text. Learning was no substitute for holiness; spiritual maturity came from praxis, not simply from study. The point was to attune ever more sensitively to God. Practical, contemplative, and spiritual knowledge were inseparable from each other, the one building on the other. Biblical heroes were examples to be known intimately, figures to be understood allegorically, ethical challenges to guide actions. The prophet Jonah works effectively to show the appropriation of the Scripture for early Christians who worried over whether their sins could be forgiven by God. Cassian told of such a query by a soldier to an Abba; the monk asked him if, when his cloak was torn, he threw it away, to which the soldier replied that of course he mended it and used it again. The teacher, drawing upon Jonah 4:10, replied, "If you are so careful about your cloak, will not God be equally careful about his creature?" Another tale of repentance would seem to have Jonah 1 as backdrop. A brother was once expelled from a monastery for being tempted; after a time, Abba Antony wanted him back, but his brothers refused to receive him. Antony posed them this narrative question: "A boat was shipwrecked at sea and lost its cargo; with great difficulty it reached the shore; but you want to throw into the sea that which has found safe harbor on the shore." Once they realized what Antony was teaching them, they accepted the man back into their midst.[10]

The Pre-Modern/Pre-Critical Period: The Middle Ages

There is substantial continuity between antiquity and the Middle Ages: a continued fascinated wrestling with the multiplicity of meaning in a text, a somewhat simplistic confidence in God's authoring of Scripture to the near-exclusion of human participation, and a commitment to the partnership of sanctity and study. The grounding assumptions remained constant: Scripture as God's word, given to human beings to facilitate understanding of and participation in the divine plan of salvation; minimal interest in and attention to biblical history as genuinely important in itself; the Old Testament as supposedly not so much about the dealings of God with Israel of the first millennium B.C.E. as concerned to tell in a sort of indirect code how God has dealt with the Christian community. The senses of Scripture were summed up in an efficient set of words that suggest the state of interpretation in the

---

[10] Douglas Buston-Christie, *The Word in the Desert: Scripture and the Quest for Holiness in Early Christian Monasticism* (New York and Oxford: Oxford University Press, 1993) 276.

period: *"Littera gesta docet, quid credas allegoria; moralis quid agas, quo tendas anagogia."*[11] A standard interpretive key was "Jerusalem": literally taught is Jerusalem as a city of the Jews; allegorically to be believed was that Jerusalem stands for the Church of Christ; morally addressed and exhorted for praxis was the human soul; and anagogically referenced was the heavenly homeland for which all were striving. Two Jonah-commentators allow us to glimpse both the continuity and certain vectors of change.

Hugh of St. Cher

Dominican Hugh of St. Cher (1190–1263) shows us continuity: doctor at Paris, a cardinal of the church, twice Provincial and eventually Vicar General of the Dominican Order. Hugh urged that Jonah be seen as a figure of Christ, and yet he cautioned that not every detail in the book ought be pushed to fit such a pattern. He moralizes a bit when talking about Jonah's declaration of being a God-fearer, finding fault with Jonah for an attitude more characterizing a slave than a son. Hugh sees Jonah's prayers from the whale as reminiscent of Jesus' cries to God while still among the dead; and he holds the whale itself as similar to the Red Sea, providing safe access for God's people and projects on a three-day schedule. Hugh also points out resonances between Jonah's prayer and various psalms (e.g., Psalms 15 and 87). He sees Jonah's sleep in the ship's hold as the sway of sin, which attempts to disregard God; the sheltering vine is Israel, shading the prophet as he awaits the conversion of the Gentiles. Hugh warns against any inference that the use of lots was condoned, and in general he exonerates Jonah of any misconduct, likening the prophet's anger to that of Jesus from the cross (e.g., Luke 23:46)—surely a stretch. Hugh's ease in correlating Jonah and Jesus at the level of discourse indicates that words themselves, rather than motif clusters or plot, remain quite central.[12]

Andrew of St. Victor

A distinctive school of exegesis and interpretation developed around a group of canons attached to a cathedral in Paris (established in 1110), a foundation that would lead ultimately to the universities emerging distinct from the monastic schools; with it we can associate Andrew of St. Victor

---

[11] Translated: The letter (literal level) teaches deeds; allegory (the allegorical level) is what one is to believe; the moral aspect (tropological level) is what is to be done; and the heavenly (anagogical) level is where all are tending.

[12] Bowers, *Legend of Jonah,* 56.

(d. 1175).[13] The Victorines opposed the medieval tendency to work primarily with exegetical commentary rather than with the biblical text itself. This practice, growing for some time before the twelfth century, was to focus upon the interpretative words (glosses and commentary) around the biblical text, which became almost—or functionally—canonical themselves. Like all ancient practitioners, the Victorines assumed that *lectio divina* (prayerful study and reflection on Scripture) was done to assist learning and charity; Andrew often punctuated his reflective studies of biblical texts with short prayers addressed to God.

Though he made the literal sense of the text the grounding for something else—and that meaning often christological—Andrew was quite remarkable for his interest paid to the literal sense itself. Not himself a skilled Hebraicist, Andrew relied on Jerome's texts with occasional disagreements about details, disputing Jerome more critically and originally than did many others; his Jonah insights, however, do not go beyond those of Jerome. Andrew studied with contemporary Hebrew scholars and was, comparatively speaking, appreciative of their interpretations. He was not particularly interested in theologizing or moralizing from the text, sticking rather with its plainer meaning when he could do so. His work on the prophets is unusual in its interest in the actual circumstances of their lives.[14] He did not deny predictive and christological relevance to figures like Jonah but was willing to consider more immediately Israelite contexts as well. Medieval scholars take care to stress that Andrew's interest does not exclude the spiritual, so he is not "rationalist" or "modern" in any sense. But his interest in the literal level overcomes the dichotomy that others of his era sometimes assumed between the literal and the spiritual, since Andrew held that words, events, and details open onto the transcendent and offer access to the presence of God.[15]

By the end of the period certain key shifts are discernible: First, the biblical text has survived the glossing procedure begun in earnest around the mid-eleventh century, but barely; the glosses on the Bible and lectures on those came near to being more important than the text. Second, though the

---

[13] Beryl Smalley, *The Study of the Bible in the Middle Ages* (3rd ed. Oxford: Basil Blackwell, 1983) 83–195. For St. Victor see also Steven Chase, *Contemplation and Compassion: The Victorine Tradition* (Maryknoll, NY: Orbis, 2003) 13–16.

[14] Andrew discussed how Jeremiah could claim that God had known him in the womb, querying what sort of relationship the expression implied; the Victorine decided that specific and detailed foreknowledge was not required, simply the sort of commitment that would see Jeremiah through a troubled ministry (and also release him early from the effects of original sin, Andrew supposed). When Andrew came to the passage in Isaiah 7 where the young woman was to conceive a son, Andrew found quite congenial the literal sense of the text: The prophet's wife will conceive and bear an eighth-century child.

[15] Chase, *Contemplation and Compassion,* 38–39.

processes of systematic philosophical thought are comparatively young, and their traces not so evident in the interpretive practices sampled here, still the seeds of the "divorce" between systematic exposition and biblical spirituality have been sown.[16] The new interpretive practice is far removed from the pitching of the text against the urgent circumstances of its practitioners that we saw with the desert monks. Third, under the double onslaught of philosophy and a renewed sense of the literal/historical meaning of text there began a slow erosion of the confident assumption that God was the author of the Bible in an uncomplicated way. Not without gain, this move nonetheless will produce, in time, an unease between the historical and religious senses of the Bible. In the long run scholastic philosophy is not compatible with allegorical reading, but the sway of allegory had become such that the split will not show up seriously for some time—perhaps not until the scholastic energy itself is all but spent. Fourth, it seems that the centuries-long discussions and debates over the ways in which meaning is present and may be extracted from texts has run its course and collapsed in exhaustion, with scholars reiterating rather than freshly rethinking the issues. Such conversations will not cease, but they will be more sterile on the whole. Finally, fifth, the professional matrix for biblical study has shifted from the houses of prayer to the halls of learning. Even if we populate those halls with the young candidates for priesthood whom Hugh of St. Cher addressed, to educate men for clerical careers—however benignly conceived—is not the same as learning the Bible "by heart" to draw ever-closer to God. All of these issues will explode in one way or another in the next era of Renaissance and Reformations, some running even into the modern period.

The Modern/Critical Period: Reformations

I have to assume that the periods of the European Renaissance and Reformations are familiar to you, since they resist ready summary here. The two exemplars selected—one Protestant and one Roman Catholic—are useful here primarily for what they say of Jonah; however, as we listen carefully to their words, the reform-linked and interpretive tug of war is discernible as a subtext.

---

[16] The primary catalyst for what is called scholastic philosophy and theology is Dominican Thomas Aquinas (1225–74). His thought cannot be included in this short essay, but see W.G.B.M. Valkenberg, *Words of the Living God: Place and Function of Holy Scripture in the Theology of St. Thomas Aquinas* (Leuven: Peeters, 2000); James A. Weisheipl, O.P., *Friar Thomas D'Aquino: His Life, Thought, and Work* (New York: Doubleday, 1974); Aidan Nichols, O.P., *Discovering Aquinas: An Introduction to His Life, Work, and Influence* (Grand Rapids and Cambridge: William B. Eerdmans Publishing Co., 2003).

Martin Luther

Martin Luther (1483–1546) spent his "Roman" years as an Augustinian monk, a doctor at the University at Wittenberg, and a commentator on Scripture. His early writings disclose struggles with a God who seemed to demand of him a near-impossible perfection, and with a stern and judgmental Jesus who found him always deficient in his efforts. Luther's question: How is any human being justified before God? His eventual insight: God does not expect humans to earn their salvation; rather, it is given gratuitously, as a mercy from God. Luther argued the necessity and possibility of a relationship of deep trust and interdependence between God and human beings rather than one based on threat and contestation. He struggled with and eventually left a church that promoted many things Luther had found most deleterious and false: an economy of indulgences, the impossibilities of penances often imposed, the zeal of certain authorities to uncover and extirpate heresy.

For Luther the Bible was God's word, spoken quite clearly on the whole, comprising one simple solid sense. It was to be read by all, studied, expounded in knowledgeable preaching, and of course experienced. Luther opposed a number of things in regard to Scripture: solipsistic mystical interpretations, allegorizing readings not specifically demanded by the text itself, scholastic methods and categories. But he also questioned the automatic value of patristic commentary, which seemed to him to have too great a grip on the quest for meaning. The Bible's authority was not rooted in the centuries of traditional interpretation or, of course, in a flawed ecclesiastical institution. The events of the Hebrew Scriptures anticipated Jesus, Luther held, and were important primarily in that regard, certainly not as events in themselves.

Luther preached and wrote on the book of Jonah, and his commentaries show his general teachings in a gracious genre.[17] Jonah functions for Luther as an exemplum of a sinner—fearful before God and determined to flee, but able to be brought to return as well and to acknowledge his own unworthiness. Jonah learned. He was also considered by Luther to be a powerful preacher, delivering an effective word—more effective a preacher than Jesus, Luther dared to say! As explicated by Luther, the small book also shows God: eager and active to effect the salvation of all peoples, gracious to all and

---

[17] Luther wrote twice on Jonah (1525 and 1526), but I will treat both texts here as simply his views on Jonah. Hilton C. Oswald, ed., *Luther's Works. Vol. 19: Lectures on the Minor Prophets: II: Jonah, Habakkuk*, trans. Charles D. Froehlich (1525) and Martin H. Bertram (1526) (St. Louis: Concordia Publishing House, 1982) 3–104.

merciful. The small book's reference to idolatrous sailors provides Luther occasion to comment on similarly hopeless works of various monks and nuns, and burden-imposing popes, by which they tortured themselves (and others!) in hopes of being saved. And yet, Jonah's confession in 1:9 was the start of his return to God. Luther speculates whether Jonah's flight was a sin, concluding that it was; Jonah did not deserve to be saved, but God cared for him nonetheless. Luther comments comparatively extensively on Jonah's reasons for initial flight: He did not wish to leave his family and homeland; he was afraid of the king of Nineveh, or disliked him; he feared both that his words would come true and that they would not; he thought God was only concerned with the Jews. Luther also speculates that Jonah must, with his bad conscience, have dreaded the fall of the lots.

The episode regarding the whale signifies for Luther God's capacity to save humans from anything; the reformer wondered whether the prophet expected he would be consumed in the great digestive system. The three-day sojourn elicits from Luther not a speculation on the relevance to Christ in the tomb but rather on utter reliance upon God and on the value of prayer. And yet Luther perhaps had this part of the story most in mind when he offers the following outburst in the midst of discussing Jonah's prayer: "That must have been a strange voyage. Who would believe this story and not regard it as a lie and a fairy tale if it were not recorded in Scripture?"[18] Utterly practical, Luther's comments on Jonah 3:3 include wonder about Nineveh's size— "great to God"—which Luther construes as meaning God was concerned about it. The fasting of the Ninevites occasions from Luther a discussion of works and grace, since some of his "sophist-like opponents" quoted the moment against him. Luther points out that works were not demanded by the prophet when he preached, nor by God, who sees the heart. Luther finds pointless all discussion about whether God can be said to change the divine mind. When speculating on Jonah's reactions in ch. 4, Luther's prescription is that the prophet—whom he at one point called "a queer and odd saint"— had basically underestimated God's power from the start and had, not to his credit, continued to resist God's gracious will; but God was able to rise above Jonah's deficiencies, indeed to deal with them generously as well.

Teresa of Avila

Roman Catholic Teresa of Avila (1515–1582) was a contemplative, a founder-reformer, a writer and poet, a teacher. She lived in Spain at a height of its temporal power and struggled with national and secular matters as well as

---

[18] Oswald, *Luther's Works,* 19:68.

with the issues within the Carmelite order, with which she was involved from the age of twenty-one. Her writing stresses Scripture's role in the transformation of the human person into God, the way in which humans enter as deeply as possible into the life and love of God. To live thus and to help others in their life toward God occupied Teresa in her activities and her writing, surely in her own prayer. God, Teresa experienced, is present to us all the time, and our part is to become more aware of this reality and allow it more and more to transform our lives. The fruits of such a growth will be evident in acts of love and service to others. *The Interior Castle,* produced toward the end of her life, describes the journey of the soul toward the King who dwells at its center.[19] It can exemplify for us her appropriation of OT texts for her broader purposes. As her address is intimate, so also her language is vivid and studded with images and analogies to help her make her insights clear to others. When drawing on the OT, her references remain allusive, since she counted on her readers/hearers to know the source and context of a given image. Assuming her interlocutors would follow, she recontextualizes the experience available from the brief referent for discussion of the journey toward God and the process of allowing God to dwell more intimately with us. Scripture grounded her experience and her writings thoroughly; though she excerpted snippets to sustain points, they were never detached from the whole.

Teresa does two things of note with Jonah. The first is traditional: She revolves briefly the question about Jonah's various fears in relation to the Ninevites, notably his concern that the city might not, even after the prophet's bold words, be destroyed. Her discussion, however, moves to discuss a basically unrelated point: various ways in which locutions need to be heeded by those who receive them, diverse traps in which such souls may be caught. The second reference is more original, though also rather ancillary to the issues of the Jonah story itself. Teresa describes to her readers the work of the worms, who feed on mulberry leaves and then spin the cocoons in which they die (metamorphose, we would say), so that what emerges is a creature transformed. It is a stunning image for the journey of the human toward God, and of course is nonbiblical. But Teresa follows it up with a brief reference to other worms, such as the one in Jonah 4:6-7, which under cover of night gnawed its way through Jonah's protection. Somewhat out of context for the book and making the opposite point from the silkworm image, she speaks of the worm analogously to the way in which virtues can be destroyed by the "worms" of self-love, self-esteem, a judgmental spirit, lack of love.[20]

---

[19] Kieran Kavanaugh, O.C.D., intro. and trans.; Otilio Rodriguez, O.C.D., intro. Preface by Raimundo Panikkar, *Teresa of Avila: The Interior Castle* (New York: Paulist, 1979).

[20] Kavanaugh and Rodriguez, *Teresa of Avila,* 122, 99–100.

My hunch is that these "early moderns" do not sound particularly modern to you, a point with which I would not disagree. And yet Luther's resistance to much of the authoritative tradition and Teresa's fresh and indeed brilliant appropriations of Scripture signal a new road ahead, where virtually all the pre-critical ideas will be called into serious question.

The Modern/Historical-Critical Period: Early Phase

Though critical reflection on the Bible has its roots entwined with the Renaissance and Reformations, we can recognize it more clearly when we see overt interest in rational causes of things, an absorption in history and facticity, and a keen sense of analytical process. Our last two exemplars of Jonah commentary come from early Modernism—that is, from the eighteenth and nineteenth centuries. Their writing is imbued with a historical awareness that has been absent before this moment, and you will detect struggle to reconcile religion with the rationalism that characterizes the modern period.

Jonathan Edwards

Edwards (1703–1758) was a Congregationalist minister, a scholar and preacher, briefly president of what would become Princeton University, and actively involved in the Great Awakening of the mid-eighteenth century in North America.[21] Though deeply conversant with the nascent Modern period and its issues, he remained committed to a more classical vision of biblical matters, showing a primarily rearguard action on behalf of ideas whose time had actually passed. Edwards struggled over the implications of some of the ideas he articulated: cautious and conserving about what was being challenged, intensely aware of what might be swept away too quickly. But his erudition, honesty, and powerful articulation make him important for insight into the factors of the struggle of the Modern period with its antecedents.

Edwards had a conversion experience as a young man, and his life project was to communicate to others the possibility and urgency of experiencing a glorious Divine Being whose powerful purposes unfolded harmoniously with all creation. For him, God was at the center of all that exists and needed to be acknowledged as sovereign in every realm of culture. He was convinced of and eager to show the basic compatibility of biblical religion with

---

[21] For the life and work of Jonathan Edwards see Robert E. Brown, *Jonathan Edwards and the Bible* (Bloomington: Indiana University Press, 2002), and George M. Marsden, *Jonathan Edwards: A Life* (New Haven and London: Yale University Press, 2003).

the currents of his day. He sensed the need to correlate historical and scientific matters with religious ones, seeing them all as rooted in epistemology—the way in which humans come to know what we know. He concluded that, though the Bible was not known and understood with a naïve immediacy, it was not thereby to be jettisoned as completely unreliable. Recognizing the inadequacy of its historical framework (biblical creation and fall, redemption and the expectation of an eschatological finish), he continued to insist upon the biblical schema's basic relevance. The key question for him was how to re-articulate a deeply and authentically biblical vision with the presuppositions of his own age as they were emerging from the mouths and pens of various opponents—notably for him, those Christians who undermined Calvinist tenets (e.g., radical human sinfulness and need for God) and Deists (allowing God a merely absentee or even passive role in human affairs). Edwards' challenge was great, since the presuppositions of the era favored the rationally discernible over what was merely asserted, grounded authoritatively, and humanly inexplicable.

The issues perhaps clearest to discuss here are not the basic philosophical ones or the emergent scientific ones but certain historical matters.[22] Edwards considered it important for the Bible to be able to show itself historically respectable, and the criteria by which it needed to do so were fairly clear. The matters of historicity had to be enjoined at several levels, and we can pose from Edwards' work the key questions. At the textual level: Are manuscripts and readings reliable? At a more abstract level of reliability, philosophy, almost cosmology: How can certain matters in the Bible be shown congruent with rational science and thought? How is faith linked with scholarship, revelation with epistemology? The truth of any narrative, including the Bible, was now closely bound up with factual historicity. Could biblical scholarship show that the named authors were in fact the writers, and hence reliable authorities, or were such works forgeries? Were the said authors in a position to know the things of which they wrote, so that they could claim the rights of eyewitnesses? Had they themselves experienced the matters of which they wrote? Or had they, perhaps, worked with reliable archival material, so with empirical evidence of some sort—documents, monuments—that later scholars might access as well? Could their works be corroborated by other documents? Was there any correlation between other religions—especially ancient Near Eastern ones—and the Bible? Could the narratives themselves sustain the sort of incipiently rigorous scrutiny that was the lot of all other documents, ancient ones in particular?

---

[22] Robert Brown, *Jonathan Edwards,* ch. 4, discusses these at some length, not simply Edwards' view but that of the era.

Edwards studied Scripture his whole life and wrote on it, though typically in notebooks rather than finished pieces.[23] One of his basic hermeneutical struggles was the correlation of the two testaments, and one of his chosen strategies was typology, a classic mode that the Modern period was struggling to transcend. Edwards adopted it as a mean between the excessive literalism of some of his peers and the egregious allegorizing of his forebears, maintaining that the strategy itself was Bible-based and hence legitimated from within (in contrast with contemporaries who insisted it was not one of the meanings inherent in the Hebrew Bible text). Edwards extended the interpretive process to the natural world itself, again urging that to speak in types—or better, in symbols—was one of God's accustomed ways of communication. Thus not only biblical persons, events, or things were disclosive of God—often specifically of Christ—but nature was as well, assisting the imagination to a deeper apprehension of God's being and workings. Related: Edwards preached with vivid metaphors that also helped his hearers to ponder imaginatively the words of Scripture Edwards was expounding, and to the divine meaning he held was contained within such words. His comments on Jonah are in this vein: The ship and sailors are like the church, saved by one who was himself plunged into sorrows, swallowed by death and hell for three days before emerging victoriously.[24] Edwards thus offers a sort of Janus-like view of the biblical text, in one instance bravely looking to the issues of verification demanded by his era but also inclining back in time to note a basis for the OT's ability to speak usefully for Christians.

E. B. Pusey

The work of Anglican priest and scholar Edward Bouverie Pusey (1800–1886) brings us even more solidly into the Modern period. His relevant context is England's Oxford Movement of the nineteenth century.[25] The movement, which sprang from and was named for that university in the 1830s, was concerned to revitalize Anglican presence in England by re-sorting what we might call issues of how the sacred and secular can best interface. Hoping to avoid the excesses of both Roman Catholic monarchism and Protestant congregationalism, the reformers of England's established

---

[23] Conrad Cherry, "Symbols of Spiritual Truth: Jonathan Edwards as Biblical Interpreter," *Interpretation* 39 (1985) 263–71, characterizes this aspect of Edwards more succinctly than do the longer works on Edwards' thought.

[24] S. J. Stein, ed., *Jonathan Edwards: Notes on Scripture* (New Haven: Yale University Press, 1998) 78.

[25] For some background on the Oxford Movement consult George Herring, *What Was the Oxford Movement?* (London and New York: Continuum, 2002).

church wanted to see clear and visible ecclesiastical commitment on the key issues of the day (e.g., on Catholic emancipation and effects of industrialization), to maintain an established position (and not dissolve into small units of individual believers), to preserve ecclesial and episcopal structures (rather than splinter into de-centered entities). By turns "liberal" and "conservative," the movement took various stands, which were rehearsed in its organ of information, *Tracts for the Times,* written by various individuals, running to many pages, and securing eventually a wide readership.

Pusey provides us with some writings on Jonah, a commentary prefaced by a more general discussion of urgent issues of the day.[26] The prefatory remarks are more valuable to show the viewpoint of the era, while the commenting notes rely on traditional points more comfortably. Pusey begins by explaining Jonah's historical context: eighth-century Israel. He talks briefly about the natural religion of Jonah's sailor companions, a matter of some interest by then in the center of the British empire. He maintains Jonah as author of the book, observing that all major and minor prophets wrote of themselves in the third person. Pusey praises the form of the book, and opines that no one beyond criticism's babyhood would be bothered with issues rising from the book of Jonah—perhaps a whistling in the dark to disguise some evident nervousness. He assesses by eight criteria that Jonah is a good, simple, well-written narrative.[27]

The miracles in the book are reliable, e.g., the survival of Jonah within the fish, because they were narrated at the time by an eyewitness: the prophet himself. Were they not true, they would not have been included, Pusey argues. He observes that the eighth-century Hebrews were simple folk who knew little of maritime matters or of the ways of sea creatures, but he brings forward as well a piece published in 1758 that told of how a large fish almost devoured a human being. His point is both to counter, with contemporary and reliable evidence, any who found the Jonah tale incredible and also to reinforce the confidence of those who believed its testimony. The book also advanced historical knowledge, Pusey claims, and is presented realistically. For example, it makes utter sense that, tired from a hard journey, Jonah would go below-deck for a nap. Once overboard and swallowed, Jonah would easily articulate the psalm-like prayer of Jonah 2, familiar as he would have been with the Hebrew psalter. Again the note of authenticity: Only one who has suffered as we can imagine Jonah did would be able to recite such a prayer.

---

[26] E. B. Pusey, *The Minor Prophets: A Commentary,* vol. 1 (Grand Rapids: Baker Books, 1950) 371–427.

[27] These points occur in no particularly clear order in Pusey's preface, pp. 371–80; they are in certain instances ramified a bit in the commentary itself.

Pusey amplifies certain points that Jonah, authoring his biblical book, did not tell us: e.g., details about Nineveh available from later historical researches. The commentary contains a map of Nineveh, information on who the Assyrians were, speculations on the name of the city's responsive ruler, and a biological drawing of the plant that temporarily sheltered Jonah, identified as *ricinus communis*. Pusey also comments on the animal sackcloth as not so very different from the customs of others who clothe animals on special occasions. Pusey misses Jonah's explanations of his own anger with God, which the Englishman supposes rises from the prophet's knowledge of what God was planning to do and what the Assyrians themselves would do to harm Israel between late-eighth and late-seventh centuries. For Pusey the deity in the story is powerful and providential. God provides what is needed: a storm, a fish, a plant, a wind. The Western classics, Pusey reminds his readers, have many similar motifs: Ovid's tales, for example, with humans, monsters, and various transformations. But, he breaks off: None of these reaches is necessary, since the psalms themselves testify to such phenomena. Jesus quotes the book, which enhances its reliability and the confidence all ought to have in God's protective presence.

With those points established preliminarily, and in a number of cases repeated and expanded in the commentary notes, we may observe a few of Pusey's other kinds of concerns, which he mixes—without apparent discomfort—amid the more historical and scientific assertions. In notes to Jonah 1, Pusey speculates on the reasons for the prophet's refusal to obey, raising both a tendency he notes for the Jews to disregard their prophets (cf. the responsive Ninevites) and the possibility that Jews fear the consequences for themselves once God begins to deal mercifully with Gentiles. Pusey reflects at some length on this matter of human struggles to obey God in face of a clear human propensity like Jonah's to disobey. He also discourses on God's power over nature, human beings, and even dice, noting (with St. Augustine) that there might be rare occasions when lots would be licit. Jonah 2 occasions from the Oxford scholar the observation that it is Jonah's suffering that makes him similar to Jesus, though Pusey also notes that one of them embraced his struggles more willingly than the other. General comments on human suffering are supplemented both by a quotation from St. Irenaeus and by citation of an item from the London *Times*. But the Englishman also offers us access to the dispositions of the fish, which he says swallowed Jonah unwillingly and released him with the same disposition. His comments on Jonah 3 detail specifics of the manner in which the Ninevite king brought his people—and animals—to effective repentance and discusses the various factors of the prophetic pronouncement itself: what was intended by God, said by Jonah, heard by the Ninevites, and ultimately effected. That Jesus approved the repentance of these Assyrians indicates, for Pusey, its remarkable nature. The last chapter is taken up with considerations of Jonah's anger, God's patience dealing with it, and the challenges other angry souls face in conforming to God's will.

We can see in Pusey's writing the urgent questions of the era: How is the (Hebrew) Bible and its recital of sacred deeds reliable? meaningful? If Edwards' typology is not the way for the deeds of God to seem coherent, what was that way? Pusey's words on Jonah suggest that the book's value rested on its relevance, plausibility, and authenticity. The biblical words needed to be and could be certified as reliable by reference to history. But once those issues have been set forth prefatorily, the commentary itself returns to what we can call general religious or spiritual questions as well, mixing them with apparent ease amid matters of geography, climate, botany, ichthyology, and natural religion. That the Bible was meaningful many continued to assert; the question was to explain how. A literal level became increasingly lexical and grammatical, historical and factual, with other more "theological" points earnestly asserted as though they were obvious. Pusey's work is not bereft of religious meaning, but he asserts it without much evident concern for methodological basis. Biblical theology of a certain sort would step in here, struggling but uncomfortably to bridge the gap between the historical and the religious.

The high modern period is more familiar to us, since we have lived in it ourselves. And it is well represented in some of the discussions ahead of us here: Chapter 3 will include brief reference to psychological interpretation; Chapter 4 will draw on contemporary historiography; Chapter 5 will discuss the fresh appreciation for the literary and reader-centered aspects of the Bible. The purpose of this chapter, selecting nine representative scholars out of Jonah's long and rich interpretive past, has been to suggest some trends, some emphases, some convictions, and some procedures that can help us accomplish more fully our own project of doing meaning with Jonah.

CHAPTER THREE

Locating Biblical Jonah Historically

Now that we have laid groundwork for our study—named our itinerary, set up some frameworks, and sampled the astonishing diversity of what other readers have done—we are ready to look more deeply and carefully at the Jonah story itself. I hope you carried away from the previous chapter of this book the impression that, although specifically historical questions and workings were not valued much until recently, modern scholars have lately promoted such inquiries, to make up for neglect! And I trust you got the sense that, after a couple of centuries of steadfast historical work, the tide is turning once again to some of the "old" language- and literature-related topics neglected recently while history has had its innings; some fresh questions about reading and readers have emerged as well. The best of contemporary biblical criticism tries to make integrated use of the kinds of questions and pursuits relevant to what it wishes to know, utilizing whatever is needed. A byproduct of such a situation is the admission—implicit or explicit—that definitive studies that "do it all" are neither possible nor desirable. Another gleaning of our long study of other interpreters was the recognition that readers can only really ask the questions that are part of their imaginative world and track them with the tools at hand. Even if we seem now to go back to some classic questions, our available tools and insights render our interpretive task quite fresh and distinctive to our post-modern selves. All reading is located.

Our Current Project

My hope for this chapter is to ask some "new" historical questions and to probe them with the assistance of "new" literary methods and contemporary interpretive strategies.[1] We will showcase the work of a skilled

---

[1] I have placed quotation marks around those words to indicate that though there are technical efforts called "New Historicism" and "New Criticism," I am not engaging those here.

Hebrew Bible historian, Ehud Ben Zvi.[2] His book on Jonah is neither a commentary nor a monograph but a collection of essays that achieve a rough coherence when edited together between a pair of covers rather than speaking their various minds from diverse places. The work is rich in bibliographic suggestions where various points can be followed up by those with interests Ben Zvi does not have time or space to detail. In that sense the book is a tangible reminder that every effort of interpretation is partial and that every reader needs to draw together what works for him or her, abandoning any illusion of completeness or even substantial adequacy.

My questions for us, influenced by those pursued by Ben Zvi though not restricted to his, are the following: *Who were the original and intended readers of the Jonah story—those for whom the story was constructed to work well? How will they have read and reread the story: with what processes and what outcomes? What will their reading and interpretive conventions have been and what consequent insights are they likely to have drawn from their engagement with the narrative? Why will they have been responsive to the prompts that influenced their reading? And how will their reading of this book, with its various features and in the circumstances pertaining when they read, have influenced their meaning-making?* These are all questions about which Ben Zvi is explicit. But I have some additional questions that he leaves largely implicit in his book, partly since he has dealt with them on other occasions: *How can we now know who the intended readers were, can we hypothesize how and why they read, and in what set of ways can we begin to unsnarl the many possibilities with which they can plausibly have been presented?* Put a bit differently: *Is it likely that we, at least two millennia later and living in such a wholly different world from any early Jonah readers, can get at their interests?* And most important: *Why should we want to do so even if we think it is possible? What is the gain for our reading to have known how the most ancient of the Jonah readers read the story?* If you think back to our frameworks for a moment, you will recognize their structure from our Chapter 1: *How will we, now, query the processes of certain of the composers of Scripture? And how does the world behind the text make its contribution to our knowledge? How does the narrative itself guide us? And to what extent is our reading more our own than it is ever likely to be theirs?* These "worlds" will criss-cross, making their appropriate contributions. Our frameworks will help us keep track of what we are doing.

Because the task of this chapter is complex, let me try another analogy from U.S. history and from our likely shared experience before we turn

---

[2] Ehud Ben Zvi, *Signs of Jonah: Reading and Rereading in Ancient Yehud* (Sheffield: Sheffield Academic Press, 2003). He characterizes his book on pp. 3, 11–12.

back to the much more mysterious and unknown biblical story. Having already drawn on the Civil War and its battle of Gettysburg, let me shift a bit to draw our interpretive skills to address a film that is set—though of course not produced—in that same era: *Gone With the Wind.* I am going to assume you have seen or can easily view that film in order to assist with reading Jonah. First, we can and must ask many kinds of historical questions about the mid-nineteenth century when the Civil War was fought; in some cases we can learn what we seek, though our insight is liable to fall somewhat short of complete, no matter how skilled we may in time become. I could list the sorts of historical questions we would need to investigate, but so can you by now! And we will need to inquire into the making of the film, so that we can get an accurate sense of when, why, and for whom it was produced. Of course this is not a narrow question, at least in terms of the movie we are thinking of. We can know that it was produced in the 1930s for U.S. audiences. But we will need additionally to ask: for white people? for African-Americans? for rich people or for poor? I think we will easily and correctly conclude that the film was for whites rather than for blacks and for affluent audiences, not the indigent. We can next ask how the film details the story of Civil War Atlanta, what the intended audience is "supposed" to see, think, react to. To paint in broad strokes simply to clarify the point: Is the film meant to be a model for race relations, or a feminist manifesto, perhaps a study in nonviolence? I think we can say no, those are not its purposes or effects on most of its intended viewers.[3]

We can scrutinize the "story world" of the film, its component persons and events, ask whether they are accurate to history or not. We may conclude, after significant study, that many of them are not very historically precise, but they exist in a powerfully conceived and visualized narrative and so become believable, "true," whether or not they are accurate. The film tells a story of the Civil War, regardless of facticity. And we can pick up some strands of it readily: The resourceful Scarlett O'Hara is more admirable than the noble but dispirited Ashley Wilkes, and the South's future will build on her and not on him. The (ex-)slaves we come to know best side with their (former) "owners," suggesting that slavery was not so bad after all. The Ku Klux Klan is to be thought of as an understandable effort by vanquished and desperate southern men to protect their families from evils unloosed from the North once the war was over. There are many details we could underline that build up these rather baldly-stated "literary" or story-world features of the

---

[3] Information on the film can be found in Herb Bridges and Terry C. Boodman, *Gone With the Wind: The Definitive Illustrated History of the Book, the Movie, and the Legend* (New York: Simon and Schuster/Fireside, 1989) ix, 3–7, 24, 40, 187–204.

film. Other viewers than the original or intended audience will construe matters differently, but that is another subject for study. If we are interested in the original groups to whom the film was most sympathetically addressed, we need to understand how they will have responded and why. We could get that information, though it would require some tracking.

But it may be quite difficult for any of us, now, to undertake to study sympathetically the original circumstances of the film: the tragic story of the war over slavery and federal union, the unfortunate debacle of Reconstruction, the persistent blight of racism so thoroughly embedded in a society that steadfastly resists looking at evidence of it, to this very day. We may decide that the past forty or so years make *Gone With the Wind* so obscene, so harmful to our health, that we cannot go back prior to our experience of the Civil Rights era, which at least partially opened the eyes of U.S. citizens, and that we are thus unable to bring adequate understanding either to the production of the film or to the reactions of its first viewers. Such a thing is impossible and in any case undesirable, we may conclude. Or, alternatively, we may decide to use the film to disclose the racism of the 1930s as well as of the 1860s, perhaps even our own times and our participation in race relations. But in any case, the viewpoint we are exercising is primarily our own twenty-first-century angle, whatever it is, and the interests we are pursuing are substantially our own rather than those of earlier eras. I hope this analogy reminds you of the framework we developed in our Chapter 1: past/present emphases to be balanced, and three worlds to be queried: behind, within, and in front of the text. When we map our Jonah issues onto that hypothetical interpretive quest we find ourselves facing a vast and interlocking, mutually constructing and reinforcing set of interpretive factors. If we must settle for provisional readings, even with a fairly recent film about an era of history on which there is vast data, all the more when the material at hand is more sparse.

The project of this chapter is to consider what we can of the historical circumstances that are plausibly part of the production and reception of the book in its first circumstances. The work of Ben Zvi will offer us some good possibilities about these things. It will also show us suitable and sophisticated contemporary historical methodology, which has traveled far since the struggles of the early and even late modernists we sampled in the chapter previous to this one. We will be able to observe the skill with which a biblical scholar makes use of literary and reader-oriented strategies even to deal with thoroughly historical questions. These first two projects will rely substantially on Ben Zvi. But additionally we will ask why such information—either the process or the result—is important, necessary, salutary for our contemporary selves. Ben Zvi self-identifies as an historian of ancient Israel, so his project makes perfect sense for him.[4] But I venture that none of us can make that claim. *So why do we need to know about the reception of Jonah in Persian Yehud?*

(Re-)constructing Pertinent Historical Data for the Book's Production

Our first step will be to get from this very learned scholar an accurate sense of some of the information he wishes to communicate to us. The task is made slightly more complex than it might otherwise be, since we are dealing with nine somewhat overlapping essays rather than with a book that builds its argument rather more deliberately and efficiently. But his chosen genre simply gives an opportunity to read more attentively and to resist too simple a conclusion from what he says!

Ben Zvi's Questions

Of his many questions several are most persistent and hence foundational.[5] First: How does the book of Jonah offer access to material relevant to the historical study of ancient Israel? Second: Why do prophetic books like Jonah exist, and what basic work do they accomplish? Third: How do they do it? Specifically, how does the composite identity of Jonah (including both his mention in 2 Kings and in the book named for him) function for a rich set of rereading possibilities for its intended audience?[6] Fourth: How did the original or intended audience read: with what assumptions, strategies, expectations, and results? Fifth: What could they learn from the book—and what can we much later readers suppose they learned? Sixth: How did the intended audience see and challenge themselves, not so much as individuals but as a class? And finally, seventh, Ben Zvi asks how interpretation works with such consistency, generally speaking, as well as with not inconsiderable variety.[7]

Ben Zvi's Foundational Assumptions

The book, like any, builds on assumptions both implicit and explicit. Though it is not always immediately clear which points are assumptions to

---

[4] Ben Zvi, *Signs of Jonah,* 3, 5.

[5] These are derived mainly from *Signs of Jonah,* ch. 1, which serves as an introduction to the whole set of explorations, though they are nuanced at other places in the book as well.

[6] This question about Jonah's complex characterization is perhaps the one that is unpacked most thoroughly at various places in *Signs of Jonah*'s several chapters.

[7] See *Signs of Jonah,* ch. 9.

be taken for granted and which are theses to unpack and demonstrate—since these categories cannot be hermetically separated—I will attempt to make a suitable division here. Key among his explicit assumptions are again seven: Ben Zvi assumes, with relatively little discussion, first, that the book of Jonah as we have it is basically a product of post-exilic Persian Judah/Yehud (i.e., of the mid-sixth to mid-fourth centuries B.C.E.).[8] He suggests that Israel's experience of exile was a watershed event, such that life *with* kings before the exile to Babylon would have been quite different from life *without* them once the community had resettled in the land.[9] He also claims, second, that the "name of the game" is rereading, rather than initial reading.[10] This is a valuable point, since the key challenge of classics is not to dazzle with a first cleverness but to continue to sustain readers who come to know them quite well. Related but deserving special mention is, third: What will make such a familiar narrative continue to be effective is not only its authority but also its felt relevance for readers—and that feature is itself a product of many factors. The relevance is not abstract but urgent and particular.[11] And fourth, among factors of pertinence will be a sort of "limited strangeness," odd enough to catch the eye of its audience but not so bizarre that it can be easily dismissed as foolish and meaningless.[12] A book like Jonah thus, fifth, shapes its readership, but their needs and expectations also help determine the book. So the expectations and *mores* of narrative and audience are mutually constructing.[13] We can make some progress in discerning some of these tangled facets of the book by attending carefully to various of its linguistic cues. Since, sixth, the production of books is always costly, we should assume that this work will serve the interests of those whose resources sustain "book-making."[14] Ben Zvi asserts that the book of Jonah will have been assumed by its Judean readers to provide reliable information about God's ways, for example, God's basic control over events.[15] Though Ben Zvi often uses the word "message," a term I find unhelpful in the extreme, he nonetheless is clear that, seventh, what is gained

---

[8] *Signs of Jonah,* 5–7, 50, 82, 93–94, 116, 127–28.

[9] Noted in *Signs of Jonah,* 9.

[10] This emphasis is explored often, e.g., *Signs of Jonah,* 9, 32–33.

[11] *Signs of Jonah,* 3, 9–10, and really *passim.*

[12] Ben Zvi initiates this discussion in *Signs of Jonah,* 2, and refers to it repeatedly (pp. 81–89, 96), taking care to help us negotiate what would be slightly odd to the audience under consideration in this book.

[13] See *Signs of Jonah,* 2–3 and 31–33, 65–79, 98, 109, 113–15.

[14] This point is taken up in *Signs of Jonah,* 4–7, and 116, 130, and developed in various ways.

[15] *Signs of Jonah,* 4, 18, 29, 134–35, and the whole of ch. 3.

from rereading and reflection is insight, not some simple apophthegm.[16] There is, rather, a series of possibilities available from the narrative, depending on choices made. A plurality of voices, a textual polyvalence, is part of the basic nature of biblical narrative, and any attempt to reduce it to even a few clear points should be resisted. But the narrative is not endlessly open to any construction one might wish to derive.[17]

Among implicit assumptions is Ben Zvi's conviction that he is able to reconstruct the mindset of the first Jonah rereaders, and also his sense that if we do not bother to "meet" and come to know this first readership or make imprecise assumptions about them, we are likely to misinterpret at least some of the book; hence careful historical work is part of our responsibility.[18]

Ben Zvi's Theses

The thesis, as you know from your own writing, is the main point to be argued. In a taut and trim monograph, the thesis should be able to be stated in a couple of sentences, even if the book takes many pages to unpack it. In Ben Zvi's collection of articles I think there are several thesis points, all harnessed to shed light on a particular facet of exilic Israel: its infrastructure of interpretation. First: The book exists and functions to socialize, educate, and challenge in a particular way its readership, which, as stated above, is the literati of Persian Yehud.[19] A second thesis is that *a,* if not *the* major "spring" in the Jonah story is the fate of Nineveh, actually two fates, operative concurrently: The story of Jonah indicates the city was spared when the prophet preached and the citizenry repented; but the book's intended readership will know as well that Nineveh was destroyed and not rebuilt.[20] Packed within this thesis is more than simple facticity—Nineveh thrives or

---

[16] "Message" is part of the popular religious language used about the Bible, with the assumption—explicit or implicit—that biblical material is readily reducible to pious platitudes or moral maxims, gleaned and offered by the one speaking. It is a vastly reductionistic enterprise pursued with minimal process or controls. You might listen to the next ten homilies you hear and count how many "messages" you are offered as coming from biblical texts. Ben Zvi explains in *Signs of Jonah,* ch. 9, where "message" is a product of what author, main narrative characters, and recipients of the book understand in a more complex way.

[17] *Signs of Jonah,* 10, 28–33; chs. 2–5 demonstrate certain possibilities implicit in this claim that the book's language offers multiple legitimate pathways for reading, each with its own set of implications: multiple, but not arbitrary.

[18] This is one of the places to see the difference from pre-critical studies, which virtually ignored the question of the book's intended readers, assuming rather that meaning was universal.

[19] See his discussion in *Signs of Jonah,* 5–7, 50, 82, 93–94, 116, 127–28.

[20] The point is made many times in *Signs of Jonah,* e.g., ch. 2 in fullest detail but also on 111–15.

does not—but a tangle of theological assertions about God and God's ways. God knows or does not know the future? God controls events or does not? God is merciful or inclined toward reprisal? God is changeable or not? God communicates rather adequately with prophets or does not? For Ben Zvi these are vital issues to be pondered as the story is reread by the group for whom it was produced.[21] A third thesis unpacked at length is that—and how—the very complex and somewhat subtle characterization of the figure Jonah is the key to how readers will read. The book functions as a study of how prophets (and surrogates) work, and the figure of central interest in the book is Jonah, not the Ninevites or the sailors, as so many other commentators have supposed.[22] Fourth: The book of Jonah is a meta-study of prophecy, not abstractly, but featuring Jonah and his adventures. Recognizable as a prophetic book, it also functions as a key for understanding prophecy and other prophetic books.[23] What is prophecy when uttered? Does the prophet necessarily understand "his own" utterance, or might he mistake it and bungle the process rather egregiously? A fifth thesis to be unpacked is the specific self-image of post-exilic Yehud and its leadership, the particular "hooks" upon which that group's reading will hang: notably their own identity as "brokers" of the word of God, different in some ways from a "pre-exilic" prophet like Jonah, but (un)comfortably resonant as well.[24]

Constructing the Fit: The Book of Jonah and Its Intended Audience

Ben Zvi's Method/ology for Explaining and Sustaining His Theses

We will now work with evidence submitted by Ben Zvi, though I have supplemented it from elsewhere in his writings and rearranged it to make it

---

[21] See *Signs of Jonah,* chs. 3–5, though again, the point is explored throughout the book.

[22] Again, it is easy enough to see how interpreters who assume unproblematically that their own sense of things was intended by the author—or the Author—can make a too simple deduction here. It is only when particular readers have become important and scholarly confidence in universals has reduced that we can proceed in a different way. It is perhaps cautionary that Gentiles tend to focus on the sailors and the Ninevites and to valorize them often contrastively with Jonah or "the Jews" who are only implicit in the book; Jewish readers are typically not so interested in Gentile reactions! Note: The communication of the story is not determined by or restricted to its originating audience, but nor is that group irrelevant, as has been long supposed.

[23] *Signs of Jonah,* 10–11 and 80–98.

[24] The best summary of this point is in Ben Zvi's *Signs of Jonah,* ch. 7, though markers of the group's identity are sprinkled elsewhere as well. See also his "Introduction: Writings, Speeches, and the Prophetic Books—Setting an Agenda," in *Writings and Speech in Israelite and Ancient Near Eastern Prophecy* (Atlanta: Society of Biblical Literature, 2000) 1–29.

communicate a bit more assertively. The project, as you will recall, is to tease out *the*—or *a plausible*—set of mutually-constructing relations between what the text permits and what the intended audience ostensibly needs and wants to consider. Ben Zvi is a historian, and his methodology in this book is to discern, or suggest, the fit between the first or intended readers he hypothesizes and the Jonah character he urges they are given for negotiation. It is that process we will look at.

Summary of Ben Zvi's Intended Audience:
Identity, Concerns, Reading Processes

Ben Zvi has already announced, on the basis of earlier published work, that the Jonah audience is the literate leadership of post-exilic Judah (i.e., Persian Yehud), specifically of Jerusalem. What can be known about that group? Their composite identity includes several features. First, it is a mixed community, comprising those who experienced exile in Babylon and those who did not.[25] They live in a Jerusalem much shrunk from monarchic times, perhaps from 25,000 to 1,500 or fewer persons.[26] The community centers around the worship of YHWH within the Jerusalem Temple.[27] As sketched, this group is signally shaped by the experience of exile and its ramifications—not simply by the experience of "being in Babylon," since not all will have been there, but all are radically shaped by the experience of devastation of their "nation," a trauma not wholly overcome.[28] These "literati" are so named by Ben Zvi because they, within their group, can read. He says: "In Yehud, prophetic and other written texts were composed, redacted, studied, stored, read and reread by the literati of the period as YHWH's word and teaching."[29] Their role and responsibility, additionally, was to "broker" the word of God from written texts. These leaders bear the main charge of producing such texts: to compose, redact, and edit them, to read and reread them, to explain and teach them. Ben Zvi calls them "animators" of the community's tradition, an accumulation that at that time is coming to exist in written form.[30]

---

[25] Ehud Ben Zvi, "What's New in Yehud? Some Considerations," in Rainer Albertz and Bob Becking, eds., *Yahwism after the Exile: Perspectives on Israelite Religion in the Persian Era* (Assen: Van Gorcum, 2003) 36–37. Not every scholar is as sanguine about such a mix as he, but for the moment his view can stand, since it is not immediately relevant to our Jonah project.

[26] "What's New," 42–44.

[27] "What's New," 36–44.

[28] "What's New," 36–37.

[29] "What's New," 45.

[30] *Signs of Jonah,* 10–12, 62, 91, 100–06.

The main concerns for the literati, as Ben Ziv constructs them, are three. First, he suggests that no earlier group can have been so "grasped" by exile experience as the people of the late-sixth-century community.[31] The cataclysmic defeat and humiliation suffered by city, community, temple, leaders, and even deity in the early sixth century, culminating in exile, is not easily transcended, but remains live and painful. That the community has "returned" and re-established itself in Jerusalem does not resolve the many issues compacted in the experience. Jerusalem and its leadership—accused and guilty of many things, repenting and reversing but not effectively in the short run—is now reinstated. A "wrath-deserving city" was overturned, and then the overturning itself overturned. More practically: how is such a negative experience to be avoided in the future? Can a rerouted and reversed fate itself be overturned? Might a misreading of God's character and actions lead to another such catastrophe? Will God's people relapse?[32] Second, of signal concern was their relationship with the past, specifically the matter of failed or flawed leadership, the clear assertion of the heritage that even the best of the heroes from the past can be said to have failed in some way.[33] Third, the matter of prophecy itself: How are God's purposes to be discerned and embodied by all citizens, not simply the elites? If communication is not unequivocal and direct, then how is it to occur? Once the community's traditions are preserved in and on-call from written texts, then to know about such texts is necessary but perhaps not quite sufficient. Put slightly differently: If the brokers of God's word are no longer prophets who received clear commissions, how will such intermediaries manage the process of communicating and enabling divine purposes? Is it enough to have texts at one's fingertips, so to speak, to be able to cite them as wanted? So the question, which we can sense as ever-ripe, is that of the nature of prophecy in its widest sense of intermediation between God and the cosmos. Here Ben Zvi observes well that we need not call the intended audience of Jonah "prophets." It is enough that they share some responsibility for the communication of God's word, as indeed we know others, like the priests, will have as well. If the question is not pondered abstractly, but concretely, then a story about a quirky prophet will be apt. The Jonah narrative, at least at the surface, clothes itself not so much in dress of "the exile" as with the garb of earlier times. Reflection

---

[31] "What's New," 36–37. I am not sure I agree that the worst catastrophe has the biggest impact, but that is not really what this argument is about.

[32] See discussion in *Signs of Jonah,* 51–53, 58–64, 118–22, and visible on every page of the study.

[33] "What's New," 32ff.

and insight will not occur didactically and in a straight line but more sug-
gestively, imaginatively, and indirectly.

We can gather from Ben Zvi's analyses five nested points of interpretive infrastructure. First, the literati read analogically, referencing most
basically their own situation. They are concerned to ground their identity
in the past that they narrate, though they do it indirectly. They read for
links, and to legitimate their own situation. Second, and related, is what
Ben Zvi calls the process of marginalizing their own present in favor of
both the heroic past and the idealized future.[34] That is, though their concern
focuses on their own circumstances, they do not narrate these, but past
events that ground their identity. Their reading is analogical, with themselves and their institutions and events set small in the shadow of a valorized past. Third, though we might see that there is no small amount of
death and disaster in the stories of the past, such a "biographic optic" is not
the lens for post-exilic reading; rather, the possibilities for return, renewal,
a fresh start are implied in the narratives as well and in conjunction with
the failures. The future opens ambivalently from apparently truncated stories. Our historian sketches the importance of a post-exilic audience able to
discern, even amid the diverse themes and genres of the traditional material, patterns of similarity: Many of the materials start in the past and come
up to the present—hence inviting participation.[35]

Fourth, for Ben Zvi the literati of Yehud would accept and even identify with the authoritative, authorial voice of the tradition in a particular
way. Though as a result of contemporary literary theory we have come to
understand the collusion between authorial voice and readerly community
as implied (actually, as our inferred) author and reader, there is no reason
to confine the relationship to modern times. "Just as the voice of the author
resonates in the book, so their [the receivers'] voices become animators of
that voice as they read and reread a text that conveys—and creates—divine
knowledge," says Ben Zvi.[36] He suggests that Jerusalem's post-exilic
literati would have identified with this voice, would have seen themselves
as aligned with it, sharing the role of "brokering" the word of God.[37] Fifth,

[34] "What's New," 47, and "Looking at the Primary (Hi)Story and the Prophetic Books as
Literary/Theological Units within the Frame of the Early Second Temple: Some Considerations," *Scandinavian Journal of the Old Testament* 12 (1998) 35–36.

[35] "Looking," 26–28.

[36] This point is developed in *Signs of Jonah*, 47, 87, 97, 100–07, 116.

[37] Relevant here once again is the sense, expressed by Ben Zvi and numerous others recently, that "biblical" texts are highly likely to have been produced by those whose interests
they expressed and who had the resources required for this expensive task. So the compatibility being argued for is not simply ideas—theology—but is a matter of social location as well.

Ben Zvi offers an unusual claim about intent and "messages": "The end result of the process is a far more nuanced net of positions than any isolated
claim by itself."[38] A book like Jonah is not "aimed at" outsiders, but is constructed more sympathetically to convey insight to "insiders," its ironies
and parodies developed for and about themselves. So the point, as Ben Zvi
hones it, is not to send barbed messages to others but to initiate a "critical
self-appraisal of the group within which and for which the book was written. This message [sic] leads to, and reflects, a nuanced self-image within
the literati themselves and a awareness of the problematic character of the
knowledge they possessed."[39]

Converging the Book and Its Intended Readers

With this still general characterization of the intended readers of Jonah
in mind, let us now imagine the various features of the book of Jonah in the
hands, on the lips, in the hearts of these leaders. What, specifically, are they
reading, discussing, coming to understand, and teaching? To illustrate
rather than demonstrate completely, let us consider seven features. Though
I will characterize so as to suggest the fit, I will resist making blunt matches
between the identity and needs of the group sketched above and the story
they are now about to read. That is your task: to refine the links!

First, biblical Jonah has a dual identity.[40] Many commentators have
converged the eighth-century prophet of 2 Kings 14:23-29 and the prophet
of the longer narrative, though rarely with such benefit as does Ben Zvi.
Reminding us elsewhere that it is not unusual for later communities to
shape new adventures for older named heroes, Ben Zvi gets a bit more
mileage from the topos. The Jonah of 2 Kings 14 has enough identity to
make a contribution to "book Jonah," though his figure is not filled in so
decisively that he hardens into utter specificity. "Kings Jonah" is a prophet,
serving under a wicked ruler (Jeroboam II), involved in that royal rene-
gade's achieving something perhaps unexpected, undeserved: an enhance-
ment of his territory, a reclamation of land lost. There is no suggestion that
Jeroboam repented, as did some other named kings in that same chronicle.
But God acted nonetheless, speaking a word through Jonah when Israel's
distress became apparent and there was none to help (2 Kgs 14:25-27). Just
how the prophet assists is left opaque. "Book Jonah" is also a prophet who

---

[38] *Signs of Jonah,* 99. Ben Zvi's chs. 7–8 present the material I have reorganized for my
own purposes in this section of my work.

[39] Refer to *Signs of Jonah,* 98–100, 131–37.

[40] The point is made several times, *Signs of Jonah,* 40–64, 90–91, 95.

assists an unlikely monarch, unexpectedly for both, with the issue at least partly that of deservingness. For good reasons the book of Jonah cannot talk about the sixth-century exile, which in Jonah's story setting has not yet occurred. And yet, as Ben Zvi points out, Jonah is *an* exile, *in* exile.[41] The "two Jonahs" exemplify in their ministries the limited strangeness that should catch later rereaders' eyes: A pre-exilic Northern prophet becomes a hero for a post-exilic Southern community.

Second, "book Jonah" is, as virtually all have observed, in the dark about something entangled with his own relatedness with God. The question is the specific nature of his problem. As Ben Zvi sees it, the Jonah character is to be queried not so much for his original flight—a matter that absorbed many pre-critical commentators—but for his anger in the second half of the book. Our historian supposes that Jonah's basic miscue is about his "broker" status with God, the extent to which he himself—officially, not simply personally—is important in God's actions. Ben Zvi urges that the prophet Jonah overestimates his "official" importance in God's economy with other human beings.[42] Jonah is able to cite various aspects of God's actions and personal characteristics, but citing is not wholly adequate to the challenge he faces. Counterintuitively for his kind, this prophet rebels and yet succeeds, preaches but is understood by his hearers better than he understands his own utterance. His anger, according to Ben Zvi, is because whatever God is doing goes right over Jonah's head, apparently need not really pass through his own brokering hands.[43] Jonah is less important than he had supposed: hence his anger.

A third related and relevant feature of Jonah is his reductionistic way of reading God. If, as is evident in the Hebrew biblical tradition, God does any number of things and also their apparent opposites, then to select one side of the slate and disregard the other is a monologic reading of the deity.[44] That is, the tradition itself is richly multivalent about the divine nature, capacities, and behaviors, not simply from book to book but often within a book, a chapter, even a verse. To read one-sidedly is an interpretation error that shrinks insight and hence theology. For Ben Zvi, Jonah's narrative incapacity to contemplate God's response to repentance, alleging reproachfully the string of qualities Jonah names in 4:2-3, is inadequate for a prophet. A prophet able to allude to many places in what is now Scripture as adeptly as Jonah does while faltering over the question of whether God will

---

[41] *Signs of Jonah,* 95, 127.

[42] Among other places, consult *Signs of Jonah,* 25, 30, 57–58, 87–88, 109–10.

[43] See the case made in *Signs of Jonah,* 14–21 and 87–90.

[44] *Signs of Jonah,* 21–22, 107–15.

be merciful or not is rendered provocatively problematic. More than knowledge is required, and Jonah is shown deficient in his understanding.[45] The flurry of episodes at the end of the book—the sheltering plant, the gobbling worm, the desiccating wind—all point out the prophet's lack of familiarity, at least in his own situation and experience, with what God might do. Jonah is shown deficient by a storyteller who knows better, who draws the deity as taking the prophet in hand, patiently, to help him see where he lacks perspective. And insight, self-knowledge is what is on offer, rather than "messages" to send to others. Jonah is parodic, though not grotesque. He can be critiqued by rereaders without needing to be ridiculed, at least by those with experience and self-knowledge. Jonah is recognizably a broker of God's word, in fact does very well in some senses! And yet his capacity to miscue despite his knowledge, to founder in a situation where God's mercy flows even to those who might not quite deserve it—or, conversely, to some who may in fact be good candidates for it—hints at a risky myopia about God's ways. That the Jonah character becomes so distracted about his role in what is evidently a wonderful moment for those to whom he preaches highlights a situation that cuts close to the bone for Jerusalem's leaders. If insight is to arise somewhat indirectly for Jerusalem's literati from the story of Jonah, the catalyst is plausibly a character with whom they can identify somewhat sympathetically while still seeing room for "his" improvement. Those not too smug or self-righteous could see in Jonah's experiences their own questions and in his flailings their own uncertainty. There is no extractable "message," but there is insight available for those open to it.

A fourth situation of relevance rises, this time not from the prophet himself, but from the narrative's plot, specifically the question of time. Remembering all too vividly the many painful issues of defeat and exile in the sixth century—the critical existential issues of their day[46]—the intended readers would readily engage risks of slippery repentance, the question of entitlement to divine mercy, the likely possibilities of God's ways with sinners. And here the double ending of the book is apt. When will Nineveh's destruction for wickedness take place? Not until the sentence has been called out, apparently. And not even then, since it may be deferred or reversed. As the book of Jonah ends, the destruction has not occurred. Jonah has gone to sit outside the city to see what will happen, apparently without

---

[45] *Signs of Jonah,* 19–26.

[46] We understand from the chronology that few if any of the citizens of Persian Yehud will have been actual refugees from Judah in the first twenty or so years of the sixth century. If we accept that return from exile cannot be earlier than the 530s and quite possibly later, it is a matter of a next generation reflecting on the bitter experience of their elders somewhat as children of Holocaust survivors continue to be haunted by its issues.

utter assurance that there will be nothing to view. We need to recall that the news of the reprieve is shared with readers by the narrator, not overtly with characters (3:10); Jonah is angry over what does not occur at once, though he need not be construed to grasp fully that the delay is longer than the forty days he has announced. The Ninevites themselves—as those "deserving" punishment—are best construed as not knowing for sure what is their fate. They articulate uncertainty (3:9) without ever being reassured in our hearing. As we can see, the book moves on to distract Jonah with other things that upset his own sense of comfort as he waits. And yet relief is temporary in the case of Nineveh, though outside of Jonah's awareness, since it experienced a reprieve, but then eventually a permanent overturning. Overturnings can be overturned. A threatened city can be spared and a doomed city given a fresh start. The question is *how,* in God's economy. Two tales of one Assyrian city, and in fact of at least two of Jerusalem. Time is a wildcard in the divine-human economy. There is no comforting "shelf-life" for prophetic words, no "expires by" date after which those involved might relax a bit.

Ben Zvi is distinctive among Jonah scholars in calling attention to a fifth feature, the possibility that the prophet, God's servant, was depicted as running away from his master when first called. He argues carefully and convincingly that such a descriptor cannot be positive, since in both the social worlds we can investigate and in the world of the biblical text, runaways were almost never condoned.[47] Only in Deuteronomy 23:16-17 is an escaped slave not to be returned to his or her legitimate owner; in the case of the slaves who run successfully away from Pharaoh, the point may be offered that they were not legitimately *his* slaves or servants at all. So there is an additional negative valence on Jonah that we might miss, were we disregarding completely the putative circumstances of production of the book and the likely values of its intended readers. Insofar as the exile and return from it are cast in biblical texts to resemble the exodus from Egypt, the short Jonah narrative presents us with yet another tale of how Israel will sort its relationship with God.

A sixth point of attention, closely interwoven with the others, draws readers to watch Jonah where he contends with God verbally, as we see in ch. 4. Misunderstanding is the key, not ignorance. Jonah has, notably in ch. 2,[48] been shown familiar with the language of theology. But such skill does not, apparently, help him act wisely. Ben Zvi raises the provocative ques-

---

[47] See *Signs of Jonah,* ch. 5, where the case is made.

[48] Reading Ben Zvi reminds me how comparatively unimportant the fish adventure is for historical critics!

tion of specifics: If Jonah is demonstrably angry over God's forbearance with the people of Nineveh, is it a general irritation or a particular one that Jonah raises? If Nineveh is reprieved, is "Nineveh" the issue, or "reprieve"? So, Ben Zvi inquires, would Jonah have been equally impatient had God chosen to have mercy on the sixth-century Jerusalem, which had been threatened by prophets and reformed, though ultimately ineffectually (e.g., 2 Kings 22–25)? Ben Zvi has suggested that, though in scholarship much is made of the many sins of Assyrians—and Nineveh is (sometimes) the capital of that empire, in the knowledge of the post-exilic readership—such a datum is not so obvious as we may assume. Reminding us that the likely source of knowledge about long-ago events would be the written text (not eyewitnesses, a library, or an Internet), our historian points out that in the books of Kings the Assyrians are not named malefactors until *after* the time of Jeroboam II, under whom the "first" Jonah served. So, unable to benefit by the historical knowledge to which *we* have access—that in fact Assyria had earlier and longer innings against ancient Israel—we see that Nineveh may in fact be a rather innocent city! The city of Jonah's ministry is neither the notorious Babylon nor Sodom and Gomorrah. It is a most interesting point, and a neglected one, at least in my researches on the book. It makes a vivid reminder that our categories are far from natural or normal, even when they are presumably well-informed! Ben Zvi supposes that Jonah's intolerance for God's change of mind—however aimed and timed—was to be critiqued. Jonah does poorly as an intercessor when compared with Abraham and Moses.[49] And yet those two worthies were not without their own flaws, so perhaps there is hope for wee Jonah!

A seventh point is really a reminder about how insight arises when texts are read and reread as hypothesized here. Meaning accrues as readers negotiate, repeatedly and perhaps differently over time, the many nodes of potentiality. As Jerusalem's leaders write, teach, pray, redact, re-copy, and preach even this one short narrative, not to mention its fellows, there are endless invitations to reflection, to self-knowledge, to transformation into deeper relationship with God and God's people. Ancient tradition is made freshly relevant and is itself enhanced while it strengthens new readers. The fit is plausible, coherent, even compelling. The processes of socialization, education, and formation go on creatively and imaginatively, but not without constraint. For example, I find it difficult to find room here for "evangelization" to non-Jews, or for a text that scolds about narrow exclusivity. It is not that the story cannot be read that way; but in the community

---

[49] For various points concerning Nineveh, consult *Signs of Jonah,* 51–53, 58–64, 118–22.

Ben Zvi has constructed, it is unlikely. A particular set of "hooks" works best for the rereaders for whom the story is crafted.[50]

A Final Set of Questions

Have we, in your appraisal, made substantial progress in understanding more about the society of ancient (at least sixth-century) Israel? Do you feel less vague about the time and circumstances of the production of the book, and perhaps less concern with the circumstances when the story's action may have occurred? Do you have a better sense of how such post-exilic readers would proceed, a feel for what particulars of the story might have been most relevant to them? Is it clearer to you than before how one might "get perspective," change, be transformed from one awareness to another? I hope so, and feel well-enriched myself, after these strenuous reading efforts. But is this *re*construction *probable* or is it rather a *plausible con*struction? *That is, can we, some twenty-five hundred years later, claim to retrieve the specific circumstances of Jerusalem's reading community, rely on historical accuracy for our reconstruction?* Or is this whole interpretation venture too circular? *Another way to ask that question is to think about whether we are picking up on proffered implications or rather drawing inferences.* Part of my reading here is resistant. I remain leery of anything like certitude, because it seems to me there is way too much we do not know.[51]

But even supposing that my caution is well-founded, is our exercise fruitless, despite Ben Zvi's careful work? Not at all, and for several reasons. First, his reading has disabled, or at least called into question, a good deal of the standard viewpoint on Jonah, specifically that which is inherently if subtly anti-Jewish. Even if "plausible" remains the best word for Ben Zvi's work—and it may be too stingy an assessment—he has performed an invaluable second service by making visible for us the impor-

---

[50] See *Signs of Jonah,* 84–85 and 101–02. Even if we do not construe the local Persian Yehud leadership as hostile toward non-Jews, Gentiles are unlikely to be for these Jews the medium of deep insight about themselves. Ben Zvi refreshingly excuses his "Jonah audience" from active hostility or xenophobia toward others by asserting that insofar as Gentiles are thought of, it is as potential or nascent Jews, perhaps someday fortunate enough to be able to share the Jerusalem Temple heritage. But not yet.

[51] Though he does not address this specific point in the material I have presented here, in other writings on this same period Ben Zvi allows the possibility of quite radically differing scenarios. See his "Inclusion in and Exclusion from Israel as Conveyed by the Use of the Term 'Israel' in Post-Monarchic Biblical Texts," in Steven W. Holloway and Lowell K. Handy, eds., *The Pitcher Is Broken: Memorial Essays for Gösta W. Alström* (Sheffield: Sheffield Academic Press, 1995) 95–149.

tance of particular reading. It has taken biblical scholars a long time to recognize that reading is not universal; when we suppose it to be so we are actually mapping our norms onto the universe. Ben Zvi's book says bluntly that Jews of the sixth or fifth century B.C.E. will have read the book with particular experience, frames of reference, expectations, and burning questions. And he demonstrates that a number of those factors are quite unfamiliar to us many centuries later, and perhaps not of great interest. All reading is particular, and meaning is constructed primarily on site. Ben Zvi has also done us the favor of reminding us not to assume ignorantly or lazily that the story setting of a book is the whole of its interpretive horizon, and that there are other issues to raise, even if we are treading on uncertain ground. Part of the critical reading demanded of (post-)modern scholarship is the bringing to bear of as many lenses as are appropriate.

But still, are we right to question, at least, under the rubric of "circularity," whether Ben Zvi is not doing his own reading, primarily, reconstructing his own eye while claiming it to be that of Yehud's literati? That he is a trained and experienced historian might slow us from concluding that in his case. If we are not able to claim his credentials, and especially when we are not guided by skill like his, we may be suspicious that the view we are discerning is more our own than we may like. But is it a bad thing, if true? Can our reading be *both* highly attentive to what historical and literary cues beckon to us and *also* deeply alert to our own interests? If we move back, briefly, to our *Gone With the Wind* project, we can see that this is the case, granted one is a film (and a novel) and the other Sacred Scripture! What they share is the medium of symbolic representation, which is complex rather than simple. If we go to the library or rent the video of the work in question, assuming uncritically or determinedly that what we are seeing is a factual representation of an era bygone, we will miss a lot of possibilities: If the O'Haras, the Butlers, and the Wilkeses never existed, is the movie rendered valueless? Is the story about Southern ante- and post-bellum society accurate, and from whose angle? Was it meant to be historically accurate, or did its creators have other purposes in mind? Is the film perhaps a commentary on the "Jim Crow" South of the later nineteenth and early twentieth centuries, detailing a society whose means of oppression were not much less powerful than those of the days of antebellum slavery? What effect would the book or film have had on its various audiences: on wealthy white women, or on angry black men? On educators in the Northern states? On people with active social consciences? On racists? Who criticized the book/film, and how were their words received? Who valorized it, and why? How might a player like "Mammy" (Hattie McDaniel) have come to view her own role in the decades since it made her famous? These matters do not detract from our appreciation of the artwork, unless we are seeking merely entertainment. They should enhance our participation in it and make us more alert to the presence and power of violence, sexism, and racism in our midst.

So it may be right to suggest that the main or nearest viewer when we read is ourselves. We are not at all disregarding the many prompts we have, thanks to the scholarly reconstructions handed us to ponder. But still, when *we* read a book and a character like Jonah, our closest referent is our own circumstances. Without at all brushing away all we can know from the past, another context cannot function for us in the way it did for its own/the book's intended readers. But the gain for us is still tremendous. Even if we remain skeptical that we have retrieved Jonah's intended readers and suspect that we have re-inscribed our own interests, there is still a reason for our researches and our pondering. We have entered the text and sorted its issues energetically, actively, critically. We have been presented with layers of possibilities for our own insight—too many to review in this final paragraph of this chapter. Any one of them—e.g., the question of the endurance of prophetic words—is rich enough to sustain us for quite some time. The very processes or socialization and formation under discussion here have reached out to us from Scripture, granted our needs are very different from those we have been entertaining. Additionally, we still have been presented with a problematic in reading that we may learn from as we engage with imaginative skills as well as more factual information. Ben Zvi's supposition, you may recall, is that Jonah is not a sufficiently skilled interpreter. We may think he has other deficiencies as well, but what we have been offered is a broker of God's purposes and plans who reads reductively. Whether the intended Jonah rereaders can remedy the problem, Ben Zvi has hinted that others may have been able to do so. He himself has diagnosed Jonah's malaise—or designed it. The challenge remains to us to read the tradition skillfully. Ben Zvi's work with Jonah intertexts has made clear enough that the story and its biblical matrix are composed like a symphony, where motifs and phrases are continuously evocative of each other, where "melodies" and chords resonate richly in relation to many other themes. Can we read as skillfully as our text allows, even begs us to do? The narrative does not offer us a simple message about fantastic fish or foreign foes. But it does challenge us to read its central character—God—with appropriate attention to all that is said. *What does the story mean? What are you asking of it?*

CHAPTER FOUR

Ancient Analogical Readings

In the previous chapter we did a rather thoroughly historical reading of Jonah. The point was not to discover the factual details of an *originating Jonah incident* but rather to ascertain or assay the historical circumstances pertaining to the *book's production and reception* by its first and intended readership. What you will have noted, I hope, is that though surely historical methods featured prominently as we worked to understand Persian Jerusalem and its leadership, methods that were also literary- and reader- centered were well integrated. That is, our historian reconstructed the concerns of a particular period not so much via archaeology and macro-history, but from social-scientific reconstructions of the period and from a sensitive reading of many biblical texts, including Jonah; and he asked centrally the question of what would have been particularly meaningful for actual readers for whom the book was meant and who actually held it in their hands. Though I pointed out the inevitable circularity of the effort—in order for Ben Zvi's claim to work, one part of the analysis both generates and also assumes the other—still the exercise is a useful one. It may be that we have a construction rather than a re-construction, but there is value in the exercise. Not being a biblical historian myself, I have scant confidence in what can be known with certitude. But I respect the work of a careful scholar like Ben Zvi and can see that his reading prompts us to acknowledge that, insofar as his reading is accurate, he disallows some scholarly efforts to read the book a-contextually. It is not that readers cannot produce readings that disregard originating conditions; obviously they can do and have done. But context, and specifically intended audience, is a powerful cue, and we do well at the very least to consider it.

Again, I suspect we can see this from our own experience. If we take a date like the well-worn September 11, 2001—or name November 22, 1963, or June 6, 1944—and ask what would have been predominantly in the minds of U.S. citizens on those days, we can reconstruct those audience expectations. I think I need not explain the most recent of those dates, and so if some "alien" were reading literature which presumed that context without detailing it, and the "alien interpreter" did not know what had happened but construed abstractly, ignorant of three airplane catastrophes and about loss or forgiveness, it would be an inadequate reading. If you recognize the other two dates I gave, you can again anticipate that the overwhelming contexts and frames of reference will have been obvious to many people at the moment, and literature "prescribed" for such readers will have counted on their urgent concerns. If we do not know what happened on November 22, 1963 in Dallas, Texas and read a poem about evanescent hopes untimely withered, we may interpret quite thinly. It is not that we are *wrong,* but we have missed an opportunity to be much *more right,* to grasp the apt circumstances much more precisely. Our remarks are not invalidated if we do not know what was on the minds of virtually all U.S. citizens on that November day, but they are vastly enriched if we do know. So if we have been angled correctly as to the dominant concerns of Persian Yehud's leaders when they read their Jonah, we are helped in our reading as well, not limited. So the historical, the literary, and the readerly collaborate to help us find, or make, meaning.

The last reminder before we begin a new reading adventure is that in our Chapter 2 we saw that for most of the long story of interpretation of Jonah (and other classics, including biblical) scholars were not much alert to history, for a variety of reasons. They assumed that the events narrated had happened, or they did not seem to suspect that they need not have actually occurred. It was not until nearly the seventeenth century in the West that "properly" historical questions emerged, and then they came to dominate and even to swamp many other interests. Without denying that description, I want to nuance it a bit, to show it slightly less true than many have supposed. That the ancients did not ask "our" modernist historical questions does not mean they did not attend to history as best they could while interpreting with other ends primarily in view. It is our challenge now to investigate some of their readings.

The Present Task

We will go back to the third through fifth centuries and look at some of the comparatively early readings of the story of Jonah, those that read it analogically. That term covers several possibilities, all of which prescribe a basic and discernible fit between the better known and the less known, between what the story is ostensibly communicating and the life circumstances of readers, as we will explore shortly; but all of them assume that the meaning of the text is most profoundly the product of reading some level other than its most obvious one. If we compare that claim with the work we did thanks to Ben Zvi, you will recall that he struggled to read the text's referential meaning as acutely as possible without going much beneath it.[1] So this will be a basically different procedure. And we will find that, for the scholars of antiquity, the needs of the reading communities are assumed to be somewhat universal and perennial to the spiritual lives of intentional religious persons rather than specific to ordinary lives of diverse people. Saint Jerome's work will be our main focus, though we will look in some detail at the influence of readings that are called allegorical, specifically at Philo and Origen (both of Alexandria), and next we will sample those that are called typological, taking up Theodore of Mopsuestia, who represents the school at Antioch. Our aim will be to understand what those scholars did, how they did it, and what meaning they found as a result of their particular work. We will critique their efforts and outcomes in the sense of appraising the benefits and deficits, the strengths and the weaknesses. And most important, we will be asking how we can make use of these readings—method and results—and where we need to be wary.

Some Entry Questions

I want to start with a question we might have asked earlier—and in fact, perhaps you have been asking it! *Why do we rely on an old book for significance, in the way Christians (and Jews and Muslims, among others) draw on Scripture for basic and profound meaning?* In so many other spheres we could name, new is best. Our life circumstances and points of view are so different from those regnant when the Bible was produced. Might it be more helpful and practical to get a new set of normative texts? *Why keep reusing old words?* A second question is related: *How do we get fresh, or current, existential meaning from old words? If we do not agree with others as to how to proceed—what strategies and techniques to make use of—and especially if we derive significantly different or discrepant meanings, are we in fact reading the same texts as others? Is there a set of correspondences we can agree upon as basic or given in some way?* Another way to get at that same issue is to ask how meaning got into the Bible in the first place; perhaps knowing that will help us know how to get it out! But the base question is, again, about meaning: *How do we read so as to render our basic narratives responsibly meaningful?* These are questions that have occupied many readers prior to

---

[1] However, recall that Ben Zvi's Judeans also read somewhat analogically, though with reference to socio-cultural factors rather than to generic spiritual ones.

ourselves, and they are bound up with the earliest readers of Scripture, though their insights will likely differ from ours. But their views are well worked out and worth our scrutiny, since they were influential for a long time and have produced some excellent readings.

Gathering those questions together brings us to these: *What did the ancients do, and how did they proceed? What were their assumptions about the Bible that led them to proceed as they did? What was productive, and where were the limits or weaknesses of their modes of interpretation? What remains from their strategies for us, and what are we best off leaving aside? And what from their readings is most insightful for us?*

Our Process

Since we already have a historical sketch (our Chapter 2, which I will presume here, and which you may need to review in order to recall the general context of antiquity), we will now proceed differently. We will start with Jerome, who is my favorite reader of Jonah, and ask what is his coherent "take" on Jonah, his particular reading of Jonah's journey. Then we will factor his work, as it were, make a representative list of what he gets— a sort of geography of Jerome's Jonah moves. Then we will bring him into dialogue with the others of the era who theorize about interpretation, in order to get an adequate sense of the hermeneutical moves.

Jerome: An Itinerary of His Jonah

Jerome's commentary is available in English with only some difficulty.[2] His particular insights are quite persistent in works that come after him, credited or not. Jerome thought, as did others after him, that to repeat in one's own work the views that others espoused reinforced them and confirmed their value. On such a scale, Jerome's readings rank high. So I am not the only admirer of his interpretation! But let me start with what appeals to me most, which comes at the level of characterization.

Jerome's basic appraisal of virtually all the characters—save death and hell, which he associates with the fish—is that they are well-intentioned, gracious, struggling to do well toward others, and equipped with complex and generous motives, not simplistic venal ones. This persistent empathetic drawing comes out as Jerome adds explanations of why characters act as

---

[2] Timothy Hegedus, "Jerome's Commentary on Jonah: Translation with Introduction and Critical Notes" (M.A. thesis, Wilfrid Laurier University, 1991). Hegedus has in publication process his translation, which he kindly advanced to me; page numbers refer to that manuscript.

they do and even when he adds discourse so that actors can explain their moves. For example, Jerome's Jonah is made explicable as a prophet caught on the horns of a dilemma: If the Gentile Ninevites do well—repent and believe—Jerome's Jonah infers or assumes that the Jews will be lost. So Jonah's initial flight from his assignment and later his subsequent anger are explained, not because the prophet is mean-spirited, but because his love for his own Israelite people makes him shrink from being a catalyst for their harm. He does not so much begrudge the Gentiles as yearn for the good of his own people; he regrets deeply that the price of salvation for Gentiles is loss for Jews. Jerome can acknowledge that Jonah is avoiding his responsibility when he boards the ship and goes below for a nap. He sleeps through the storm, not callously or lazily, but from grief (Jerome recalls Jesus' disciples in Luke 22:45), not wanting, Jerome says, to see the weather effects he knows he has brought on his current companions. Jerome insists that Jonah remains magnanimous throughout the whole ordeal of ascertaining the boat's guilty passenger, and he does not resist in any way the ultimate choice of the sailors, who are also deeply concerned for his fate as well as their own. When questioned later by God over his demeanor, Jonah puts his quandary slightly differently: I could have come to Nineveh preaching God's views gently, and no one would have heeded; and yet if I preached a God of harshness, it would not have been true! So Jonah feels angry at being made to look, or feel, like a liar, and he is grieved at being successful with Gentiles, to whom he would rather not have been sent.[3]

In Jerome's view, God also is benign. Jerome does not seem to feel the need to explain or diagnose further why God is "turning" from Jews to Gentiles, an assumption we are unlikely to share. But God's ultimate strategy with the prophet is gentle and pedagogic. Given that Jonah must go to Nineveh, the storm to bring him back to shore is a necessity, and the great fish, whether just created or brought alongside the heaving ship at the crucial moment, is a sign to Jonah of God's care. Jerome says Jonah experiences God's anger during the storm but divine mercy at the moment of rescue. But once Jonah is on dry ground again, God makes the Nineveh reassignment without needing to scold Jonah for disobedience; there is no need for God to mention what Jonah has just been through, Jerome says. Similarly, when God deals with Jonah after the Ninevite conversion it is not to upbraid him but to ask him questions. As we have noted earlier in this book, questions themselves have a different "geography" from answers, let alone from accusations. Jerome seems to understand that when one feels as bad as Jonah does and for the serious reasons he is sad, there is no need for reproof; to

---

[3] See Hegedus, "Jerome's Commentary," 5–10, 13–15, 21–25, 57–60, 66–69.

elicit insight is better. And when discussing God's plans for the Ninevites, Jerome notes that God is compassionate by nature and ready to save by mercy those he cannot save by his justice, and he prefers the repentance of sinners rather than their death; "he joyfully changed the sentence, since he saw the changed works. Or rather God, desiring from the first to be merciful, persevered in his intention, for none who wish to punish someone warn them of what they are going to do."[4] It is not that Jerome denies that Jonah stands in need of improvement; that Jonah is inarticulate at God's promptings signifies to the commentator that the prophet is in the wrong. But he will not gain by being scolded.[5]

I have already commented on the sailors' own graciousness, as Jerome renders them. They treat their passenger with respect, even once they understand that he has brought them into danger. And once it becomes obvious that Jonah must leave the ship if it is not to be destroyed, they take care with him and are alert to the danger of wrongdoing on their own part. Now you may say that the text itself urges that construction, and so it does. But the sailors themselves, especially the captain who speaks, are shown more harsh and heedless in other interpretations of the tale. It is the hearts of the grateful sailors that make vows to God, Jerome notes, not their hands making literal sacrifices on the slippery deck of a depleted boat. Similarly, the Ninevite king is exemplary in his choices. Though the last to hear Jonah's proclamation, he acts promptly and personally. And he understands that his own monarchical moves are not sufficient; his people must turn as well, and their animals. Jerome does not say much about the great fish as a character, since it is the anti-pole of the good. But with the possible exception of it—and its evil is not unduly stressed—all the characters strain to do well, go out of their way to be concerned for others, as Jerome gives them to us. Not every commentator does the same. It is my sense from a fair amount of reading that Jonah is more criticized than sympathized with. So the marvel here is that Jerome sees good will and sincerity as driving this whole narrative. You can decide for yourself: Do you do better when criticized and carped at or when dealt with respectfully and empathetically? Our human relationships are always the best analogue for thinking about our dealings with God. What is being described is actually an economy of relationships, and this one is generous, not mean.[6]

---

[4] Ibid. 56.

[5] God's treatment of Jonah can be sampled in ibid. 28, 42–43, 46, 59–60. John Calvin later will scorn Jerome's mollycoddling of Jonah!

[6] Hegedus, "Jerome's Commentary," 15, 19–20, 23–27, 50–55. Jerome also advises that the "Assyrian king" is not the epitome of evil, is not the devil, and there is no point in persisting in such an explanation.

With that main point made, let us look at some other moves that Jerome makes, strategies or tactics that can be distilled or separated out for consideration as is typically done when his work is discussed in the context of other interpreters of his time. Recall some structuring that we have already done. We have explored the balances of emphasis available to a contemporary reader grounding in an ancient classic, making a distinction between those who read to know primarily about the past and those whose interest is more in their own present. Similarly, we have made the behind-, within-, and before-the-text distinctions. In this present chapter the discussion centers on how meaning is best communicated between the divine author and the Christian readers of Scripture, the relation between what the text seems to say at its surface (comprising for Jerome and his peers both its historical and linguistic referents), and what it proffers if one moves from that level to something deeper. Jerome does all these things, and in fact moves seamlessly among the various strategies: He reads drawing in historical-materialist information; and he is attentive to the text in a variety of ways. There is no doubt that he is concerned for readers of his own day; his particular situated interests are evident to us, if perhaps not to him. Jerome reads both allegorically and typologically: He sees Jonah as a type of Jesus, Jesus as the true Jonah, and he derives various levels of insight— moral and spiritual—from the narrative. Let us pull his best examples, so we can both recognize his moves and appreciate some of his points.

At the level we can call literal or historical, Jerome makes several exemplary observations. It is difficult to define this level in a way that will cover all cases, but it is perhaps easiest to say it is the obvious or entry-level meaning, the things that the text seems plainly to refer to. Though it is customary to think the ancients had little regard for this aspect of the narrative, I do not have that sense here. Jerome clearly has other points to make but spends not a little time giving us several clear bases for our understanding. He situates "our" Jonah both in terms of the prophet in 2 Kings 14 and of the child raised from the dead by the prophet Elijah in 1 Kings 17; Jerome reminds us of the Tobit (14:3-4) link as well. Thus we can locate Jonah in terms of biblical history, which Jerome would assume to be accurate. Jerome tells us where Joppa is, where Jonah's tomb is. He notes how experienced sailors have come to know what storms do and so recognize the particular danger of the one they are caught in. He speculates on the question of survival for three days in the intestines of a large animal. He makes the connection between waters familiar to earth-dwellers and those of the abyss, which are much more terrifying and dangerous. He discourses, though less than some others, on the size of the city of Nineveh, the time required to cross it. And famously (since scolded by Augustine) Jerome renames the plant and tells us about it: Translating the Hebrew, Jerome calls the plant an "ivy." These are points he takes time with and that he apparently thinks we need to understand as we deal with the narrative.[7]

Related to this same "entry level" are some points we would consider language-based rather than cultural, but in the schema of the ancients they are still "literal." Jerome is the translator par excellence and spends his considerable skill and experience rendering the Hebrew and Greek into Latin. In addition to his classification of the plant in Jonah 4, we get from him the explanation that what the Hebrew calls a great fish has been converted into Greek—both the Septuagint and the New Testament—as "whale." The commentator indulges in an outburst when translating 3:3-4, declaring it incomprehensible to him how "forty" (Hebrew text) and "three" (Greek) can have gotten mixed up, since he sees no apparent linguistic grounds for it! Jerome helps us get the flavor of the adversative or concessory tone of 2:5, the "nevertheless," and he reminds us that the completed action (we would say perfect or past tense) of the verb in 2:1—"he cried"—urges us to see the prayer Jonah utters as a retrospective effort, not necessarily an utterance in process.[8] A couple of other points show us Jerome's textual or literary skill: To those who find utterly unrealistic the string of questions the sailors hurl at their mysterious passenger in the midst of the storm Jerome recalls a similar passage in Vergil, where Jerome says the point is to ascertain a stranger's relevance to the scene being played out, not simply to bandy useless words. He comments usefully that in Hebrew anthropology and diction, anger and grief are not neatly distinguished. In a couple of instances Jerome comments that narrative order reverses, e.g., 1:10; there is no reason for the sailors to feel more afraid after Jonah has uttered his name, rank, and serial number. Though he does not do much with his observation except help us see that logic is not crucially affected, it is in fact a characteristic of the Jonah-storyteller that others will later exploit usefully.[9]

Jerome makes many moves that we would now call intertextual. That is, he makes frequent use of tiny literary details to uncover related and sig-

---

[7] The English words are, of course, Hegedus translating Jerome's Latin translation of Hebrew and Greek words. For literal-level details consult Hegedus, "Jerome's Commentary," 61–66.

[8] Many commentators worry how Jonah can be saying all the phrases of the prayer of Jonah 2 while in the sea or in the sea creature.

[9] For a good summary of Jerome as a translator see Dennis Brown, "Jerome and the Vulgate," in Alan J. Hauser and Duane F. Watson, eds., *A History of Biblical Interpretation. Volume 1: The Ancient Period* (Grand Rapids: Eerdmans, 2003) 355–79. For miscellaneous language-related comments by Jerome, see Hegedus, "Jerome's Commentary," 17–20, 28–30, 38–41, 61–64.

nificant points. Most famous, perhaps, is Jonah's name, which by its spelling relates him to all Bible passages with doves (Hebrew for dove is *yonah*), and to those linked with oppression (since the three consonants of his name also relate to a verb with that meaning), and the patronymic (son of Amittai) is also explained with reference to wordplay.[10] Jerome comments on the value of Jonah's self-identifying as a Hebrew (root letters *ʿbr*) rather than as a Jew (or an Israelite), which opens out on any number of other texts where the root letters of the verb for "crossing over" (Hebrew root *ʿbr*) are used. Jerome twice mentions Psalm 103:25-26 in reference to the large sea creature. He links Jonah to other famous intercessors, especially those associated with forty days: Moses, Elijah, Jesus. That Jonah goes east of where he was recalls Cain for Jerome (Genesis 4). And like many others, Jerome sees interpretive possibilities between the story of Nineveh's destruction and that of Sodom and Gomorrah. Though this mode of reading is more associated with Jewish than with Christian interpretation, that distinction is less firm than many suppose (see our Chapter 6 below). The assumption common to both Christian and Jewish biblical interpreters was that the text signifies as a system and that its infinite detail is there to help us get at the fullness of meaning available from this short narrative and its biblical matrix.[11]

The analogical interpretation that is the direct concern of this chapter can be viewed in a number of ways. Without denigrating the literal meanings we have just noticed, Jerome has interests that transcend them. He is not writing primarily about geography, animal digestion, or botany, though such points are not dispensable. I think his most consistent move is to see the Jonah story in terms of the life of Jesus. That is, he matches every moment of Jonah that allows it to a place in the New Testament, even at one point making Jesus the real Jonah: "In the belly of the whale the Lord prayed these things which we read above under the person of Jonah."[12] In other words, Hebrew Jonah rehearses various moments of what we see later in the life of "Christian" Jesus. The most famous example is the parallel of the three days and nights spent "below": In the Jonah story Jerome calls the place the realm of death and evil, and in Jesus' case the descent is both the Incarnation itself[13] and then Passion, death, and descent of Jesus to the abyss. Jerome

---

[10] The "surname" is related to words for reliability, faithfulness, certainty, also connected to our liturgical affirmation "Amen," by which, whether we know it or not, we are reinforcing the value of what we are responding to.

[11] Hegedus notes certain of these links on 1–3.

[12] Hegedus, "Jerome's Commentary," 44–45.

[13] The Incarnation is obviously not an evil, but from a certain point of view it might be seen as a condescension of God toward humans, a "coming down."

mentions the link more than once and spends some time being sure that readers who are counting understand how the sum of days in both instances is three. It is worth noting that though Jerome spends some time on the comparison, especially on the more troublesome aspects of Jonah's descent, he does not lose sight of the main point: prayer in distress. In other words, the parallels are not simply noted; they are to be helpfully exploited for people in trouble. But there are other christological places as well, less famous and obvious. Jerome notes that Jesus, like Jonah, grieved over the nonrepentance of his own Jewish people and that he, too, delayed to preach to Gentiles as was his charge to do. As Jonah preferred not to go to Nineveh, Jesus preferred not to die as he sensed was imminent on the eve of his arrest. Both eventually did as commanded. Like Jonah when going over the side of the boat, Jesus was willing to expend his life for the good of others.[14]

There are other points that Jerome makes from some of those same passages, explanations that are not so much christological as more generally allegorical. For example, though Jonah's flight prefigures the Incarnation, it also resembles human resistance to doing God's will, a sort of blindness that God is quite able to correct, here by a storm. Jonah's flailings when overboard signify struggle and near-despair, the sort that prompts reaching out to God; the issue for Jerome is not whether the prophet was in the sea or in the fish, since the fish itself was certainly in the sea.[15] In some—even most—cases we may detect what is sort of a moral or behavioral valence on Jerome's comments: When discussing whether the Ninevites learned from Jonah's single sentence whether they had three or forty days for a change of heart and life, Jerome opines that for sinners, forty is much to be preferred, allowing more time for what is needed. He also lectures briefly on the licitness of living according to lots and of being complicit in the ending of one's own life.[16] Jerome's longest note in this quite succinct commentary concerns the view (attributed occasionally to Origen) that all sinners will ultimately be saved. Jerome says that point of view is not to be indulged, and that God's mercy does not necessarily include the forgiveness of *all* souls! But Jerome cautions against any need to derive morals from every part of the text, suggesting that the book's last

---

[14] Jerome cites numerous places in the gospels: for Jesus' supposed delay and avoidance see Matt 27:45; Mark 15:33; Luke 23:44-45; Matt 26:39; cf. 15:26; Luke 19:41. The christological readings are in the Hegedus translation on pp. 1, 4, 8–9, 21–23, 29–37, 41–42, 46, 57–58.

[15] Allegorical interpretations emerge in Hegedus, "Jerome's Commentary," 12–13, 25–26, 38–44, 61–65.

[16] Lots are rarely permissible and suicide to be indulged only in truly dire circumstances.

two verses in particular are resistant to it. However, he makes a valiant try by bringing forward the parable of the father and his two sons in Luke 15.[17]

The last set of Jerome comments I wish to single out here are what I would call readerly, in the sense we have discussed earlier in this book: It matters who interprets, and that all of us do it with our own interests and experiences at the forefront, whether we recognize and acknowledge it or not. Though I said above, and continue to think, that Jerome is as generous in his constructions as any I have seen, he is nonetheless dismissive of Judaism and Jews. It is clear that Jerome is convinced that the Jews were at fault in their dismissal of their own Christ-linked salvation, and that the fact of it is not much to be regretted by Christians. In the zero-sum game that Jerome supposes, once the Gentiles are responsive, inevitably the Jews lose out. Jerome's Jonah grieves over that equation without ever questioning it closely. "For the condemnation of Israel Jonah is sent to the Gentiles, because while Nineveh repents Israel perseveres in its evil."[18] So though this sense of regretful Jonah and "guilty Judaism" is a taproot of Jerome's interpretation and benign characterization of all involved, it is basically anti-Jewish, as would have been the norm, even for one like Jerome who knew, studied with, and learned a great deal from Jews. On more than one occasion Jerome polarizes the sailors and Ninevites over against those who call for the crucifixion of Jesus—leaders and people.

Influences on Jerome

OVERVIEW

Having begun by looking at the actual readings that Jerome did and then by factoring his approach a bit, though still descriptively, we have reached the moment when we need to ask what specifically he is doing in terms of the interpretive strategies of his contemporaries. In a sense we are asking who his ancestors in interpretation were, and we are looking at his siblings too. The main thrust of this chapter is to talk about analogical readings, which are commonly called the allegorical and typological. But though that is the main exploration, I want to keep insisting that Jewish midrashic and substantially postmodern intertextual reading remain a strong third component here as well. Since there is a sense in which all can stand beneath the large umbrella of analogy, let us start there. Let me offer three visuals to distinguish these three named modes, since they have al-

---

[17] For tropological or moral points see Hegedus, "Jerome's Commentary," 11–12, 17, 21–23, 47–49, 50–55.

[18] Ibid. 5, 49–50.

ready been characterized in our Chapter 2. *Intertextual/midrashic reading* leaves a track that looks like a zigzag. It can start almost anywhere, as we have seen, perhaps with some small quirk or anomaly in the text, or with a question; and then as the interpreter visits other textual sites, selected by various criteria, new light is shed on the original question or anomaly. This procedure is familiar to all computer-users who browse from one site to another, as prompted by the flexible question they are tracking. *Allegorical reading* is more like an excavation site, where one starts at the surface but digs ever deeper, with more interest in the lower than the upper strata, not disregarding what one has moved but not stopping there either. And *typological reading* seems best envisioned as a sort of chain or arc, starting in one place and moving forward or, in fact, starting at a later text and arcing backwards. These visuals are important so that, while alleging similarities, we can also recognize distinctions among these strategies. But since earlier discussions seem to segment them too rigidly, we will see how they share a good deal and are best seen as dialogue partners.

What are the general assumptions common to readers—Jewish and Christian (and even sometimes Muslim)—who read intertextually, those who read allegorically, and those whose interpretations are typological? We can name several. First, at least for ancients, all such reading counts on texts that are considered inspired and recognized as such by the relevant community. Though that may seem natural or obvious, it is actually our old question: *Why use old texts instead of getting new ones?* And the implicit claim of all such reading is that old texts are and can indeed be made relevant for now, whenever now is.[19] A second presupposition explains the first, for the texts are considered as authored substantially by God, however that claim may be understood by the various groups who espouse it. That means that the texts say what God intends. Third, the process of study and interpretation is driven by the quest for holiness, again variously conceived. The point of reading the texts is to transform the reader in the direction of the Authority of the Scripture: to facilitate return to or union with God. Reading's goal is to find meaning, enact it, be shaped by it. Study is not simply a quest for knowledge. The fourth point is related: The ancient texts are for now. Though old, and though written for "their own" times, they also continue to function for present readers.[20] Reading is not simply a visit to a museum.

[19] Jon Whitman, ed., *Interpretation and Allegory: Antiquity to the Modern Period* (Leiden and Boston: Brill, 2000) 4. Hence readers are not restricted to the original contexts of the passages under study—whether those be historical-cultural or textual-literary.

[20] Alan J. Hauser and Duane F. Watson, "Introduction and Overview," in Hauser and Watson, eds., *A History of Biblical Interpretation. Volume 1: The Ancient Period* (Grand Rapids: Eerdmans, 2003) 5.

Fifth, the basic quest is to uncover meaning that is hidden, or less than obvious. Such potential is present in the sacred texts, if not always easy to find. The depths need unlocking, a process that starts, though it does not end, at the surface of the words and proceeds by one (or more) of the strategies under consideration here. The letter is not unimportant. Sixth, the base for such a search and the payoff is a basic similarity between one text and another more urgent one, a match between an existential situation and something else. Analogy of some kind makes all these projects work. And seventh, the "grail" of the reading quest was—and in certain ways continues to be—for the inherent, ontologically given, non-arbitrary, and reliable base or code that establishes the meaning as coherent.[21] This is not a search for a single meaning; meaning is basically affirmed as multiple, if not always in so many words. The interpretive cipher or key, over time, has been claimed to be the human mind, the cosmos, the structures of language, the mysteries of symbology or mythology, certain features of human culture—or some combination of them. Jerome had many images for Scripture that reflect these assumptions, notably that it was as an ocean and a labyrinth of the mysteries of God, as a forest of meanings.[22]

And just to get these points out clearly before we look in more detail: The charges against these reading strategies include: Such practices are alien to the text, imposed artificially onto it, they are non-historical and disregard the cultural context that gave rise to the text; they are contrived, abstract, and universalizing—disdaining the material/cultural world on their way to making their affirmations of eternal meaning and significance.[23] There is some truth to those charges, at least on occasion. And it has become clear in the past quarter of a century that all these analogy-

---

[21] In an earlier draft of this chapter I included a discussion and critique of psychological readings of Jonah, specifically the work of André Lacocque and Pierre-Emmanuel Lacocque, *Jonah: A Psycho-Religious Approach to the Prophet,* foreword by Mircea Eliade (Columbia, SC: University of South Carolina Press, 1990). That book, though modern, works in a way not wholly dissimilar from the works under discussion here. Though the insights of modern psychology are surely crucial for our reading, on the whole the Lacocques fail to make good use of them, in my view. Among other flaws, their reading is insufficiently attentive to the historical-social factors of the book, merges the nuanced view of various psychologists too readily, reaches for universal explanations of human behavior without sufficient attention to the cultural, and overlooks certain of the factors of language and interpretation that are under current discussion. I appreciate their basic instinct to read a book like Jonah with the assistance of psychology's insights, but I find their particular effort in need of revision.

[22] Hegedus, "Jerome's Commentary," xlii.

[23] Martin Luther called allegory a harlot's embrace and said at one point bluntly, "I hate allegory," in Jon Whitman, ed. and introductory essay, *Interpretation and Allegory: Antiquity to the Modern Period* (Leiden, Boston, Cologne: Brill, 2000) 3.

based readings have substantially disregarded particular readers and the constructive role of reading, as we have seen previously.

PHILO, ORIGEN, AND THE ALLEGORICAL METHOD OF ALEXANDRIA

Part of Jerome's formative influence comes from the interpretive practice at Alexandria. As already described, this center was noted for its distinctive readings of Greek and Roman classics as well as the Bible.[24] Philo of Alexandria (25 B.C.E.–50 C.E.) is its most famous Jewish interpreter, and Origen of Alexandria its most brilliant and controversial Christian reader. The precise details of Alexandrian hermeneutics lie beyond this study, since the center's purposes, practices, and even terminology were not utterly consistent. For example, David Dawson usefully points out that Philo might interpret as he did (primarily the Pentateuch) to counter or curb excessive *allegorizing*, whereas Origen wrote against excessive *literalism* " . . . which, he argues, leads to disbelief among Jews, false belief among heretics, and reprehensible belief among simple-minded Christians. All three forms of misreading stem from an inability to discern spiritual meaning beyond the 'bare letter' of scripture . . . . "[25] Philo, drawing from Stoic ethics and a Platonist cosmology, presumed as basic the transcendence and ineffability of God; Origen's grounding absorption was the return of all created reality back to God after a primal fall and the pedagogical role Scripture plays in that process.[26] Both Philo and Origen borrow a basic analogy from the human person, suggesting that as humans have a body, a soul, and a spirit, so a text has its physical properties and literal meaning, its more ethical or tropological aspect, and a deeper spiritual or even mystical level of communication.[27] Origen pushes the analogy farther: " . . . [T]he spiritual life is an exegetical process [in] which religious experience, especially mystical experience, is

---

[24] Whitman, *Interpretation and Allegory,* xi, calls allegory "one of the formative interpretive activities of the West."

[25] David Dawson, "Plato's Soul and the Body of the Text in Philo and Origen," in *Interpretation and Allegory,* 102, discussing *Concerning First Principles* 4.2.4. Though Origen eventually settled in Caesarea, he traveled widely enough so that he wrote in relation to a number of vexing situations and threatening interlocutors: Gnostics whose esoteric teachings were not grounded in the biblical text; Greco-Roman philosophers (e.g., Celsus) who disdained Christianity on various grounds; Marcionites who wished to discard significant portions of the Hebrew Scriptures; Jewish exegetes who were resistant to christological moves by Christians; and literalists who were content—determined—to take the biblical passages at face value.

[26] Dennis Brown, "Jerome and the Vulgate," 365; Peder Borgen, "Philo of Alexandria as Exegete," in Hauser and Watson, eds., *History of Biblical Interpretation,* 119.

[27] Dawson, "Plato's Soul," 93–96.

realized in the act of making the language of the Bible at its deepest and incommunicable level into the soul's language. Origen's most intense religious experiences took place within the work of exegesis itself . . . ."[28]

Origen is particularly useful for understanding Jerome, not only because both are Christian but also since Origen theorized at some length about the systematic process of interpretation of the Bible (his *Concerning First Principles*), thus bringing methodological unity to textual, critical, and philosophical studies. It is important to name the bases on which Origen claims to rely since in some instances they will be condign with our own, though in many cases likely not. Origen held the Bible to be authored by God, who arranged it down to its last letter as it needed to be (Origen acknowledged human involvement in the process, but saw it quite substantially controlled by divine inspiration). That is, Origen presumed a very literal process of inspiration that brought in its train a matched assumption about inerrancy. With God as author there could not be mistakes (Origen did not include the textual transmission problems as errors); if there appear to be inconsistencies and discrepancies, especially where there are awkward anthropomorphic elements, these invite deeper study. Origen taught that in some cases certain mysterious items were placed there by God to challenge us to cope in more sophisticated ways than we might otherwise have done. He taught that the purpose of the Bible was to mediate to us salvation, the gifts offered to us by the Logos of God. Bernard and Patricia McGinn write of Origen: "For him scripture in its entirety is nothing else than the Logos, or Word of God, teaching each believer in and through the church. The Logos, eternally begotten from the Father's self-emptying, who in turn emptied himself by taking on flesh, now becomes present and active in us through the mediation of his presence in the inspired words of the scripture."[29] Divine truths are available in the Bible, and made accessible to all of good will, though in a graded way, the more deeply to those able to apprehend the spiritual truths that are hidden in the text. This process of drawing ever-closer to God reverses the ruptured experience of the human community. Origen, though accused of importing an interpretation process foreign to the Bible into its pages, claimed (not without warrant) that the Bible itself, by its own richly allusive nature and interpretive processes, grounds such interpretation.[30]

---

[28] Bernard McGinn and Patricia Ferris McGinn, *Early Christian Mystics: The Divine Vision of the Spiritual Masters* (New York: Crossroad, 2003) 28–29.

[29] McGinn and McGinn, *Early Christian Mystics,* 23–24.

[30] Frances Young, "Alexandrian and Antiochene Exegesis," in Hauser and Watson, eds., *History of Biblical Interpretation,* 335–36, gives as the standard warrants Prov 22:20-21; Ps 77:2; Gal 4:22-26; 1 Cor 2:7-8; 9:9-10; 10:1-4; Col 2:17; Eph 5:32; Heb 8:5; 10:1.

How did Origen manage and demonstrate his processes of interpretation? The first thing perhaps to say is that his procedures varied, depending on the genre of text he was working with. But we can, although schematically, characterize Origen's process of reading by naming its most consistent steps. The first is a tremendous attention to the *philological and even physical* sense of the text.[31] As a prelude to interpretation the text was read aloud and made sense of, with punctuation inserted and made definitive; we can see here his insistence on the relevance of the text's particulars, none excessive, none able to be overlooked in the quest for meaning, each needing to be established as carefully as possible. That done, Origen moved on to the levels he typically found in biblical passages. The first level of meaning he called the *literal or historical,* comprising, besides events, data like geography and botany. Though a good deal of criticism rages around the famous Alexandrian here, it is worth noting that he most likely took most biblical events as historical, i.e., he assumed, perhaps unconsciously, that they had really happened. It is an oversimplification to charge that he does not respect the literal sense, since for some readers (among whom he listed Jews and the unlettered) further progress would be unlikely. The literal was to be first sought and in fact retained, though gone beyond if possible. Perhaps it is helpful to say that for Origen a historical event stood *behind* the biblical narrative, though the point would not be to reduce the narrative to the fact. And the recognition and classification of figures of speech, e.g., allegory, was part of grappling with the literal level as well.

Another level was called the *moral,* and comes closer to what we would likely call psychological or ethical. A third crucial level was for Origen the *allegorical or spiritual.* It is from this level, accessed ordinarily via the first two, that the divine mysteries about God and human beings become available to those able to attend to them. The process he envisioned here wants nuance. Since Origen held that the action made available within Scripture is that of the Logos (we can say the person of Jesus the Christ) instructing the soul, then the gift for us—it is always present readers that Origen is thinking of—is salvation: contemplation, divinization. The process he described was thus a way in which a reader entered a text to participate in the reality of *paideia*/formation that the text mediates. Hence the referent of the biblical text is not a historical event but the pedagogy of the Logos, which was made available via the biblical text.

---

[31] Young, "Alexandrian and Antiochene Exegesis," 338–41, stresses that the interpreters we are dealing with are experts in language and that for us to understand them as interpreters we must take proper account of their care for all the physical aspects of coming to know a text thoroughly.

But, though Origen elaborated rules and procedures, he did not follow them consistently, since his allegorizing went rich and multiple, adapted to the text under consideration. Young notes that Origen most habitually worked with two levels, but she stresses that his "undersense" included, richly, what we might parse as psychological, mystical, moral, ecclesiastical, christological, eschatological.[32] Scholars diverge on these complex matters considerably and inevitably, given their own presuppositions and training. But it is best, I think, to see Origen as not so much husking the literal (and moral) to get to the fruit of the allegorical as counting on a process of transposition via previous levels toward something ever more profound. The literal and moral senses of the text seem points of departure for the spiritual. The spiritual sense re-enacts the transcript of the literal sense in a parabolic or enigmatic way, not as an end in itself; what was rendered present for the later reader was, for Origen, the saving activity of God. The process of discerning the spiritual meaning through (again, not usually instead of) the other senses was certainly a matter of study, but also centrally of holiness and discernment. In some cases allegorical interpretation, as this method is commonly called, will distinguish a fourth level of meaning called heavenly or anagogical, orienting the reader to the final goal of Christian life and praxis.

If we keep in mind that these analogical procedures do not consist in anyone's—Origen's, Jerome's, or our own—taking a text and making its communication fit a predetermined sequence, then we are liable to get farther than some studies of allegory do. Origen and Jerome start their exegesis and interpretation already seized by the utter and overriding importance of the gift of Life offered in Jesus and the effect participation in that reality has in the experience of every creature. To help others see what riches are available, thanks to Scripture, is what animates the reading of an Origen or Jerome, not an obsession for classifying details. It may also (and almost incidentally here) be the case that the centrality of the Christ event, its galvanizing character, is what pushes Christian use of these reading strategies into a different quadrant than the less "anything-centered" Jewish readings will go.

THEODORE OF MOPSUESTIA AND THE TYPOLOGICAL METHOD OF ANTIOCH

Another way to appreciate the contribution of Jerome to interpretive theory as well as to actual reading is to consider "his Jonah" in terms of commentators at Antioch. Antiochenes share a good deal with what has just been described, differing perhaps more in emphasis on the compo-

---

[32] Young, "Alexandrian and Antiochene Exegesis," 335–36.

nents of interpretation than in kind of reading done. Young suggests that the basic differential between the groups is not measured by a regard for history or even by attention to multiple meanings, but by their respective focal interests in philosophy (Alexandria) or in rhetoric (Antioch).[33] And even there the lines are not really so clear, since rhetoric and philosophy share, by differing roots and routes, a concern for right living. There are differences, but before getting to those let us see what was common.

The Antiochenes shared with Alexandrians a basic interest in the multiple workings of language, and in fact a good deal of the terminology of the classical training. Fundamental would be the sort of work with text and "punctuation sense," with figures of speech—including allegory—with cultural particularities like flora and fauna, city size and location. The Antiochenes had an interest in what we might call the plausibility of the narrative (comprising storyline and speeches), its capacity to be of service to religious meaning. The Antiochenes were more likely than the Alexandrians to exploit the biblical context of a passage than to rush it to a new and later context. This is not so much a historical interest in the modern sense as it is an insistence on the originating circumstances as relevant in themselves.[34] Antiochene practice sought to clarify the subject matter of the narrative— what was to be demonstrated, what signified—the "mind" of the text. This "hypothesis" was kept clear and focal in the writings of this school. Also to be expected is a moral urgency, related to prophecy, with its capacity to speak into time, its rhetorical possibilities, and its pedagogic features. And building on this broad and carefully-established base, counting on its viability, was *theoria,* a contemplative insight based on mimetic relationships between one text or situation and another. As did Origen, the proponents of "the other school" could point to Scripture itself as the Mother of such reading; St. Paul calls it allegory, but it is the more basic figure and resemblance that we can read in his studies of Adam and Christ, of Sarah and Hagar with the synagogue and the church. The rhetorical emphasis or heritage at Antioch fostered a sense of prophets as those announcing events that had later counterparts as well as the notion of the deity instructing as a philosopher worked with students.[35]

---

[33] Young, "Alexandrian and Antiochene Exegesis," 344–51.

[34] Anyone steeped in modern historical criticism will scarcely recognize the "historical" interest of Antioch, at least not without some decompression!

[35] Young, "Alexandrian and Antiochene Exegesis," 350, and S. C. Winter, "A Fifth-Century Christian Commentary on Jonah," in Stephen L. Cook and S. C. Winter, eds., *On the Way to Nineveh: Studies in Honor of George M. Landes* (Atlanta: Scholars Press, 1999) 248–50; Winter attributes this anonymous commentary to Theodore, though that relationship has been denied recently.

The Antiochenes were not so interested in the exact wording of passages as were Alexandrians or Jewish readers; they were sometimes quite content to paraphrase a text if its meaning could thus be brought out more clearly. The vehicle of the deeper appropriation was perhaps more likely to be moral or "psychagogic" than linguistic, and there is beyond a doubt more moderation in making christological links than at Alexandria, though those few links explicitly made—e.g., Jonah named as a type of Christ—are made important. Young suggests that a salient difference between the schools has to do with time: "For Origen the Platonist, both the created order and the text of Scripture were symbolic of the eternal world of spiritual realities. Symbols and types he understood in terms of something standing for something else, so that the words of Scripture became a kind of code to be cracked by allegorical reading." Antiochenes, on the other hand, were suspicious of anything that "dismantled" the story or "turned any part of the story into a docetic charade [and] threatened the reality of salvation."[36] Before theorizing additionally, let us look at Theodore's Jonah commentary and see what it does.[37] As we consider it, the points to see are that it is a good example of Antiochene reading, it is not so very alien from what we heard about at Alexandria, and both schools can be discerned in Jerome's work on Jonah.

The commentary is shorter than Jerome's, and its choices for use of space are telling. A preface to the book makes a basic and extended "typological/christological" point: As the Exodus and the blood marking the doors of Hebrew homes made possible the escape of that group from bondage, so does the blood of Jesus accomplish a liberation; as the community of refugeeing Hebrews experienced healing when they encountered the bronze serpent raised up before them in the wilderness, so the lifting up of the savior on the cross was a source of salvation for a later group. The basic sense of later event being made tangible by the earlier one, or the earlier one underlined by recognition of the later one, is made crucial, as is, prior to these examples, the affirmation that the unity of God as author of both testaments and of all creation, humans included, is what grounds these similarities.[38] Hence typology is no "mere" literary feature, but a correspondence with creation and God's divine plan.

The Jonah similarity is suggested next, as Theodore moves closer to the biblical story from his prefatorial point. He couches the temporal contrast in terms of a polarity familiar to us from Jerome: What the Jews re-

---

[36] Young, "Alexandrian and Antiochene Exegesis," 351.

[37] Robert C. Hill, trans., "Commentary on the Prophet Jonah, " in *Theodore of Mopsuestia: Commentary on the Twelve Prophets* (Washington, DC: The Catholic University of America Press, 2004) 185–205.

[38] Ibid. 185–88.

sisted, God made available to the Gentiles; Jonah was sent to Gentiles since Israelites had a habit of disregarding prophets. That Jonah survived three days and nights in a mysterious place is mentioned, but to be picked up on, briefly, as a credential to make more likely that the Ninevites will take him seriously. Theodore urges that Jonah's disobedience is what led to the whale episode—a detail that does not work christologically for him, though you may remember that Jerome is able to make some analogies to Jesus' slowness to get going on a ministry to Gentiles! The design of this whole episode of Jonah 1–2 does not lie outside God's scope, since God cares for those who are receptive to divine purposes, notably Gentiles by implication here.[39] So Jonah is one of only a few labeled types, sent to a depraved group, to a city so large, so overpopulated, and so evil that it was known to Israel. Though we may note that there is nothing about Jewish refusal in the actual book—Jonah is the only Jew represented—Theodore spends considerable space on Jewish recalcitrance and on the motivation of Jonah's initial refusal that we have seen in Jerome: his sorrow over the later damage to Jerusalem, made know by the prophet Nahum.[40]

Before leaving this section of the story Theodore emphasizes that God's ultimate goal was not the destruction of the Gentiles but their repentance.[41] He mentions briefly the location of Tarsus and the unlikelihood that the prophet thought he was actually fleeing God—rather a particular aspect of God's face accessible in Jerusalem. The commentary is half over and we are at 1:1! God seems to allow Jonah to go his way, until the storm breaks out. Theodore takes pains to unscramble the sequence of events: It makes no sense to think of Jonah going below *during* the storm, while others are struggling against the danger; clearly he went below as soon as he boarded. Theodore is not so much interested in the prophet's feelings here, but moves on to the moment when the sailors bring him up to answer questions, since they can see from the fact that only their vessel is affected that the circle of potential culprits is small. The stress here is on the responses of the sailors to the truth of the situation, thanks to a likely assist from God. Jonah's confession of belief in and service to the powerful storm deity makes the sailors nervous of throwing him over; such a deed might be even more offensive to a God who is obviously already riled. But as we know, that is what they do, and the consequence is not simply better weather but the conversion of the sailors from their idols——that being the meaning of sacrifices they offered—not literal ones.[42]

[39] Ibid. 188–90.

[40] Jonah resembles Paul as well, who like Jesus sorrows over the "fate" of the Jews. Ibid. 190.

[41] Hill, ed., "Commentary," 189.

[42] Ibid. 193–98.

Jonah, according to Theodore, is in the water for a long time—plenty of time to make the psalm of ch. 2 sensible—before being picked up by the fish, which is not characterized as evil, but which gets the minimum attention imaginable! And Theodore, like virtually all the ancients, spends little interest on the experience of being inside a large creature. His Jonah prays from the water, and in addition to the standard text of Jonah 2, other more relevant text is dubbed in. This is a place to see that this Antiochene commentary usually gives no translation and is amazingly cavalier about the actual biblical text. Let me render the "Jonah psalm," its biblical phrasing juxtaposed with other more situated comment from the flailing prophet. A few verses will suffice to show the pattern: "You cast me into the depths of the heart of the seas, and the rivers encircled me; all your billows and your waves passed over me," to which Theodore's Jonah adds, "fleeing your service, you caused me [sic] to fall into the sea and experience a mighty storm; in the course of it the sea was whipped up, and like rivers its watery billows crashed upon me." And, biblically: "Then I said, 'I am driven out of your sight; shall I never again gaze upon your holy temple?'" is supplemented by, "With the ineluctable force of the calamity I thought myself rejected from your providence . . . and had no hope any longer of being in your holy temple to perform the worship due to you." "Waters flooded my very soul" is enhanced by "Then the sea monster took me from that place, and I seemed to inhabit some land, whence there was no possibility for the one in its grip to escape; though kept safe inside by divine providence, there was no finding any egress from there."[43]

The last few pages of the commentary go to the second half of the narrative. Theodore explains, while considering Nineveh's size, that though we have only a single terse proclamation, more was involved, obviously, Jonah spent considerable time traipsing about the city and he had to say more than a sentence; how else would the Ninevites have been responsive to a foreigner as they were? The commentator does not mention here the three-day experience, already having hinted its effectiveness.[44] God is the designer of the repentance process, and the Ninevites, like the sailors, make propitiatory offerings of their changed hearts and lives. God's care overarches Jonah's ministry. Jonah's reaction to the result of his preaching allows Theodore to retrace the issues of motivation: Jonah is sad at looking like a liar and a fraud.[45] The last chapter of the story, in the hands of Theodore, becomes the

[43] Ibid. 199–200.

[44] As Winter points out, "A Fifth-Century Christian Commentary," 246, the typology works primarily from the effective preaching and God's mercy to sinners, to which the three-day survival is subordinated.

[45] Hill, ed., "Commentary," 203.

education of Jonah, a divine effort designed to instruct him more fully about God's particular plans. Theodore seems to find the wind the last straw for Jonah—why grow old here if it will be like this? Theodore spends a bit of time on the breakdown of inhabitants of Nineveh: how many children, adults, why the mention of animals, and so forth.

An extended quotation from Frances Young makes a good close to this comparative section:

> Ancient literary criticism understood texts of all kinds in terms of *mimēsis,* that is, as representations of life intended to instruct. There was some anecdotal interest in the author and the circumstances of the text's composition, as well as in any circumstances that might eluci- date the content, but there was no genuinely historical criticism [she includes a reference]. Reading was anachronistic, for the intent of the author was simply to persuade the reader. Both Origen and the Anti- ochenes used the analytical methods of the schools, but their concep- tion of literary *mimēsis* was different. One stemmed from the treatment of texts in the rhetorical schools [Antioch], the other [Alexandria] from their handling in the philosophical schools. The differing results were not the outcome of literal reading as opposed to spiritual sense, for both knew, unlike modernists but perhaps not postmodernists, that the wording of the Bible carried deeper meanings and that the immediate sense or reference pointed beyond itself . . . . The difference lay not so much in exegetical method as in hermeneutical principles.[46]

Concluding Appraisal of Ancient Analogical Reading

Jerome and his contemporaries (Origen and Theodore, specifically, but others as well) accomplish their helpful readings by doing several things, which here I will characterize in fresh language rather than repeat what I have said before in the standard categories of theology and spiritu- ality. At base they are in every case minutely attentive to the biblical text, taking it as God's complex and mysterious but reliable communication with us who stand in need of its wisdom for our lives. They assume that Scripture's primary interest is to help us draw closer to God—who also wishes that—and to our neighbors—which God also desires. The "infor- mation," or better, the wisdom we need for that great quest is proffered re- liably from the biblical text. So the more care exercised on it and with it, the better. Jerome et al. thirst for such depth of relationship, and so they ex- ercise various strategies to expand the "react-able" surface of the text, as it

---

[46] Young, "Alexandrian and Antiochene Exegesis," 351–52.

were, the space from which we can gather the insight we need. As we have already seen, they exercise the readable material in various ways, all of which assert a fundamental similarity between some scriptural detail and our lives, though of course they do not put it quite like that when theorizing. Being Christian, they assume that a good deal of what God wants to disclose and what we need to heed is available from the figure of the Christ, not simply the details of his historical life but the many aspects of the "Jesus project" God has been effecting from eternity. Much is subsumed there, since for Christians that Christic reality makes new everything that had seemed other than it.

And then these scholars, having been driven to their readings by their thirst and their confidence in God's care, construct a grammar to show us what they have done, so they and we can do likewise. But the speech—and the thirst—precede the grammar, and we will never participate in their interpretive quest for love of God and neighbor if our main interest is the hermeneutical grammar! But conversely, we will never get what Jerome and his friends have shared with us if we cannot see some patterns in it. The key to the readings is ostensibly in the Scripture itself, as has already been shown: how words trip off rich associations, how figures can be made analogous to each other in various ways, how motifs can be mined helpfully. But we can see, I think, that the actually more relevant key is the deep experience the commentator brings to the text. Jerome might not have readily agreed to that assertion. But in fact the basic prompt for Jerome's reading of all characters, at least in Jonah, has to be his own experience of how people are, of what generates self-knowledge, of how encouragement for struggling on is best proffered. The ancients are more readerly than they know or get credit for!

To assess Jerome's specific achievement now in terms of its strengths and weaknesses, benefits and deficits, is a good next step for our study. I have already said that his reading of the biblical book is brief, balanced, full, rich. The biblical narrative is enhanced by Jerome's reading and interpretation, in that he can underline by asserting things that I, for one, would not have seen. To return to the language of Wendy Beckett, art historian and "proficient" in the matter of love of God and neighbor: Jerome deals with the characters, and by extension with his readers, so as to allow us to gain perspective somewhat obliquely rather than be bludgeoned by negativity. If Jonah's problematic behavior can be explained as an excess of grief rather than as a selfish and petty stubbornness, then my defenses are lowered so that I can see the need for redirection of regretful anger's energy. Jonah can learn, and I, standing behind him, can see as well. The christology is similarly balanced: Jesus is exemplary not only as a survivor and a preacher; he is also a pioneer who resisted or regretted the necessity of suffering when he faced it close up, though he ultimately embraced it when encouraged. And he was slow as well to take up the most radical and unthinkable of his assignments, though he did that as well, eventually. I, for one, feel in good company here, feel that I can progress in love with support where I am likely to resist belittlement. It may be the case that the persistent focus on Jesus will become short-circuiting over the centuries, but that does not occur in Jerome's work. And Jerome's many other insights into the human condition that he seems to derive from his familiarity with persons besides Jesus are helpful as well.

There are deficits as well, or weaknesses, as I add the score of Jerome's work. I think he misses an opportunity to work with the whole fish adventure, to mine the "helpful rescue" as well as "threatening danger" aspects of it. Writers who come after Jerome will become too narrow in their reading of the Jonah-Jesus analogy, omitting some of the possibilities in order to focus on a few (survivor of death, effective preacher to Gentiles, incarnated Logos) that become rote and somewhat sterile from overuse. To the extent that the Hebrew Scripture becomes trawled almost exclusively for a rather small set of analogies to the Christ-event, there is a hermeneutical diminution of its richness. Jerome is, in my view, not to be accused of that, but his method of reading is susceptible to it. And finally, and most significantly of all, the steady treatment of the Jews as failed responders to God's grace, as literalistic and carnal—i.e., blunt and obtuse—interpreters, is deeply regrettable, as it, too, piles up in the centuries stretching between Jerome and the mid-twentieth century. His particular reading of God's withdrawing from Jews and turning to receptive Gentiles is not a particularly good fit with Jonah and is massively self-interested as Christians so interpret.

Finally, before attempting one ancillary but related task in this chapter, let us return to the assumptions that ground Jerome, Origen, and even their peers at Antioch; earlier in this chapter I suggested seven. My claim here is that we—by which I mean educated and committed readers of our early-third-millennium era—can agree up to a point but not beyond. We need to reshape the assumptions of the ancients so that they suit our intellectual world and are condign with it. Consequently, our search for meaning will not be grounded on the seven I have placed under Jerome's work. I will reproduce what I said there, and then qualify the points as I see them.

First, all reading in early antiquity counts on texts that are inspired and recognized as such by the reading community, which relies on them for deep relevance. Many now still accept the basic premise of revelation and inspiration of Scripture but probably understand it with a very different anthropology than did Jerome and the ancients. In a word, the human participation in all phases of the process is now greatly expanded, which makes the voice of God less obvious to discern. A second ancient presupposition explains the first, for the revealed texts are considered as authored substantially by God. The texts say what God intends. My point here is similar to my rider to the first assumption: The means for struggling to read the Scriptures with some transparency onto God's plans are vastly more complex than had once been thought. The project remains the one to which I, with many others, am committed, but the path is much more difficult to detect than the earlier commentators can have supposed. Contemporary criticism is a vital and indispensable means for reducing our culpable naïvete.

Third, the process of study and interpretation is driven by the quest for holiness, again variously conceived. The point of studying and reading the texts is to transform the interpreter in the direction of the Author-ity of the Scripture, facilitate the return to God. Reading's goal is to find meaning, enact it, be shaped by it. Study is not simply a quest for knowledge. That I continue to think is valid, indeed crucial, though the sorts of relevant study are perhaps wider if not deeper than had been thought. The fourth point is related: The ancient texts are for now. Though old, and though written for "their own" times, they also continue to function fruitfully for present readers. Reading is not simply a visit to a museum. Again, I basically agree; but the responsibility to understand as much about the past as possible and also catch the "bend" of our own reading situations—often largely constructed from a submerged past—presses strongly. To read while remaining ignorant of the past is irresponsible and inadequate and will result in poor interpretations. And yet Scripture is not simply an old neighborhood where we once lived but now visit as jaded tourists; that it is ancient does not disqualify it from use. Fifth, the basic quest is to uncover meaning that is hidden, or less than obvious. Such potential is present in the sacred texts if not lying at the surface. The depths need unlocking, a process that starts, though it does not end, at the surface of the words and proceeds by one (or more) of the strategies under consideration here. The "letters" are not unimportant. Again, the shift is perhaps in the balance of factors. I would not see the biblical text as primarily a cipher or code, and yet its richest significance is not engaged simply by resolving its originating referents. Contemporary language study (the turn to language) is important to understand if we are not to under-read. Similarly, the reader must acknowledge the vast diversity of possibilities and choose carefully what she or he undertakes to do, since it will be partial at best. The careful choice of strategies is one of the most crucial moments for responsible reading.

Sixth, the base for such a search and the payoff is a basic similarity between one text and another more urgent one, a match between one existential situation and another. Analogy of some kind makes all these projects work. I would agree that the main prompt for us is analogy to our own lives—but not so much a finding of messages we struggle to apply to our own situations; rather, what what we need and want most urgently presents itself to our eyes. We then need to appropriate it very critically and suspiciously but not without love, empathy, and self-knowledge. We need to be similarly appraising of what others like us, with whom we are prone to agree, say; and we need to listen with attention and respect when those with whom we seem to share less—not to mention those with whom we disagree—bring forth their insights. Finally, seventh, the "grail" of the reading quest was, and in certain ways continues to be, for the inherent, ontologically given, non-arbitrary and reliable base or code that establishes the meaning as coherent. This is not a search for a single meaning; meaning was basically affirmed as multiple, if not always in so many words. The interpretive cipher or key, over time, has been claimed to be the human mind, the cosmos, the structures of language, the mysteries of symbology or mythology, certain features of human culture, or some combination of them. I have my doubts that there is a single code, or that time is well spent searching for it or advancing our claims that we have spotted "it" to the exclusion of others.

Conclusions

As we step back, now, from the specifically analogical readers and reconnect to our basic project, which is the construction of deeply existential meaning with our classic and privileged text, where are we? We can again distill seven points. First, we can name what does not quite work, though it has been helpful and productive up to a point. Meaning does not seem to be buried inside the text: not as a residue of some historical event which we must excavate in order to enter its meaning world and make it our own, nor as a treasure to be dug from the language structures, where we have to grasp the cipher in order to access a hoard that otherwise we will miss. Whether the cipher is God's specific communication to us or some patterning of our minds or culture, this search is ultimately misconceived in some way. Meaning is not a thing, hidden away, stored up, placed there in the past by someone. The scholars who have assumed that model—from the ancient patristic commentators and their heirs to the modern "psychological" interpreters—have seen some good things, some points that are useful for us. But their model is basically not workable in my view.

Second, and related: Meaning is an event, a process—not a thing. To negotiate the meaning of a work like Jonah does not at all disregard or dismiss the factors the "analogy scholars" we have studied dealt with as though they are irrelevant, but it re-balances them, correlates them in a different way. The major shift is to re-articulate more carefully the role played by the reader. The quest for meaning is more like playing a game, as has been pointed out by those working in the field of hermeneutics. To play a game is active; being simply a spectator of others' play is absorbing, sometimes, but it is not the same as participating in the game. And interpretation is not an activity like running a par course, where I can visit the stations on my own, compete with my former achievements, set my own standards for my performance. Rather, to search for meaning, at least when we are reading Scripture, is a team sport, where we are utterly interlinked with many others who are reading with us and/or who have done so in the past. Nor is the quest for meaning a one-time event—a grand Super Bowl that, once played, ends the season, except for the reporting on it. The meaning quest remains alive. Engagement is active, interactive with many others, ongoing. Not a search for a thing, interpretation is an engagement that generates and sustains many kinds of relationships and results in insight and change: the process of transformation. It is my sense that though he would not quite have recognized this description, Jerome's reading of Jonah is precisely the fruit of his particular existential choices, and he is doing basically what I have just described. Jerome worked his set of strategies not as though he were solving a complex math problem and had to manage his moves with formulaic exactitude. His engagement with the figure of Jesus prompts a good deal of patient insight about Jonah's moves; his own insights into the workings of human nature and God's grace seem to induce him to see that relationship as persuasive rather than punitive; and his theology of Christian election opens up from him a well of compassion for the Jews, who he thinks have been abandoned by God.

So a third point: *What does work?* At base, as many have supposed over the centuries of interpretation, there is an analogy sensed—by a reader—between one text and another, one situation and another, between the life experience of one group and that of another. The analogy is not, at best, simply one thing: three days in a fish belly, three days in a tomb or in the underworld. It is perhaps not ideally named bluntly in the text, though some detail of it may be tagged to give us a head start. It is not *not* a specific detail, but it also opens on much more. It is best, when negotiating meaning, to look for a set of factors, a cluster, even a sort of field of elements that resonate for us as readers. Then we, interpreting, discern the fit, elicit its details, construct bridges, invest in possibilities, select what is provocative. Note the active language here and the claim that the reader is virtually a co-player with the biblical authoring processes. The resemblances sensed and negotiated are rooted not simply in a past event behind the text, not merely in words that comprise the text in some artistic arrangement, though these are not incidental. The letter surely signifies. But the root resemblance is how a community of "biblical people," some thousand years worth with all that wise know-how, wrestled into language their experience of dealing with God in their common and personal lives; and we, insofar as we are engaged in a similar experience, can sense a fit with their experience. It is not the same, since the differences among us over three millennia are not small. The language of the biblical people will, of course, make use of their "history" and their cultural contexts; what else would they draw upon? But their expression exceeds, overflows history. And they will have cast their insight in the depths that their Hebrew language held out to them; what else? But what they are communicating is not simply clever discourse. So though we need to plumb the world in which they lived as they engaged God, we do not live there, so we cannot stop there. Their language is crucial but not stagnant.

And this leads to a fourth point, which actually simply unfolds the analogical base a bit. We started out noting that the effects of intertextual reading, of allegory and of typology—all basically mimetic—work on the fit between one "player" and another. So far so good. What makes the results of those readings good is the *frisson* of recognition when we find the readings the ancients have suggested and recognize that they work for us as well, not simply because they have to, since they are old and respected, but insofar as they actually do offer us insight and relevance in some way. The ancients were more right than they often get credit for. Accusations that allegory and its kin are inevitably alien, artificial, a-historical, abstract, contrived, disdainful and dismissive of context, imposed and overly universal need not be true, though of course they may be; some analogical reading is poorly done.[47] Scripture—the biblical corpus itself—is brimming with invitations to us to make sense of things analogically and by resonance. Such readings can be forced but need not be; good readers can remain fully alert to many kinds of context when reading analogically. If the dead were voting, such reading would have more "delegates" than many modern efforts that have reduced their quest pretty much to the ascertainable facts and originating referents.

Fifth: But as readers take on this highly participative and almost frighteningly responsible role, we need to stay alert to the place where our particular feet are placed and not claim more than we can do or undertake less than we must. We cannot insist that our readings are adequate for all times or all people, or reduce the power of our narratives to our own insights, claim our grammar as the be-all and end-all. That way lies arrogance, and reductive reading. We need not, cannot, and must not claim that we have solved our texts for all time. Now, most scholars would not say such a thing directly, but often the claim is implicit in the way their readings are set

---

[47] Whitman, *Interpretation and Allegory,* 13–15.

forth. Related: We need not pronounce for those whose experience differs from ours, especially for those we don't know very well. They may pick up on our readings, but then that is part of their negotiation. When we read we want to consult widely, borrow what seems right, but not take over what is not authentically our experience. We need to be as self-aware—and growing—as we can be when reading, so that we do not easily simply project our preferences onto the text. Part of the process of getting perspective, of finding or making meaning, comes as we see suddenly and perhaps with shame or compunction something about ourselves that we wish were not the case. As Christian readers (e.g., Jerome) have "their Jonah" regret that God abandons the "undeserving Jews" when the Christians repent readily, we now can see how self-interested that assumption is, granted it results in a sympathetic reading of Jonah. And when Christians insist that the Jewish authors and authoring communities are exhorting their benighted fellows to a greater universalism, we may recall the centuries of Christian exclusivism and persecution that culminated in the atrocity of the mid-twentieth century. Whose is the challenge to greater generosity toward the perceived "other"? So part of our negotiating meaning involves being alert for what we would rather not see but perhaps need to contemplate. Our meaning may come indirectly and ambush us from some unexpected place.

As we think about meaning, point six, it is not so incredible that, rather than a search for a difficult-to-find thing, "Scripturing" is an ever-expanding process. No one can complete it or exhaust all the possibilities. The Bible, when "handled well," does not wear out! If what vitalizes biblical narrative is the ongoing engagement with the mystery of God in the Jewish and young Christian community, and insofar as we center our lives around that same process, there is no limit on what we may discern. Even if we are simply looking for rich human insight, that will not be lacking, since the lives of the "Bible generations" were nothing if not richly human. To expend a life searching for God and being found is deeply human. The language that articulates the experience is rich and diverse. You will have noticed, carrying your Bible around, that it is not a small book! Our own struggles to relate with our various others to a vast and complex deity are not readily solvable, are not winding down into easy puzzles. *Why use old words?* First of all, the words are not merely old; they are also wholly fresh and current for us. And they are not simply "now words," but in fact have done long service, have worked well for many, and so are proven reliable. Finally, seventh, we must decide what we are asking of Scripture, of the story of Jonah, as we search for meaning. Do we want to explore the experience of anger, of jealousy, of resentment, of conflicted love, of danger? It is all available, and more—much more.

CHAPTER FIVE

Literary Features

We are halfway in our Jonah study, at least this project we are doing together. We are in pursuit of meaning, as well as needing to know how we are engaging it. We have discovered that meaning is ours to construct actively, as so many have done before us. Meaning-making is an event rather than a thing, and it is a collaborative task that we must do communally. If we are to search well, we must read with other people: living and dead, past and present, similar and dissimilar from us. Our meaning will be customized to suit the factors of our own location or situations, but it is neither sought nor found privately. We also have seen that the process of discovering meaning involves both some sense of what we are after but also an openness to what we may not have anticipated, an alertness to consider what comes our way unbidden. We have spent the last three chapters engaging ways in which other seeker-interpreters have worked, a journey that has taken us into the long past of mostly Christian interpreters, has given us the chance to ask about the construction of the original Jewish audience of the book, and has led us to consider some analogical readings of the story. In every case we have needed to think about historical matters, literary issues, and actual readers, but the balance of each of those projects has differed, as we are by turns stressing what lies behind the text, within it, or before it. Though so far we have seemed to be more interested in the views of other readers, I hope you have been honing your own sense of what you are asking this wonderful tale.

Present Task

In this chapter we will shift gears in several ways. First, we will work primarily with readers, readings, and interpretive processes generated within the past quarter-century or so, all intent on the literary features of the book. If you read some of these sources along with this discussion of them you will find that these writers are generally hesitant to talk directly about meaning;

perhaps it is more accurate to say that they will be more chary in what they claim, will offer tentative suggestions rather than pronouncing firmly and untroubledly, as have some of our earlier "consultants." These contemporary interpreters will also seem more interested in literary processes and dynamics than in religion. As you watch, you will find that any religious meaning arises for them specifically and explicitly from skilled negotiation of narrative features. After examining five literary strategies, we will turn a corner and consider one additional aspect. And in this chapter I will be less concerned than before to coordinate the insights brought forward and more to present them so that you can glean from them what you want. We will continue to let questions guide us: first to isolate the question that lies behind the presentation of a particular literary feature, then to represent the best summary of the point we can do; as we evaluate the benefits and deficits of the particular point made you need to be asking how the information assists you in your particular meaning quest, as I will be doing "off-air."

Literary Features of the Book of Jonah

You may recall from the end of Chapter 2 of this book that modern literary questions about the Bible came into their own only in the last few decades of the twentieth century. You may well say to me that when we are talking about a book, the subject is always literary, and in a sense I cannot disagree. But recall as well that up until the seventeenth century or so historical questions were not very prominent, but after the rise of critical studies they were *so* prominent that the quest for "genetic factors" of the Bible pushed aesthetic concerns to the very edges of study. The literary scholars we will "interview" now are aiming to redress that imbalance by considering features of the Jonah story that do not require much, if any, historical study. One point I have been making repeatedly is that our study works best when we can blend various types of study as needed. But at this moment we will focus on what is primarily literary. And we will do it in six steps, looking at six specific aspects.

Issue One: Features of the Jonah Narrator

An excellent place to begin is with the work of Kenneth Craig, who provides in his Jonah researches a good deal of basic and useful information. Here we will consider his sense of the characteristics of the particular narrator who gives us the Jonah story.[1] I would like to avoid here the gen-

---

[1] Kenneth M. Craig, Jr., *A Poetics of Jonah: Art in the Service of Ideology* (Columbia, SC: University of South Carolina Press, 1993); useful as well may be his review article,

eral and abstract discussion of kinds of narrators and go directly to the particular features we have in this story. Some commentators, Craig included, like the words "omniscient" and "reliable" for the narrator. My sense, rather, is that whatever that voice tells us is never enough, but always generates from us additional things we wish to know; hence absolute terms (like omniscient) are misleading. Our narrator holds back. Craig's comments here can be enumerated as six. His first observation is the most general: The narrator tends to tell the story briskly and to alternate between brief bouts of direct character discourse and "traffic-directing" or confirmatory comments. That is, after commencing abruptly and with minimal introduction of the character Jonah, the narrator settles into a pattern where "he" (as I will say for the Jonah narrator) either tells us who is talking— 1:1-2, 6—or else confirms what they have said;[2] occasionally the narrator sums up for us and presents some information we might not have known without him (1:3; 2:1; 3:10). The narrator can offer an "insider" view for a character, e.g., at 1:4 where the ship has a point of view, and at 1:10 where the sailors become panicked upon hearing Jonah speak, but outside our hearing. Craig reminds us that the narrator discloses more in this way about the sailors and Ninevites than about Jonah, at least until ch. 4.

A second useful point from Craig is that there are several instances where chronology is "deformed" or rerouted: 1:10; 2:1; the prayer of 2:3-10; 4:2; and possibly 4:5 seem to be places where, for some reason, the narrator chooses a slightly irregular path. So we are not given Jonah's explanation to the sailors, but simply see the result of it; we have some confusion of time and place of "exile and deliverance" as Jonah thrashes and prays, asks and gives thanks for rescue while still overboard; the prophet himself has apparently delayed to share a feeling he had earlier (4:2-3), though to claim that one "knew something all along" is perhaps suspect; and it is not clear what Jonah anticipates when he leaves the city but settles to await a further event. I think that, rather than simply chronological anomalies, these are all slight rifts in the text, prompting additional questions. The most odd of all is the abrupt or seemingly truncated ending, where certain storytelling conventions would have us anticipate more of a resolution. A third point Craig offers, related to what he says about translation, is that

---

"Jonah in Recent Research," *Currents in Research: Biblical Studies* 7 (1999) 97–118. For the narrator, see *Poetics of Jonah*, ch. 3. He makes some additional points in his ch. 7, and many works in your bibliography will have contributions to make on this topic.

[2] Craig, *Poetics of Jonah,* 34–35, 40–41, and ch. 3, also points out how the narrator and characters share specific language: e.g., 1:7; 1:4 and 11; 1:12 and 15; 3:2 and 4; 3:5 and 8; 3:9 and 10; 4:1, 4, and 9. That might seem obvious or natural, but it is actually a way in which the character and narrators collaborate or "bleed into" each other.

this narrator occasionally abandons standard word order for emphasis (1:4; 1:9; 3:3) and (fourth), he may use unusual vocabulary (e.g., the word for "have a care for" in 4:10-11).

The fifth point we may draw from our contemporary literary scholar's work has to do with the narrator's drawing of characters. Craig simplifies the possibilities to three: We learn about someone in a story because of narrator information (a large category, as we have already seen), from character speech (of several types), and by noting ways in which characters are seen to respond to each other. As you notice these things, recall how little we have (e.g., compared to a novel, where we can learn a great deal more, or even a lengthy biblical narrative like 1 Samuel, where we have many chapters to come to know King Saul), and yet how much we can derive from that little. So we learn about God, among other ways, from how Jonah and the sailors converse about the deity. We may think Jonah has faded out nearly completely from ch. 3, except it is his words to which the Ninevites have responded. We are given the inner feelings of the sailors and Ninevites but, contrastively, are screened from Jonah's motives and feelings until nearly the end of the story. The fact that several characters share the word "evil" (1:2, 7; 3:8, 10; 4:1, 2, 6) reminds us that we have multiple viewpoints here and that a common generic noun like "evil" will shift its referent and valence, depending on who is talking. Evil for one is boon for another. And only two of the characters have names. There are more nuances to be seen here, but this selection suffices to show us considerable texture in how we come to know these literary figures.

A sixth point concerns direct discourse specifically. Craig assists us to notice that our character sets talk (foreigners at 1:6, 7; 3:7-8; deity at 1:2; 3:2; 4:4, 9, 10-11; prophet at 1:9, 12; 3:4; 4:2-3, 8, 9), not only generating information and self-disclosure but having other effects as well. The sailors quote Deuteronomy 21:8 and Jeremiah 16:14-15; Jonah's complaint at 4:2 catches several biblical texts.[3] The words of one character (or character set) qualify our views of others, as we can ponder the sailors so reluctant in our hearing to jettison the source of their trouble, in our catching Jonah's criticism of God's permissive qualities, and in our listening to God's probing Jonah's care for the plant that sheltered him. Craig aptly concludes that the Jonah narrator is "a master at the art of indirection."[4]

One other scholar deserves consideration here, his points on the poetics of Jonah offered compactly on three pages of a packed work on the po-

---

[3] Jack M. Sasson, *Jonah. A New Translation with Introduction, Commentary and Interpretations* (New York: Doubleday, 1990) 272–86.

[4] Craig, *Poetics of Jonah*, 72.

etics of biblical narrative.[5] Meir Sternberg suggests that what works most effectively is a surprise gap which controls the reader's progress over the whole book. Sternberg claims that the narrator misleads the reader about the characteristics of the main protagonists: Jonah is drawn tender-hearted and God fierce. Only once those portraits have been etched in considerable detail does the narrator reverse them, showing that Jonah is actually resentful and God too kind. The narrative, he concludes, concerns the education of a prophet. My questions here are two: First, except for our very first reading, we cannot be surprised; if the gap is really the "spring" of the whole story, why has the book not been discarded once we have filled the gap? And second, though Sternberg's own prose presses us to read with him, his "apparently" and "obviously" and "confident" language is slightly coercive; I think he makes too airtight a case for clear portraits suddenly reversed. That many others have read the story in other ways slows us from thinking that we have to follow a certain track, no matter the brilliance of it.

Issue Two: Rhetorics and Narrative Structure

Like Craig, Phyllis Trible has written extensively on the book of Jonah, and to that work we will turn to get a sense of another literary feature—actually a set of features.[6] She can be seen as doing two main things: First, she introduces us to rhetorical criticism, the vast network of features by which a work can be said to communicate persuasively and effectively to its reader and offer the basis for constructing meaning.[7] And second, as she brings this network of observations to the well-crafted story of Jonah, she distills her work into a vast structure (or set of charts) that lays out in

[5] Meir Sternberg, *The Poetics of Biblical Narrative: Ideological Literature and the Drama of Reading* (Bloomington: Indiana University Press, 1985) 318–20. Sternberg's work was highly influential at the moment of the "turn toward language," since he reads brilliantly. He fell on more ungrateful times as the reader became more appreciated, since Sternberg is of the opinion that correct reading is quite circumscribed and depends on the reader's cuing to the formal features of the narrative. His readings are always worth considering, in my view, but not because only they are correct.

[6] Phyllis Trible, "The Book of Jonah: Introduction, Commentary, and Reflections," *The New Interpreter's Bible* (Nashville: Abingdon, 1996) 7:463–529 is her most recent; we will also refer here to work done in her *Rhetorical Criticism: Context, Method, and the Book of Jonah* (Minneapolis: Fortress, 1994).

[7] In *Rhetorical Criticism,* Part One, she summarizes for us what the term means outside the Bible, its origins in ancient Greece, its various relationships to literary studies—ancient and modern (and beyond); she reviews the path by which biblical scholars came to appreciate the field of rhetorical studies and gives some samples of Hebrew narrative that have been offered by various scholars. Her Part Two is most valuable for us, focusing specifically on the Jonah narrative.

fine detail the architecture, or floor plan, of the book.[8] She prefaces this major section of her book with directions to the participant as to how to proceed, so that we can work alongside her and also get maximum benefit from what she is able to show. The links between form and content, and form-content and meaning, are inseparable, Trible insists and demonstrates. There is no way for a summary to do justice to the detail she offers; you must study both her chapters 6–9 and the charts themselves, which, like Craig's book, provide non-Hebrew-readers with considerable usable information about the diction of the book. And she is able to make visible numerous points we would otherwise miss.

A sketch: Trible finds in the story two scenes: the first comprises Jonah 1–2, the second Jonah 3–4. Each of those major scenes is divided into four episodes: in scene one we find 1:1-3; 1:4-6; 1:7-16; 2:1-10; and in scene two she offers 3:1-4; 3:5-11; 4:1-5; 4:6-11. Immediately we can see patterns, relationships, and oddities or breaks in the patterning, whatever we decide to think about them. For example, Trible's charts help us think about the relationship between the two "episodes one," which seems quite close, and the two "episodes four," which seem more independent of each other. Her carefully deployed fonts and scripts allow us to watch the use and reuse of a motif like "great," which threads through the story persistently. We are helpfully directed to chiastic structures: small ones like 1:3 and 3:6, and larger ones like 1:15-16 and 2:1-11. These small balanced units are one of the most ubiquitous features of ancient Hebrew, and Trible helps us gain benefit from noting them. Her precise transcriptions from Hebrew into English assist us to see Hebrew word order, even if we are not proficient in the language. And she draws our attention to small rhetorical forms, like the sailors' prayer of 1:14 and the king's decree of 3:7-9. Finally, we can see what is "remaindered" or sticks out oddly when all else is in balance, as do the last two Hebrew words of YHWH's final question, mentioning animals.

It would be difficult to imagine a more useful study of literary features than Trible's, and it is a nice complement to some of the points available from Craig. As you finish your study you may wonder if all this detail is necessary for proper understanding of the story, a question on which you should have some views by now! We may fruitfully ask whether rhetorical criticism, Trible's work on Jonah in particular, is able to show us things

---

[8] These features are defined succinctly in *Rhetorical Criticism* Appendix B and illustrated throughout the book. The macrostructure occurs in ch. 5, in Appendix A; the smaller units are demonstrated throughout chs. 6–9. Other scholars occasionally offer useful structures as well, for example Jonathan Magonet, *Form and Meaning: Studies in Literary Technique in the Book of Jonah* (Sheffield: Almond Press, 1983) 57, 59, 61.

otherwise not seen (or underseen), or if it has ramified into clearer visibility some neglected poetic features? A sampling of Trible's work from each chapter of the Jonah narrative can offer us some sense of her views and possibly help our own. In Jonah 1, Trible shows the myriad ways in which Jonah differs from others: from God, from the sailors, from nature; this can be seen in various asymmetries and antitheses that characterize him and these others. The difference is presented to careful readers not simply in content but also often in form.[9] God commands, Jonah avoids; the elements obey, Jonah resists; the sailors manifest frantic and detailed concern while Jonah seems almost disinterestedly passive. We can scarcely seem to avoid the intercalating characterization as we study the rhetorics. An assertion Trible offers from Jonah 2 picks up the question of the poem's fit with its narrative matrix. She offers us a clear and balanced chiasm for the frame of the poem (2:1-2 and 11), and she presents a structure for the prayer-poem as well (2:3-10), concluding that "Someone, whether author or editor, has put in the voice of Jonah a beautifully constructed poem . . . ."[10]

As Trible lays out the skeleton of Jonah 3 we can look on the prophet's pithy proclamation of 3:5, which she says bristles with interpretive challenges: the exact implication of the forty days; the multiple possibilities of the participle from the Hebrew verb *hpk,* "overturn"; the absence of the expected form for a prophetic pronouncement of this kind; the lack of corroboration we have as to God's ordering Jonah to speak thus; the narrator's lack of reinforcing the truth of the sentence. But she concludes that by 3:8-10 the narrator has made utterly manifest the completeness of the overturning. And, for Trible, Jonah remains self-centered amid all the crisis for the Ninevites.[11] Her thorough discussion of Jonah 4 assists us to notice the prophet's prayer of 4:2-3, which Trible analyzes in itself and in relation to the rest of the book. She asks how Jonah's admission of motive in 4:2 has an impact on the earlier part of the story, notably at 1:2, where his flight might have been but was not explained. Here Trible raises the question of the variety of readings, since she quotes a scholar who reads— or fills—the gap of information quite differently than she does herself. Sternberg, a man rarely uncertain of his own readings, has seen the motivation in one way; Trible and a host of other commentators differ.[12] All read the same text, but in diverse ways.

That Trible's study of the biblical work is richly observed is clear. That she has exploited its semantic possibilities is less clear, possibly be-

[9] Trible, *Rhetorical Criticism,* ch. 6.
[10] Trible, *Rhetorical Criticism,* ch. 7, quote on 171.
[11] Trible, *Rhetorical Criticism,* ch. 8, specifically 179–80 and 190–91.
[12] Trible, *Rhetorical Criticism,* ch. 9.

cause she does not wish to do so. She seems poised on the edge of offering "the reader" a wider range of interpretation of the many cues she helps us see, but she does not quite push any to customize them. There is not much of a hint that "her readers" will run off in a variety of directions from what she has shown us about the narrative features. It does not seem much to matter who reads, except that she or he is attentive to the narrative artistry. Trible's work is solidly, brilliantly literary.

Issue Three: Genre Questions

Another question that interests literary scholars is the matter of the genre in which material is cast, or the particular forms that clothe a story's language. This is a point immediately familiar to us as soon as we stop to consider it: Is what we are considering a joke? a want-ad? a transcript of court testimony? a recipe? We know those differ in their content and intent, but also in their formal features, and surely in the expectations both their authors and readers/hearers bring to them. To mix any of these up with each other would be unlikely, though confusion often results when the genres are not so obvious. A second key point to query is more philosophical and perhaps at first seems less important: Where is genre rooted: in the intention of the author? in the formal contours of the narrative? in readerly competence and choice? Or are perhaps all of these involved? I hope you can recognize that we have stood in terrain like this before!

T. Desmond Alexander offers us a wonderful way to see what is involved in trying to identify the genre of Jonah in a piece he borrows from another scholar. He quotes us a paragraph:[13]

> The clock on the mantelpiece said ten thirty, but someone had suggested recently that the clock was wrong. As the figure of the dead woman lay on the bed in the front room, a no less silent figure glided rapidly from the house. The only sounds to be heard were the ticking of that clock and the loud wailing of an infant.

Urging us to ask what genre we have just sampled, Alexander helps us suppose initially that we are reading detective fiction: The clock is a clue, and the inaccuracy comment a red herring; the dead woman looks to be the victim and the retreating figure possibly the murderer; the crying child gives paths to numerous other questions we ask as we are trying to grasp the significance of what we have read. But Alexander next suggests that we

---

[13] T. Desmond Alexander, "Jonah and Genre," *Tyndale Bulletin* 36 (1985) 42–44.

suppose rather that the work is an autobiographical personal history, a sort of *Bildungsroman* or narrated story of the education of the writer. With that information, we can suppose that the inaccurate timepiece is a philosophical suggestion of disorder somehow relevant to the young man's life experience; the corpse is likely to have died naturally; and the wailing infant is quite plausibly the protagonist, especially if we are reading near the front cover of the book! Alexander's point is that without knowing the genre we are uncertain as to how to interpret the portion of text just sampled. Of course if we are dealing with a passage such as he has given us we will be able readily to know from the larger works how to cope: mystery or reflection—we won't be in doubt for long. The problem in the case of Jonah is that there is no "cover" to scrutinize or librarian to consult, nor is there much terrain to help us establish our footing! Scholars are not of a mind about the Jonah story's genre, and so we are missing a vital cue.

Let us take our two big genre questions together, not so much with universally prescriptive scope, but simply in terms of the book of Jonah: What are the cuing features and who makes the basic choice about their negotiation? First, if a writer makes a conscious and deliberate choice about genre, it should count for something, if not necessarily control the matter. Is there any clear signal of authorial intent? If there were, I for one would be pleased to consider it. There is some editorial (which is not quite the same as authorial, though related) data here. First, the small book has been included among the minor prophets at least since the time of the Qumran community, not so far in time from the book's plausible production.[14] If such a venerable choice is to be honored, as I hold that it is, we know that Jonah is a prophetic book! Granted, Jonah differs in a number of ways from some of the other works included in the scroll of the twelve shorter prophets; it surely shares elements with them as well. And, related: We can also relate it to short narratives of prophetic figures embedded in 1–2 Kings. Again, we might observe that few of those "narrativized" prophets have books named after them as Jonah does, and yet still our prophet resembles at least Isaiah in this pair of particulars: a story of him in 2 Kings and a named book as well. Though somewhat obvious, those two pivots of identity are important. If we are to reduce or focus Jonah to one core genre identity, it will be prophetic narrative. But though important, that does not get us very far into the question of genre. Beyond that, I see no reliable author's cue, a conclusion reinforced by the various viewpoints on the topic among scholars. If it were clear, there would be some consensus. But there is none.

---

[14] Sasson, *Jonah,* 14.

So we can move our attention to a second point, the book's literary features—the shaped language the author has left us with, whatever choices may have stood behind them when he wrote. Alexander also moves to the wider literary question, appropriately, since "prophetic" is too general a designation, though helpful to a point. He offers us, with good (though slightly dated) bibliography, a set of possibilities for Jonah's genre, including history, allegory, midrash, parable, legend, *novelle,* satire, didactic fiction.[15] His sorting of the possibilities may be useful,[16] but I would like rather to push past it toward two other questions: Does a story like Jonah *have* a precise set of genre markers, and can we usefully identify that it *is* one genre and not another? In Jonah's case, at least, we have a narrative that hosts numerous sub-genres or forms, including a psalm, questions, dialogue, and the like. So though we have already noticed that there is a clear distinction between a joke, a want-ad, a legal transcript, and a recipe—such that we will not confuse them and could offer a definition if asked—the same does not appear to be true for the narrative we are dealing with, at least at the size of item between "prophetic narrative" and its sub-parts. How can we usefully classify a matrix genre from its features? And, though we can readily take Alexander's point that we will read a detective work and a young man's autobiographical rumination differently, there is nothing in the paragraph Alexander quoted to help us know *ipso facto* which we are dealing with. So scholars, discussing the literary features of the Jonah story, have come to no clear agreement as to the narrative's specific genre in the more than two thousand years of criticism. Opinions do not lack, and they are strongly argued. But ultimately they are not—have not yet been—persuasive. So perhaps all the classifying of sub-elements in the Jonah story will never tell us what we need to know. To note these elements is important, but they will not solve our genre question, in my opinion.

Before leaving this part of the discussion, let us try one more possibility. Suppose we offered some tight and practical definitions of the genres Alexander has given us.[17] Could we then choose between history and fiction? Between history and satire? Among *novelle,* legend, and parable? Would we likely conclude that Jonah "is" not so much an allegory or

---

[15] Alexander, "Jonah and Genre," 36–40.

[16] I think you may notice, if you search out this article and consult it, that he would have helped us additionally had he provided some definitions, or at least some edges around some of the possibilities he offers us. Indeed, it might have become more apparent that some of his categories overlap substantially and others are of such different "denominations" that it is difficult to move productively among them.

[17] A useful book for certain terms is Wendell V. Harris, *Dictionary of Concepts in Literary Criticism and Theory* (Westport, CT: Greenwood, 1992).

midrash as it is readable as one if we like, or that all history is "fictive" in some basic way, in the sense of "constructed," shaped? Jonah can be allegorized. It has midrashic features, possibilities. We are about to weigh the case for—and against—its being read as a satire. Perhaps the most pregnant of the genre possibilities floating around is parable, a word Alexander defines in what seems now a very simplistic way, perhaps related to his ready dismissal of the possibility that Jonah is a parable.[18] If we were to offer an appropriate definition for "parable," my hunch is that the genre would work helpfully, if not quite adequately. But the point I want to make here is that the genre cannot, in the case of Jonah, be diagnosed satisfactorily from the heterogeneous constellation of literary features any more than they can by struggling to discern the intention of the author. Sets of features can be noted,[19] but they do not necessarily or definitively set the genre.

This last point urges back to our drawing board above. If the author does not, or has not in this instance been able to signal the genre clearly, and if those wishing to gather the genre's identity from a scrutiny of its literary DNA fail, is it simply a reader's call? We will examine this question shortly when we ask whether Jonah "is" ironic or not. I think we can conclude without spending a great deal of time on it that readers who want to progress on the question need to work with heuristic and flexible definitions. If I want to make the case for Jonah as a parable, over against the views of those who have dismissed that tag, I will need an understanding of the parable genre that can offer categories for the story at hand. Though I will not be presuming that the author of the book of Jonah had my definition in hand, my genre needs to be generally coherent with what that author would have been supposing, unless, of course, I am consciously choosing to read counter to the "culturally viable product" that we have in the Jonah story. The author does not control the genre but has influenced it, granted the demonstration of the link is now impossible. The genre definition I offer will need to include fairly well the literary features of the book. It will not be exact, of course, since art is not following formulas rigidly. But my definition needs to work with most of the elements in the narrative. Still, it will be shown effective, persuasive, and substantially illuminating insofar as I struggle to make the case, as I do the work of showing the way in which "my genre choice" produces an effective, compelling reading of

[18] Alexander, "Jonah and Genre," 38–40: He says it is more than an earthly story with a heavenly meaning, can embrace under its umbrella the forms of proverb, simile, taunt, riddle, or metaphor. We may need to ask a parable to be more than a story with a didactic point; and though Alexander does not quite say this, we may need to loosen our grip a bit on New Testament parables as setting the contours for the parable genre.

[19] Consult Sasson, *Jonah*, 18–20, and Magonet, *Form and Meaning*, 90.

the story. So though author, text, and reader remain, the most active of these now is the reader!

Issue Four: Irony, Satire, Parody

This discussion is very similar to the one we just left, though without overlapping it exactly. Perhaps it is best to say that we can track this question in a way similar to the previous one. The question is this: Is Jonah a satire, a parody, or not? Is it meant to be read ironically, tongue-in-cheek, or "straight"? Does it aim to make fun of, lampoon, or show ridiculous what it is talking about, or does it make a serious point? I have made this particular "genre" question a separate issue from our issue five, partly since it has generated a good deal of comment, of which we will sample some. We will proceed by looking for useful definitions, though we will ultimately have to settle for general ones; and then we will ask our Jonah commentators whether they are claiming that the author determines the genre or "tone" of the work, whether it lies in certain literary features, or whether it is a reader's call. You may suspect that we will end up once again with a judicious blend of these three!

The scholars I have gathered to help us here have offered definitions of the words they have in mind: satire, parody, irony.[20] Gathering from what they offer, we can work with the following useful notes: "Satire is the exposure by comedy of behavior which is standardized and, to that extent, foolish"; and "[p]arody is that breed of satire in which the standardized behavior to be exposed is literary."[21] And irony usually suggests the capacity of the need to entertain two contradictory positions simultaneously, while parody imitates and distorts another, usually serious, piece of work.

---

[20] James Ackerman, "Satire and Symbolism in the Song of Jonah," in Baruch Halpern and Jon D. Levenson, eds., *Traditions in Transformation: Turning Points in Biblical Faith* (Winona Lake, IN: Eisenbrauns, 1981) 213–46; Arnold J. Band, "Swallowing Jonah: The Eclipse of Parody," *Prooftexts* 10 (1990) 177–95; Adele Berlin, "A Rejoinder to John A. Miles, Jr., with Some Observations on the Nature of Prophecy," *JQR* 66 (1975–76) 227–35; Athalya Brenner, "Jonah's Poem out of and within its Context," in Philip R. Davies and David J. A. Clines, eds., *Among the Prophets: Language, Image and Structure in the Prophetic Writings*, JSOTSup 144 (Sheffield: Sheffield Academic Press, 1993) 183–92; Yehoshua Gitay, "Jonah: The Prophecy of Antirhetoric," in Astrid B. Beck, et al., eds., *Fortunate the Eyes That See: Essays in Honor of David Noel Freedman in Celebration of His Seventieth Birthday* (Grand Rapids: Eerdmans, 1995) 197–206; John C. Holbert, "'Deliverance Belongs to Yahweh!': Satire in the Book of Jonah," *JSOT* 21 (1981) 59–81; David Marcus, *From Balaam to Jonah: Anti-Prophetic Satire in the Hebrew Bible* (Atlanta: Scholars, 1995); John A. Miles, Jr., "Laughing at the Bible: Jonah as Parody," *JQR* 65 (1974–75) 168–81.

[21] Miles, "Laughing at the Bible," 168.

Typically involved is a composition which always assumes a pre-existing text which it imitates and distorts, often, but not always, for satiric purposes.[22] Another talks of satiric elements—the hyperbolic, grotesque, and absurd, where a dispreferred object is attacked indirectly, pointedly, externally (i.e., not simply psychologically), and says this of irony: "Irony is consistent both with complete realism of content and with the suppression of attitude on the part of the author. Satire demands at least a token fantasy, a content which the reader recognizes as grotesque, and at least an implicit moral standard, the latter being essential in a militant attitude to experience," and ". . . irony is best characterized by ambiguity of intention on the part of the author."[23] From these, we can gather the following: All tend to say or hint that there have to be two uneven or imbalanced lines of discussion that are crossed to generate the satiric or parodic genre or tone. Something serious or respected is rendered suspect by juxtaposing it with something else, with the assistance of exaggeration or distortion. There are other points we could mine from the definitions, but let us move on to the next questions.

Is the choice of satire made by the author of the story? And can a biblical editor or authority have knowingly included a satiric narrative among the prophets or eventually in the canon of Scripture? Our scholars do not, for the most part, make their sense of this matter clear, which suggests to me that they assume without much evident scrutiny that the author has a definite role to play. Even verb choices like "included," "depicts," "portrays," "inserts" betray that assumption.[24] Berlin raises specifically the question of whether satire can have been recognized and included in the Jewish canon, finding that claim unlikely and even offensive. My point here is that none has made a clear case for authorial intent; they have mostly or implicitly assumed it. If the case is not made, or if it cannot be made, then we must look elsewhere for our satire, parody, or irony.

As you might expect, most of the arguments in these articles focus on the literary narrative itself, quite appropriately. Virtually all of the writers I have assembled here, except Berlin, comb the book and arrange many instances to exemplify their definitions. A brief sampling: Jonah is parodic in his prophetic call and response; his manner of dealing with virtually all others is the opposite of what a prophet should do; his behavior is composed of exaggerations and incongruities, puns, and other wordplay; the

[22] Band, "Swallowing Jonah," 177–80.

[23] Holbert, "'Deliverance Belongs to Yahweh!,'" 60–62.

[24] See Ackerman, "Satire and Symbolism," 235; Band, "Swallowing Jonah," 182; Berlin, "Rejoinder," 227; Brenner, "Jonah's Poem," 188; Holbert, "'Deliverance Belongs to Yahweh,'" 60; and Marcus, *From Balaam to Jonah*, 95.

many intertexts, some quoted by Jonah, are ludicrous in the story; Jonah seeks refuge in dangerous places and misses the safety he is offered.[25] If we classify their observations we can see that the satire can be seen in compositional dynamics that are situational in the story, in stylistic techniques of storytelling, and in certain narrative moves made by the storyteller.[26] And we can see, I think, that the intersecting viewpoints that are necessary are in place: perhaps within the Jonah story as ch. 2 is studied in relation to the rest of the story, or more widely when other biblical intertexts are called forth; and as observed already, the "cross" may come when the story is addressed to a particular situation available from within biblical studies.

But without denying such a possibility, my question is: *Must* the story be read that way? *Is* Jonah a satire? A case can be made that the prayer of Jonah fits poorly within the narrative, but a countercase may be offered that it fits well—by various criteria.[27] Jonah may be a parody of prophets, but there are other prophetic moments, e.g., Elijah at 1 Kings 19:4-18 and Jeremiah 20:7-12, where prophets are not so compliant as our scholars ask Jonah to be! And though I am in sympathy with the point that satire or irony can be situational, that case cannot really be made from the literary text itself. We have already reviewed the careful work of Ehud Ben Zvi, who takes the book to be "straight" rather than parodic or satirical and who organizes many kinds of criteria to substantiate his case that the book was produced for the *literati* of "Persian" Jerusalem. So the case for satire cannot be made from the narrative alone, granted there are many possibilities for such a reading.

We arrive, of course, at the reader. And once again our scholars fall somewhat silent here. They come close, in several instances, to naming the role of the reader, but not quite so close as they need to come, in my opinion! They tend to remark the difficulties for readers rather than the challenges and opportunities. So Miles says it is difficult for a reader coming to a text much later than it will have been written to discern what situation is under discussion; Band notes that readers may lack the competency to respond to signals given by a text, and that a reader needs to either "get it" or resist it. Marcus accepts that at least sometimes an irony exists primarily in the eye of the beholder.[28] What they seem to avoid is the admission that the readings they offer from the literary text are, in fact, their own constructions rather than in-

---

[25] Ackerman, "Satire and Symbolism," 220–35; Band, "Swallowing Jonah," 180–85; Brenner, "Jonah's Poem," 187; Gitay, "Jonah," 197–99, 206; Holbert, "'Deliverance Belongs to Yahweh!,'" 62–75; Miles, "Laughing at the Bible," 170; Marcus, *From Balaam to Jonah,* 90.

[26] This point is offered by Band, "Swallowing Jonah," 185–88.

[27] See Ackerman, "Satire and Symbolism," and Brenner, "Jonah's Poem," for these studies.

[28] Consult Ackerman, "Satire and Symbolism," 219; Band, "Swallowing Jonah," 182–83, 191; Marcus, *From Balaam to Jonah,* 104–19; Miles, "Laughing at the Bible," 168–69.

herently "in" the text in some unequivocal way. The cases they build for satire or irony are often good ones, but without their particular reading choices, the satire did not exist. The crossing viewpoints are best seen not simply as the author and the character Jonah, or as the prophet and other characters either in the forty-eight Jonah verses or in the wider Bible; it is the reader's angles and those inferred from the text that determine the satire.[29] It is not my choice to read Jonah satirically, since I find his behaviors quite sensible against my own assumptions about the matters he is dealing with. So lacking a clear signal on the author's part, without unambiguous situational topoi and strategic narrator choices in the story itself, and without the book's production circumstances being patent, it seems that a reader may—or must—assemble a case for satire by making her or his own assumptions and intentions responsible. Note carefully: I am not saying the reader invents the satire or irony, but that the choice to diagnose it calls for a particular readerly viewpoint dialogically engaging a suitable text. Jonah surely has ironic and parodic possibilities, but they are not inevitable. An interpreter makes a strong case, not the only case. To pick up on them demands creativity and competence on the reader's part, and of course responsibility and authenticity. It seems responsible for a reader to write what she or he knows most deeply–which may be Jonah satirical or Jonah "straight."

Issue Five: Wordplay

For our last literary consideration let us do something that is fairly straightforward: a word study. As you know, when Jonah finally preaches in Nineveh his proclamation is brief (just five Hebrew words) and seems clear in its essentials: "Forty more days and Nineveh is 'something.'" You can look at your Bible translations to see how that word is translated, but let me talk a bit about the Hebrew word from which every translator began, whatever choice ultimately emerged. The Hebrew word is transliterated with the three Hebrew consonants *h p k*. This is not the place to go into great detail about Hebrew verbs, but we do need to understand that they are like, but mostly unlike, English verbs in their capacity to carry meaning. If you take the English word "turn," you know it can be a verb in several tenses (turn, turned, will turn, has turned); the verb can be transitive or intransitive (one can turn something else, like a car, or can simply turn: implied is oneself). It can be a noun (we can talk about taking turns, a turnabout), a participle—which works like a verb and adjective (turning,

---

[29] It is worth asking on what pivots such a reading rests: i.e., if one wants to see Jonah as foolish, why? How much must one overlook to build the case?

she raced away); it can take on a sort of prefix, like "return" or "overturn." Hebrew words can ring changes in a similar way with a basic root like *hpk*/turn. The question at hand with Jonah 3:4 is: What does "overturn" mean, or better, what range of meanings can it carry?

To parse the issue a bit more: At stake is whether or not the Hebrew verb root used and the particular way in which it is used—a *nifal* reflexive/passive participle—can only mean that the city will be turned over in the sense of being destroyed, routed, overwhelmed, or if it can be understood to allow also that the city will be changed, undergo some sort of conversion of manners, reverse or be reversed from its wickedness. There are at least three levels to the question: First, philosophically, do words denote or contain precise and quite clear meanings? Second, as we investigate the other places in the Bible where this word occurs, what connotations do we find? And third, as we look at the narrative dynamics, does it help good storytelling if the word ranges to include more than one thing?

You may be relieved to know that we are not going to spend a great deal of time on language philosophy! Without arguing the matter out, I want simply to stipulate that my sense of language is that we select what we need in order to convert our thoughts, feelings, and experience into language so we can grasp and perhaps share it. Though there are discourses, e.g., mathematics and science, where words have very precise meanings, in common talk it is not so orderly. So we understand that "three" means "not four" when we are working on math problems, and if we are working on a chemistry experiment it matters what bottle we reach for to add some reagent to what we are concocting. But in prosaic discourse language has a good deal more flexibility of range, and we invest words with meaning as we bring them to various "sites" of our conversation.[30] Words come to our conversation already trailing—if we wish to note it—the richness of other places where they have been used memorably. One easy way to think about this notion is music: Consider your favorite song and ask yourself in how many episodes of your life it has functioned memorably, e.g., on a special birthday, when you spent time with a close friend, after someone you loved has died. Each time you "play" or almost enact the music, it adds depth for you. Language works similarly. Another perhaps less happy but equally clear analogy can be family fights: When people who know each other well rehearse the "same old issues" that tend to come up between them, language is frequently reused and

---

[30] If you are interested in tracking this subject further, one good place to start is with the philosopher Mikhail Bakhtin, whose work with language has been extremely fruitful and creative. See Barbara Green, *Mikhail Bakhtin and Biblical Scholarship: An Introduction* (Atlanta: Society of Biblical Literature, 2000).

brings to each new round the tangible recall of rounds past. A single word, incautiously chosen, can sometimes ignite a huge row!

Additionally, when we look up our *hpk* word in a Hebrew lexicon we find that it occurs in more than one hundred places, with a wide range of meaning.[31] It can mean all the things you might anticipate: turn back—something else or oneself; restore, overturn, change, transform, pervert, turn toward, turn against, turn into. Since it can bear all those possibilities—or since it is utilized in contexts where lots of variant "turning" is under discussion—it is not feasible to restrict the meaning narrowly. Even if we inquire more deeply into the particular form of the verb as Jonah articulates it and see that he is using a participle form that implies that the city of Nineveh has some agency in the process—Nineveh participates actively in its own turning—we are not narrowed down in our understanding of the possibilities. Some Hebrew Bible words occur very infrequently, and it can be difficult to get at their semantic possibilities. But "overturn/*hpk*" is not one of them. One of the ways you could explore what the word means is to look at as many of its Bible uses as possible. It would be a good-sized task! Commentaries can help you here, but you need to read alert to the fact that the scholars may not be able to tell you everything you might wish to know. Sasson's commentary on Jonah discusses the "overturn" word usefully.[32] He tells us what it can mean and directs our attention (perhaps disproportionately) to Genesis 19, where the cities of Sodom and Gomorrah are overturned violently. He reviews with us how the earliest Jonah translations managed the word and what some great interpreters thought it best meant. Though I could be wrong in my inference, I think Sasson is not eager to let the word "overturn/*hpk*" have too wide a range of meaning, though he allows that it may exercise such an ambiguity in the Jonah story. Sasson is more interested to discuss the particular use of the word in Jonah than to roam the lexicon for possibilities.

So if Jonah's utterance is capable philosophically, historical-philologically, and existentially of bearing a wide range of meaning, let's see if such a reading is fruitful. We begin with the prophet's utterance in 3:4. Though we will say more about this later, ask yourself how you sense Jonah's demeanor as he delivers his words to Nineveh: Are the words suited to the task he is doing, to his role as a prophet, albeit a reluctant one? Note that, though scholars love to interpret Jonah's feelings here, we have little to know cer-

---

[31] Francis Brown, with S. R. Driver and C. A. Briggs, *The New Brown-Driver-Briggs-Gesenius Hebrew and English Lexicon with an Appendix Containing the Biblical Aramaic* (Peabody, MA: Hendrickson, 1979) 245–46.

[32] Sasson, *Jonah,* 94, 234–37, 267, 295, 345.

tainly and plenty of room for speculation. Whether he is simply doing his job or intent on accomplishing the repentance is left open. Second, we must note that we have not heard God instruct Jonah in these words. Specific language is sometimes given when a prophet is sent on a mission, and it may be that we are to understand that when Jonah speaks words God provided directly. But in this story Jonah appears to select his own words. We may think he knows what he wants to say, but again the matter is not so easy to close off. If words mean a lot of things and can do so simultaneously, we might want to say that Jonah does not control the meaning of his "overturn" word and we may even suppose he does not understand it fully as he articulates it. Or we may say that just because he intends and hopes for one of his meanings, the others might muscle their way forward to perform, regardless of the speaker. You may have painful experience that speakers do not fully control the impact of their words simply by intending some meaning!

Next we can think about the characters who hear Jonah, first the citizens and then their king. The people do not comment interpretively, but they act to change their behavior dramatically, enacting gestures which in Hebrew Bible culture express anguish over some situation (3:6). We might say that they respond to the prophet's "overturn/*hpk*" with "turnings over" of their behavior. And the king reinforces what they have done by dramatic gestures of his own, by proclaiming that the whole city must do what they appear to have already begun; he urges that their behaviors change from planned violence and from evil conduct in general (3:7-8) and that urgent appeal be made to God. And then the king speculates on the effect of these deeds and the fervent plea to God: They *may* influence God to a change of mind so that the city does not perish (3:9). Note here that we do not quite have cause/effect reasoning and ethics, though we have the deeds of the Ninevites alongside the words of Jonah and the plans of God. We can see that the Ninevites' hope for a reprieve seems justified from what they say and do, though nothing they heard from Jonah explicitly offers it. That is, I think the text prompts us to understand that the Ninevites hope it is not too late for their lives to be saved, but they do not know whether it is the case or if their actions are suitable. In other words, as the Ninevites hear "overturn/*hpk*" they act as though turnings may prevent overturnings. And God, we are told, changes his mind and averts the disaster that he had intended and does not carry it out (3:10).

We have already talked about ways in which hypothetical "intended readers" might hear the words. We can have no way of knowing with certitude, but we entertained Ehud Ben Zvi to suggest that the question of changed behavior turning punishment away from a city is likely a sensitive one for them, whether they are thinking of enemy cities like Babylon and Nineveh or of their own Jerusalem, turning now in one way and now in another. And what we can get some purchase on is how we choose to hear Jonah's proclamation, which ought to take account of the various factors just named. That is, our hearing should include more ears than simply our own as we factor in the various artistic reverberations under consideration among the characters. If we wish to restrict Jonah's participial verb to a single meaning, we can do that. But I think we will do better to allow it as much latitude as it can sustain. It need not lose color or strength by our permitting it some range; think of the various possibilities as jostling energetically amongst each other. In a sense all the characters and we, standing behind them, are bidding for what they wish the verb to mean, are wagering for their reputations and lives. Since, particularly with Jonah, we have many possibilities to weigh and cannot select them all simultaneously, we need to understand our own wishes and hopes and "own" them in the sense of taking responsibility for them. If we read Jonah as querulous and resentful of others' good, more intent on his own reputation than on the weal of others, then we need to see why that is our best sense of things. If we prefer to think that Jonah, like other prophets, struggles in various ways with the prophetic challenge to utter God's words such that humans can understand and accomplish them and never fully understand quite how it works, then we need to ponder the implications of such a choice. But we need to acknowledge that, since Jonah the character remains somewhat inscrutable and undecidable, when we read him definitively we are "finalizing" him ourselves.

Finally here, it is crucial for our understanding of "overturn/*hpk*" that we look at the narrated design of the book, its authoring into a culturally enduring product. Is the concept of reversals prominent in the book, and in a variety of ways? I think we can move backwards from ch. 3 to recall Jonah's going west when he was asked to go east and his being brought back from a sea voyage to dry land, via a whale that swallowed and then disgorged him. We watched him as well go below deck and then be hauled up again from his slumbers during a storm that was bidden forth and then averted by certain behaviors on the part of the sailors, some of which suggested reversal of allegiance on their part (1:14-16). And we can move ahead in the short narrative of Jonah and see that, besides his initial turnings around, he is whiplashed from silence before God to complaint, from gratitude for his life's being spared to wishing he were dead, from consolation under a comfortable shrub to indignation when it withers away. The story is constituted substantially by reversals, and so I think we are bidden to allow the range of Jonah's language at 3:4 to be broad and provocative. The dilemma on which the story ends testifies similarly. Our choices about the meaning of "overturn/*hpk*" are crucial to the reading process and must be taken with great care.

Turning a Corner

The last point to make—crucial and I hope not unexpected—is that it takes a skilled and competent reader to read an artistic narrative fruitfully. So having singled out five literary features to consider, our final move is to think again about what a reader, approaching situated, will do. A useful article by scholar A.K.M. Adam puts matters sensibly by using the analogy of the fish-eye lens, which is a very wide-angle lens (180 degrees) that produces a round image rather than the usual rectangle, magnifying the center and losing the periphery a bit, somewhat in the way our human eye does.[33] Adam introduces us to one of the earliest and most persistent reader theorists, Stanley Fish, and brings out the most controversial issue in reader-oriented theory: *Is there a text, or not?* Now, at a certain level it seems a foolish question, since we know there is a written Bible and it has a story of Jonah. But the actual point is more subtle: *Does the text constrain our reading in any way, or can readers in fact negotiate just about anything they wish?* Again to hedge the question a bit: It is not so much a matter of whether the text tells us anything; clearly it does. But the issue really is: *how much does it tell us?* Does Jonah have a wife and children in the biblical book? Obviously there is no mention of them; the narrative is silent on that point (though we can find out about them in the *Qur'an*!). We may add them if we wish to do so, and we will soon watch Jewish tradition fill in certain other textual lacunae in wonderful ways. More complex and controversial is the question of Jonah's motivation: *Who can decide what is bothering Jonah, on the basis of the various bits of information the text poses?* Is Jonah jealous of the Gentiles, or not? *Who can read him, and by what set of interpretive decisions?* That question can be factored variously, and it cannot be answered definitively from the narrative itself. Readers will differ on Jonah's reasons for his actions. To some extent the readers will be drawing on their own experience to supply for Jonah; it is inevitable, and it is desirable.

Adam's question, then, is about the role of the reader in the construction of meaning. He takes a middle position between Fish's minimalism and others who want to make a strong case for ways in which literary texts "stack" their intentions so that readers lose most options. Adam uses the image of the fish-eyed view (the camera's view), which I believe he understands we will know is different from human binocular vision (our eyes are placed in such a way as to contribute to what we see differently from those whose eyes are set on the sides of their heads, or from the fisheye camera

---

[33] A.K.M. Adam, "The Sign of Jonah: A Fish-Eye View," *Semeia* 51 (1990) 177–91. I am also indebted to GTU student David Mammola for helping me understand this image.

lens). Adam's point is that we need to "correct" for our particular eyes, that is, we need to make explicit to ourselves and others as clearly as we can the default assumptions with which we read. He maintains that it is the grounding assumptions, and I would add also our methodological strategies, that account substantially for the variations in our readings. Were we to ante these up as we go, and sort them carefully, then reading effects might be neither so obvious nor so mysterious to us as they sometimes are. Adam reminds us that we have little trouble seeing that "distorting" reality in pre-critical readers, but more difficulty in imagining it in ourselves.

Adam defuses the issue of whether there "is" a text or not, somewhat in the way I would disarm the extreme argument about whether there "is" an author. There is a rich and complex text of Jonah, and there was a skilled author who produced it. But just as we cannot rely on discovering a definitive authorial intention that would not in any case restrict our own understanding, so the fact that there is a text does not mean that it warrants any particular interpretation or method of interpreting. Every act of reading focuses on what is central for that reader, thus making the center of interest more prominent than peripheral concerns. It is the reader-of-the-text, not simply the text itself, that constructs significance. The text on its own does not mandate or interdict meaning, does not, as Adam puts it, exert "functional efficacy."[34] Reading is always a matter of selecting what is of concern to the interpreter; it is impossible and undesirable to correct for bias completely. One immediate fear is that our readings will be wrong; we rightly challenge ourselves to read as responsibly as we can. By that I mean that we need to anticipate as honestly as we can do what our interests are, and to live our lives so that our interests are worthwhile. We can, if we choose, read Scripture (or the biblical text) frivolously, falsely (to our own experience), or disrespectfully; but I for one do not choose to do that. The other important corrective to our own "fish-eye" is to read with others—the dead and the living, particularly those whose interests are not the same as our own.

So the final "literary" moment for us to visit, which actually has been hovering in the air as we talked about both historical and literary criticism, is reader-oriented (also called reader-response, reader-alert, and pragmatic) criticism. It, like the others, is a product of the world in which we now live, both springing from and reinforcing an awareness that readers vary vastly. Reader-alert criticism is not an alternative to the other two types of studies we have explored, though it brings forth from them something that most earlier theorists left unexplored. But think back to our latest historical scholar, Ehud Ben Zvi: His premise was that how the original

[34] Adam, "Sign of Jonah," 179.

Jonah readers, those for whom the story was intended, construed the narrative made a difference, even to us, whose lenses are quite different from theirs. That is, Ben Zvi urges that it matters who is reading, though his further point——not shared by all reader-response theorists——would be that our reading must take the original audience into account, insofar as the design of the story will have been crafted specially for the first ears to hear it. We gain by attending to that customization.

As we watched the literary theorists help us notice even just five artistic features of the book, they may have taken for granted that authors/texts have complex and likely preferred viewpoints, and that readers have choices to negotiate; not all readers will pick up on the same elements in the same way. Our various literary scholars did not much develop that possibility, and some may deny it, explicitly or implicitly, at least in some of their early work. But it becomes clear as the literary aspects of a book like Jonah emerge——often under the skilled work of the particular interpreters we just reviewed and others like them——that the language is not univalent but polyvalent, genuinely susceptible of multiple and diverse interpretations. Much of what may have seemed "writerly" is actually "readerly." Whatever else will be relevant, meaning is thoroughly dialogical: not wholly forced on a reader nor left utterly open. If that is the case, then it follows that we must take careful notice of the situated reader: from an initial phase where biblical studies were dominated by white, upper-class clerical males, there has come a democratization of the readers and the beginnings of appreciation for readings from the "underside" of history. We may also note, after Ben Zvi, that the particular studies over the past twenty-five hundred years of our traditions were generated for that same rather restricted audience; now the scope of readings is aimed wider.

Reader-oriented and "interested" criticisms are challenging in that they seem to democratize interpretation overly, at least in the view of some; they may seem to allow and even encourage just about any reading one might offer. But what they actually do is allow some who would not have been welcome at the interpretation table to take their place there, to have their opportunity to interpret from their own stance, skill, and experience. And they offer to readers who had assumed their own innocent objectivity the insight that such a claim cannot be sustained. A corollary of diverse readership is diverse interests or projects. The readings that will be judged most adequate need to take proper note of the best of the insights uncovered by other critical study. Those likely to be most successful over time, that is, to effect their value with readers, may well include the best critical insights of past scholars. If we look back at our various readers, those we have just studied and in fact those we will see ahead, they are all reader-sensitive, but in many cases they simply do not realize or acknowledge it. What becomes new here is the recognition and admission that the reader matters. The reader has actually always mattered, but that was less obvious in eras when readers seemed, at least by certain categories, to be more homogeneous and when they tended to repeat and be strongly influenced by what each other said. It is, at the end of the Modern period and beyond, much more obvious than before how constructed and idiosyncratic is our own appropriation of various texts.

It is difficult and perhaps not crucial to mark the genuinely Postmodern off from the Modern. If we were to name simply one huge and tangled cluster of postmodern phenomena, it would have to be the radically indeterminate nature of all reality. It is an insight that has scarcely come to be appropriated yet, but one condign with the notion that readers vary vastly in their appropriations. Indeterminacy's challenge for biblical matters is daunting, since it will call into question virtually everything that we have been accustomed to see as foundational. What is likely to emerge, relevant to present purposes, is a much richer and more tensive understanding of God and of God's ways of interacting with all of creation; there will, I hope, be a serious effort to rethink the relationship between the testaments that does not almost inevitably disrespect the Jewish heritage. The urgencies of the world of nature will be unpacked afresh, and "black holes" of all kinds will seem acceptable instead of needing to be resolved.

Adam is far from saying that anything goes, that there are no constraints on readers at all. That is always a cheap shot aimed at reader theory and misses its real challenge. His point is that we all need, now, to discern and acknowledge our own structures and strategies, to understand how they work, and in fact to become as aware as possible where such habits as our own come from. We read highly influenced by others as well as by the importunings of our own blind spots, again the point being to come to know this, acknowledge it, even exploit it in various ways. Adam helps us see why there is continuity in reading, and he also allows us to understand more fully why there are paradigm shifts, such as the ones we are tracking in this chapter and the last one.

A pair of scholars to help us with this issue of readers is two women who work within the Jewish tradition.[35] The title of their article is as enigmatic as was Adam's, and their specific mode of argumentation different; but their originating question and main insight are similar. *How do shared assumptions work, especially if they are not voiced, and how do they operate even when methodologies and ideologies vary?* In other words, Elata-Alster

---

[35] Gerda Elata-Alster and Rachel Salmon, "The Deconstruction of Genre in the Book of Jonah: Towards a Theological Discourse," *Journal of Literature and Theology* 3 (1989) 40–60.

and Salmon maintain that our operative and perhaps unconscious reading strategies, especially when not made explicit, are more persuasive than some other factors of interpretation, for example those using historical and literary building blocks. And they agree with Adam that certain interpretive conventions become "natural," are seen as inevitable, especially in groups where they are shared; it is here that they will characterize Jewish modes of reading as somewhat different from Christian practices.[36] Their particular interest centers on the general feature of oddities, apparent anomalies in the narrative: Are oddities to be fixed, resolved, or exploited and made significant?[37] Their specific text question works around a moment at or near the end of the book when Jonah sits down outside the city of Nineveh to see what will happen there. Scholars have long puzzled over the story's chronology, which seems in the view of many to work a bit bumpily. *Once he has preached, the Ninevites have changed their ways, and the narrator has shared some information with readers, what can we understand Jonah as expecting to see, and what can we anticipate is troubling him?*

Elata-Alster and Salmon argue that the norm—they might say in both historical study and in some literary study, as well as among those who simply "theologize" without much methodology at all—is to solve anomalies, or to understand them as problems that need resolution of some kind. So, as they inform us, some scholars hypothesize that the text has somehow fallen into disorder that would be alleviated if 4:5 were placed differently in relation to 4:1. That is, if Jonah has already, somehow, been told that God has had a change of heart in regard to Nineveh, then Jonah should not be camping out to watch catastrophe arrive. *Must the story proceed such that the order of telling (sometimes called the discourse order) is the same as the order events ought logically to have happened (sometimes called story order)? Is chronology the only possibility, or a sort of cause-effect chain?* Their first point is to say—and in this they are reminiscent of Ackerman— that what might seem clumsy is in fact part of a subtle strategy. But where he was interested in authorial design, they stress readerly choice. They continue to underline their main theoretical point—that we must make our reading strategies and assumptions explicit—and to work with their specific example, which is Jonah's motivation. *Might Jonah in fact be pondering some-*

---

[36] It seems important to be leery of generalizations, which actually undermine the gain from reader-specific situations. Elata-Alster and Salmon say that most Christians tend to read Jonah as a narrow zealot whose particularistic views are critiqued by the book's author (41). That is surely a common view among Christian readers, though whether of "most" would be difficult to verify; it is also the view of Jewish commentator James Ackerman, as we saw above.

[37] The question—or assumption—beneath the question is how to decide what is odd.

thing else, e.g., the loss of his own prophetic insight (maybe Jonah does not know, cannot see what is going to happen), *or his own failings* (is Jonah culpable for his near-refusal to take on his assigned task of prophecy)?[38]

The second part of their essay is amazingly fruitful, since in effect they say: Let's read like traditional Jewish scholars instead of in the more linear way of certain rationalist (usually Christian) scholars. In this way they are suggesting that the book of Jonah may not need to be forced into a "genre," i.e., to be a narrative or a prophetic book; it may be related, intertextually, to many sites within the Bible, related to each in a distinctive way. So, picking up a way both ancient and modern,[39] they do just that. The two scholars, reading "sideways" in the traditional Jewish midrashic mode (and also participating in postmodern intertextual play) here track Jonah to various sites, offering ways in which the short story is made richer when we think of it in one context and/or another: So Jonah acts to protect Israel from the dishonor that will accrue to his people if and when they are compared unfavorably with Gentiles; or Jonah is troubled by the discrepancy between what God has announced and what has in fact happened. Or Jonah has—with some creative gap-filling by the rabbis—had experience before of announcing something that does not come to pass and knows that it is hard on his reputation as a prophet.[40] We can nominate some other possibilities: stories where God's mercy features prominently; other considerations of Ninevites and Assyrians; the Sodom and Gomorrah narrative; the tree and snake of Genesis 3. The point they stress is that the text is vastly indeterminate, and readers will pick their way through the maze of possibilities in ways that differ from each other and that are somewhat dependent on underlying assumptions and practices.[41]

They have accomplished three things: First, they have shown that Jewish modes of reading privilege different things from other traditions; readers matter. And they have shown us that there is no single regimen that the book can be put through in order to be read thoroughly and correctly. Readers must choose the path they take and leave others untaken, at least for the moment. Many possibilities are at hand, and not all can be exploited. Interpretation is never complete. Readers must name what they are doing and what their assumptions are, and see a relationship between what they choose and what they get. Finally, they have given us a preview of our next chapter!

---

[38] Elata-Alster and Salmon, "Deconstruction of Genre," 41–45 and *passim*.

[39] See the next chapter, p. 107, for some discussion of this large topic.

[40] Elata-Alster and Salmon, "Deconstruction of Genre," 45–50.

[41] I experience myself reading with the Christian training I have rather than as an educated Jew when they take Jonah off in the direction of Genesis 1–3, where I have difficulty following the point (see their pp. 50–57)!

Conclusion

This has been a long and detailed chapter, and rather than summarizing it I will simply repeat what we have done. The aim was to alert us to some of the language-based richness of the story. It can surely be overwhelming, and to select even five sets of possibilities represents a compromise between showing many more options and trying to make the demonstration more taut. Our last "literary" facet was a short discussion of how readers navigate literary artistry. This chapter, as I hope you can see, proceeded quite differently from our investigation of historian Ben Zvi and took other paths than those traversed by ancient and modern analogizers. The modes of reading do not contradict each other, ideally, though it can seem so. The point is to get some comfortable purchase on the many challenges of situated reading of deep stories like Jonah.

CHAPTER SIX

Jonah's Journey in the Whale

With several interpretive strategies on the table, and with the reader's role centrally established—not independent of the text but deeply enmeshed and interactive within it—I want to shift now to an aspect of the story that is shortchanged in Jonah scholarship. It is a truism to say that "everyone" knows the story of Jonah and the whale. If you were to quiz your friends about what they know, if you said "Jonah and what animal?" I am confident that they would answer correctly. But we are beyond word association in our quest for meaning, and the significance of Jonah's experience within the "big fish," as the Hebrew text has it, has not been as much explored as we might think. In this chapter we will explore the difficult journey across the water that results in some loss but also in some gain.

Entry Questions

This is a good place for you to stop and list your own questions about the second chapter of Jonah. You may come up with something like the following: *How central to the story is the "whale experience," given the lack of reference to it elsewhere in the narrative? Why is it not exploited better—or perhaps is it, if we look a bit more carefully? How can God and Jonah draw on it better (so to speak), with our readerly help? Is the whale good or bad, a threat or a help—and better—how is it both? Why is the "psalm"/prayer of ch. 2 apparently such a smokescreen? Why is the water journey so powerfully symbolic in literature? How, of the various possibilities, will we construct it? Who is the whale? Who is Jonah while inside the whale, and who after emerging? How exactly does the water journey function? How can we best name the motif: the journey across/through the waters, with some suffering but also with resulting gain of some kind?*

Procedure

In order to track our questions in pursuit of meaning that will entail our "getting perspective," we will work with four sets of literature. First is some material that is, for the most part, much older than the Jonah story: ancient Near Eastern narrative that is plausibly background in some way for the biblical story of Jonah (and for much other biblical material as well). We will not be able to work with all of it, so after naming the best possibilities we will examine one wonderful story in detail, working with only a small portion of it. The point is not that these stories "are" the Jonah story or even that the Jonah writer borrowed from them. It is a reader's choice—mine for us and I hope one you can embrace as well—to see how knowing one ancient story in some detail can illumine another. It is not so much a matter of matching and mapping motifs as of seizing some aspect of relationship and pursuing it, sensing a gain in understanding a narrative. As before, we are not looking for a single meaning or message, but hoping to be surprised by rich and transforming insight. First we will ask how Jonah is meaning-full when seen as a survivor of the water journey, as a failure at securing immortality when he gets a second chance at it. Second, we will simply note the ubiquity and potential significance of the "water journey" in the Bible: Noah and Moses as flood heroes, Jesus as well. Third, we will revisit the Celtic story of Brendan the Navigator, which explores the journey across waters with the aid of a large fish. Fourth, we will gather from the rich Jewish post-biblical tradition its views on the fish adventure and consider the role of the Jonah narrative in Jewish Day of Atonement liturgy. How is the water journey productive, for its hero and also for others of us who participate in it, even if dryshod?

Ancient Near Eastern Narratives

In General

For hundreds of years before anything like our extant Hebrew Bible stories existed, there were "strugglous" water-adventure tales told throughout the region around the Mediterranean Sea as far as the Tigris and Euphrates Rivers.[1] Spanning a number of cultures and languages and quite

---

[1] The oldest of the stories are from the Sumerian culture and language, datable from the third to second millennia B.C.E. In certain cases virtually the same stories or clearly related ones are also available in Akkadian from the Old Babylonian culture, which is second millennium. More recent translations and copies yet appear in "Assyrian Akkadian" from the first millennium, for example in the library at Nineveh.

diverse in their general contents, these stories have to do with the deeds of the gods, the roles and proclivities of human beings, the vital nature of the physical world, and various factors of cultures. Relatively recently discovered, these materials have been ordered and grouped in various ways, often in relation to what those working on them supposed they had to do with the Bible. Though there is nothing wrong with that question—and you may sense that we are dealing with a version of it here—it is likely less intrusive to look at them within their own contexts as well, even first. Good collections of these stories are available, providing translations, brief introductions, notes, and bibliographies.[2]

THE GILGAMESH STORY

The story of Gilgamesh is the most useful of the ancient Mesopotamian tales for present purposes, picking up in its narration the story of the flood, though providing the hero with another name: Utanapishtim.[3] Though this long story has suffered less than other epics at the hands of those interested primarily in its affinities with biblical material, it, too, needs to be able to stand on its own when being discussed rather than being forced at once into a biblical map. We will stick to the narrative as offered by Andrew George, specifically for tablets X and XI, which tell the adventures of Gilgamesh as he searches for immortality and learns the flood story. The story is spacious, concerning human relationships, experiences, and feelings: loneliness, love, loss, revenge, regret, and the fear of oblivion that comes with death.[4] Stephanie Dalley characterizes Gilgamesh as a human being with a tremendous capacity for friendship, endurance, adventure, joy, and sorrow, a man of weakness who loses a unique opportunity in what she

[2] See Bernard F. Batto, *Slaying the Dragon: Mythmaking in the Biblical Tradition* (Louisville: Westminster John Knox, 1992); Richard J. Clifford, s.j., *Creation Accounts in the Ancient Near East and in the Bible* (Washington, DC: The Catholic Biblical Association of America, 1994); Stephanie Dalley, *Myths from Mesopotamia: Creation, the Flood, Gilgamesh and Others* (Oxford and New York: Oxford University Press, 1989) for three studies angled differently enough to give you a good introduction to what might be useful to you.

[3] We will be using the work of Andrew George, who has produced both the critical editions of the Gilgamesh story: *The Babylonian Gilgamesh Epic: Introduction, Critical Edition and Cuneiform Texts,* 2 vols. (Oxford: Oxford University Press, 2003) and a more popular and relevant (for us) edition: *The Epic of Gilgamesh: The Babylonian Epic Poem and Other Texts in Akkadian and Sumerian* (London: Penguin Books, 1999). George constructs a standard version for us with the help of seventy-three extant manuscripts, *Epic Poem,* xv–xxviii. Of its approximately three thousand lines, about 575 are still missing.

[4] Maureen Kovacs, *The Epic of Gilgamesh. Translated, with an Introduction* (Stanford, CA: Stanford University Press, 1985) xvii.

calls a moment of carelessness. She finds it basically a story of human freedom, where the hero can occasionally thwart the gods, who are themselves
involved in human affairs.[5] George summarizes it as "one man's struggle
against death—first for immortal renown through glorious deeds, then for
eternal life itself; of his despair when confronted with inevitable failure, and
of his eventual realization that the only immortality he may expect is the enduring name afforded by leaving behind some lasting achievement."[6] It is a
story of humanization, of wise acceptance of mortal limits.[7]

The narrator opens the poem with praise of Gilgamesh, who has left,
in the city wall at Uruk where he was king, written in his own hand, testi-
monies to his exploits—the story we are about to read. A composite of divine and human, young Gilgamesh was abusive of Uruk's citizens in
various ways until the gods created for him a peer, Enkidu: First a wild
man who runs with the animals, he becomes tamed and humanized when
he loves a mortal woman. Enkidu and Gilgamesh at first contend with each
other and then adventure together, slaying Huwawa, the guardian of the
Cedar Forest, so that they can cut down the forest and win eternal fame;
and then they kill the Bull of Heaven, an adventure that involves Gilgamesh's spurning the goddess Ishtar. As they move through these exploits
various characters caution them against overreaching, warnings which they
disregard, each distinctively. We, however, are alerted that such deeds as
theirs cannot be done with impunity; we can see that the narrative is a wisdom tale even before water crossings are involved. Enkidu becomes aware
of the gravity of the pair's various quests before Gilgamesh does and
wishes to turn back, but his royal friend has no such scruples or forebod-
ings. Once the violent deeds are done, Enkidu is smitten with a serious dis-
ease and dies a painful and pitiful death, with his companion in frantic
attendance. Gilgamesh is devastated by the loss of the friend he loves and
rails against the limits of mortality. In this context—whether to find eternal
life for himself and others, to restore Enkidu's life, or simply to experience
something other than angry grief in the face of death—Gilgamesh travels
toward the dwelling of the flood hero.[8]

We pick up the story in more detail at tablet X, as Gilgamesh, clad in
a lion-skin, approaches the dwelling or business place of Siduri, the

---

[5] Dalley, *Myths from Mesopotamia*, 39–40. Gilgamesh is actually part human and part
divine, but he is clearly "less divine" than some of the deities with whom he contends.

[6] George, *Epic Poem*, xiii.

[7] Ibid. xxxiii–xlix.

[8] This summary is from George, *Critical Edition*, 505–28 and 869–97, and *Epic Poem*,
75–100.

alewife (tavern keeper). She registers fright at his appearance and tries to bolt a door between them, but Gilgamesh threatens to destroy it, so desperate is he for information, and so accustomed to accomplishing purposes by violent engagement. She questions him, giving him the opportunity (as will happen twice more) to recite his case: His friend with whom he killed has died, and Gilgamesh is now afraid of death, fears that he, too, will lie down never to rise again. He announces that he would find his way to Utanapishtim, "of whom men tell," though without explaining how such a quest is sensible or relevant. Siduri both attempts to dissuade him from his quest and then also assists him with it, advising him how to approach the man he seeks; she directs her visitor to Urshanabi, boatman for Utanapishtim, who evidently continues to ferry for him as needed.

Gilgamesh races off to find Urshanabi, weapons drawn. He throttles the ferryman and then smashes "The Stone Ones," dropping their fragments into the water.[9] When he hears his visitor's desire Urshanabi remarks that Gilgamesh has himself made difficult the very thing he wants by having destroyed the Stone Ones. The alternative involves punting poles, which Gilgamesh cuts: three hundred giant tree trunks, each to be used but once and then discarded, so lethal are the waters they are negotiating.[10] Gilgamesh wields the poles, using them up before he arrives at his destination and creatively improvising a sail from the garment of the boatman. It is thus that Utanapishtim sees his boat coming but notes it is piloted by a stranger who has managed an extraordinary feat. Questioned as to his deeds and needs, Gilgamesh responds much as before, but adds that he wants to escape his present suffering and embark on a new phase of his life.

George carefully comments on Utanapishtim's reply to Gilgamesh, which he considers quite important to our understanding the matter under negotiation in Gilgamesh's journey to wisdom. George's reading is that the flood hero lectures the wandering king on the responsibilities of kingship, which are not being met by the one to whom they have been entrusted. Though Gilgamesh is son of a goddess and of a king, he looks and is acting like a fool, not least in his searching for something he will never achieve. While so doing, he is neglecting the charges that are his, specifically provision for gods and mortals; Utanapishtim rebukes him for expending his en-

---

[9] No one is sure what these are, with opinion dividing for some sort of crew or the tackle needed for passage. In a class I took many years ago with a famous Akkadian scholar, Anne Kilmer, she suggested that they were the pulley and cable apparatus needed for one particular kind of regular water crossing.

[10] The waters of death are the most dangerous part of the ocean needing to be crossed to get to Utanapishtim; presumably they are negotiated as well by the dead on their way to the Underworld (George, *Critical Edition*, 499).

ergy on a fruitless quest rather than using it for what is within his grasp: You "fill your sinews with sorrow."[11] George summarizes: "The old man's reproachful words underline the plot of the whole latter half of the epic, in which Gilgamesh strenuously tries to escape his destiny but finally must learn to accept it."[12] Utanapishtim then ruminates on the lot of mortals, contributing as he does so some lovely images for human fragility: the reed snapped off in a canebrake, the mayfly's transient existence on the water. But he moves on to the story of the flood (tablet XI). After surviving the flood, Utanapishtim had been removed from other humans to stand in the assembly of gods, apparently inexplicably. But this is the secret matter Utanapishtim will now relate. Gilgamesh registers surprise that one so much like him in appearance has a story to tell and that it apparently does not need to be wrested from him by force.

The specific reason for the gods' decision to call for a deluge is unclear in Utanapishtim's rendition of events to Gilgamesh, though it is unquestionably their decision. All involved are sworn to secrecy, but Ea, god of wisdom and friend to human beings, tells the plan to a reed fence or wall of some sort, perhaps his or Utanapishtim's house. The fabric of the house or temple becomes the medium for Utanapishtim's learning of the threat and helps him discern what he is to do, which is to construct a vessel within which he can escape the death that will result for all the rest. The hero is shrewd in his calculations about how to manage his quest without riling his subjects or making them suspicious—since in fact he needs their help. His ruse, which also becomes prophetic, is the explanation that he is to go off and live with Ea, a move that will benefit his people, since Ea will shower various things upon them. Of the various matters he might have stressed in the telling, the flood hero details the processes of preparation, including the provisioning and launching of the vessel at the evening of the sixth day of its building. The impact of the flood itself is communicated by noise imagery and by the description of its effect on the gods who had wanted it: They are shocked at its violence and forced to refugee from their own dwellings; finally, they are described as "lying like dogs curled up in the open," or cowering like dogs who have taken shelter under a wall.[13] After some six or seven days the storm abates, and eventually Utanapish-

---

[11] George, *Epic Poem*, 86.

[12] George, *Critical Edition*, 504–05. I am not so sure that the point is so neatly comprehensive but agree it is part of what is under discussion.

[13] Ibid. 515, unpacks the line for us, noting that the impact of describing gods as dogs is stunning. What should be—normally would be—revered are despised; and beings who ordinarily are cared for are turned into classic scavengers. The common denominator may be parasite, he suggests. It is a pert and efficient comment on the deities.

tim ventures to unfasten the boat's hatch and peer out. Seeing clearly that
he and his wife are the only living beings to survive, he weeps. Once the
boat has come to rest on Mount Nimush, Utanapishtim initiates the bird-
sending process (familiar from the biblical flood story) to ascertain the dry-
ness of the region and the schedule for debarkation. When this has been
done the flood hero immediately prepares a fragrant sacrifice to draw the
gods to it, like flies, the hero narrates. The Mother deity, Belet-ili, who had
decried the destruction of her offspring when she experienced the flood
and rued the divine choice, holds up her necklace, strung of amber flies,
both to recall her days as a young lover of the god who gave the piece to
her and to name a new signification of it: Henceforth, she says, it will remind her of what they have all just suffered.

When the god Enlil arrives (though he had not been invited), he is angered that a human has survived and immediately suspects Ea of leaking the
plan. But Ea rebukes him, suggesting that the flood was improvident and
unfair; to have sent lions and wolves, famine and plagues would have been
less devastating. Enlil apparently concedes the point and decides that
Utanapishtim and his wife should be granted immortality: perhaps for their
feat of survival, perhaps to keep such a clever player off the scene in the future. So all the gods are witness to the blessing that makes the survivor-pair
immortal and sees them resettled at the mouth of waters. The next question,
as Utanapishtim asks Gilgamesh, is "Who'll convene for you the gods' assembly, so you can find the life you search for?"[14] Though we may now
sense that the answer is "no one," that the journey traversed by Utanapishtim is not repeatable by another, Utanapishtim challenges Gilgamesh to stay
awake for six days and seven nights. But no sooner is it suggested than he
falls dreamlessly asleep. The flood hero's wife feels sorry for the visitor, but
Utanapishtim pronounces tellingly about Gilgamesh: "See the fellow who
so desired life! Sleep like a fog already breathes over him."[15] Utanapishtim's
wife wants to wake the mortal, but her husband dissuades her. So she bakes
a bread-loaf for each day the human hero sleeps and sets it at his head, while
the couple tally the days on the wall. As she places the seventh offering, Gilgamesh awakens, insisting it was only a momentary nodding. But the flood
hero and the spoiled bread dispute him. Gilgamesh cries out, "'O Uta-
napishti, what should I do and where should I go? A thief has taken hold of
my [flesh!] For there in my bed-chamber Death does abide, and wherever
[I] turn, there too will be Death.'"[16]

---

[14] George, *Epic Poem*, 95.
[15] Ibid. 96.
[16] Ibid. 97.

But all that remains is for Urshanabi to ferry his customer back, after assisting him to wash and get clean clothes. The last chance for Gilgamesh comes when Utanapishtim's wife reminds her husband that the man has come a long way and endured a great deal to go home with nothing; so the flood hero tells him of a rejuvenating plant that he might acquire as he retraces his journey. Gilgamesh seems to know how to proceed, tying stones to his feet and diving into the sweet-water Apsu in search of the prickly plant. He finds the plant, takes it, surfaces and talks about it excitedly, naming it, planning for its use. But shortly thereafter he sets it down while he takes a refreshing dip into another pool of water; a snake comes by, smells the plant, and carries it off, shedding its own skin as it goes, thus testifying to the qualities of what Gilgamesh has once again not managed to secure. The story—at least this selection of it—ends as Gilgamesh regrets some of his choices and returns to Uruk and shows the boatman Urshanabi the venerable walls and foundations of his city. By returning to the opening lines of the poem which indicate that Gilgamesh has acquired wisdom, the ending affirms it.

In order to illumine our Jonah story better, let us plot a few coordinates where the heroes Jonah and Gilgamesh—and Utanapishtim—share some features. We go right to the end of both stories. After the main events seem over—Jonah has converted a wicked city and Gilgamesh has survived his encounter with Utanapishtim—a final episode occurs. Each hero is given unexpected access to a plant with fertile qualities, but just as he is rejoicing in it—perhaps too proprietorially—he loses it to a reptile. The heroes react with frustration but seem more reconciled to death than previously. Jonah calls for death, again, and Gilgamesh resigns himself to it. For the older hero we can see it is the last of a string of adventurous quests, and we are perhaps ready for him to accept his status as a great mortal and return to his city and write his royal memoirs. There is no hint in the Jonah story itself that the plant is more than a shade shrub, except that it sprang up quickly and without human labor. But as we read Jonah over against the Gilgamesh quest, and especially if we appreciate that Jonah has already avoided watery death twice, then losing the plant can seem to cap his quests as well. Each hero's last and perhaps decisive if enigmatic learning comes from failure to hold on to the specially vital plant. To find and then inexplicably lose this object is cautionary. The fuller Gilgamesh story suggests that whatever his life-related quest is, it will not be accomplished: not the restoration of Enkidu nor a reward from the gods like Utanapishtim's. Practically speaking, to hear the flood hero's tale is pointless for him. But if the quest is actually to produce wisdom, Gilgamesh does better, learning limits from his failure to grasp what is not his to secure. Jonah's elliptical story gains depth here.

Both stories, as scholars note, end abruptly, indecisively. But with Gilgamesh in mind, Jonah is not quite so anomalous as it has seemed. The story of the human on a quest for immortality cannot end in any way except that he learns something important about death and life, killing and its alternatives. Gilgamesh has been instructed already as to his responsibilities as king, has heard afresh the story of how humans with limited success rebelled against the order set down for them. That hierarchical arrangement was adjusted: Two of the mortals gained immortal status and have told him how it happened. Since his last opportunities for immortality surpass his grasp, Gilgamesh can only go home—thus achieving an immortal fame of sorts, since we are at this very moment thinking and talking about him! His story ends with a question: "'For whom, Ur-shanabi, toiled my arms so hard, for whom ran dry the blood of my heart? Not for myself did I find a bounty, [for] the "Lion of the Earth" have I done a favour.'"[17] At this moment Gilgamesh regrets his experience, a topos that was also true of Enkidu in tablet VII, when he faced his own imminent mortality. What, then, is the learning about one's own projects, the needs of the "earth," the gifts of the gods, of failure and the acceptance of limits? Against that backdrop Jonah's tale simply quits as well, and also with a question that can only be answered by readers, for or with Jonah. As Jonah is angry at God's change of purpose, God poses him an analogy: You cared for the shrub, which was yours only briefly; what about deeper bonds such as God makes with a city of persons and animals who seem caught in their own ignorance and weakness? Has Jonah toiled for them in any substantial way, and is the gain for himself or for them—or for both? Regret at failure is transformable to a wise acceptance of limits, surely one of the crucial lessons for humans to learn from the divine world. The question may seem inapposite but actually is not: Is Jonah's final anger an opportunity for himself as well as for God and the Ninevites? What is good, what evil, who has done which, and who can discern it? What is Jonah's final stop to be, and how is it related to the beginning of his journey?

Backing up from those two coordinates, we see they are, in both cases, approached by the journey of the hero through the waters—in no easy itinerary—to get to the place where his final learning occurs. Gilgamesh finds his way to Utanapishtim with difficulty and suffering, apparently only to hear the story of the other man's journey through the waters and how he survived, gaining immortality as a result of how he coped. Jonah, as you recall, has had two water journeys: first from the seaport of Jaffa, the boat trip that led to a storm and his being dropped overboard, and

---

[17] Ibid. 99.

second, the crossing inside the big fish that returned him to land. In both cases the hero needs assistance, and yet his response to aid proffered is a further test of him. Something is achieved by the negotiation of the water—though here the stories go very uneven, as we are told virtually nothing of what Jonah experiences inside the whale. But, in fact, we are told of his feelings as he fights the water: That he survives a dreadful experience he does narrate, whether biblical scholars are properly appreciative of the fit of his words or not. In a certain sense it is exactly what he ought to tell us: what he was fleeing he now urgently desires, calls out for. God, with whom he was contending, is the one who will save him. To brush near death, as Jonah tells us he does, whether in the water or in the whale, is to revalue what is important.

One last pivot to set in place: In the *Gilgamesh* story we have the beginning of the flood story itself. The gods have decided on a flood, reactive as they are to the noisy rebellion of their subordinates. None of those privy to the dreadful plan is to tell, since the point is that humans are to be wiped out. The secret leaks out indirectly, as one deity recites it to his dwelling, evidently enough of a ruse so that he has said the secret within the hearing of the one who needs to know, but indirectly. The flood hero then dissimulates to his peers as he makes plans for the flood, pretending to do something else while in fact doing the bidding of his god. Jonah is routinely scolded in biblical criticism for doing the opposite of what he was asked: told to go to Nineveh, he abandons his home and "acquires" a boat, which in fact—if indirectly—takes him to where he needs to go. That Jonah resists is clear enough, but his resistance is set in a fresh and more complex matrix if we listen to Utanapishtim's story. Jonah's journey opens before him in the company of and under the ultimate guidance of his deity. And as we hear that hero instruct Gilgamesh on the responsibilities of being king, which is to say, as he reproaches him for neglecting the task that is rightfully and responsibly his to do, we are perhaps given a different angle on Jonah's struggle to be a prophet in the normal way of things. His quest is re-angled. Please note: I am not claiming that these points of similarity are definitive or intended by the Jonah storyteller. I am simply suggesting that to read the longer Gilgamesh story is to situate some of the Jonah story issues in a richer setting. My plan here is to ask what we see if we can read Jonah as a flood hero of sorts. And I have just suggested several reasons why that may work.

Biblical Stories of Crossing the Water

With this wide ancient Near Eastern vision of water struggles in mind, I want here to call attention to the presence of component water motifs in the Bible. There is no claim to completeness here; the allusions are suggestive. To investigate these passages in detail would take us far afield, nor would the gain be much more than will be the case if we carefully notice the presence of the topos.[18]

IN THE OLD TESTAMENT

The Hebrew Bible opens with the apparently effortless separation of waters into their own realms (above, on, below earth) as well as the emergence of land from water (Genesis 1). The Bible's story of the great flood, clearly cognate with what we have been considering, is related as part of primordial time (Genesis 6–9), before the Hebrew people appear on the scene. The Hebrew patriarch Jacob (Israel) bounds his exile from home by water feats: first at the well at Haran and then many years later at the River Jabbok, where he wrestles with a divine being before returning home (Genesis 29, 32). The most famous of the water stories is the escape of Israelites from enslavement in Egypt (Exodus 13–15 tells the climax); the journey is anticipated in miniature as the hero Moses struggles at the Nile (Exodus 1). The desert itinerary of the refugees from Pharaoh can be named as a chain of watering spots (Numbers 33), and indeed certain painful wrestlings between God and the people struggling toward Canaan are characterized as battles over water (e.g., Exodus 17; Numbers 20; 27; 33). To have crossed the water once, however dramatically, is neither decisive nor sufficient in setting a healthy equilibrium between God and people. The crossing together, with God aiding the humans to survive, simply identifies a new, shared intimacy that will need working out as their journey together continues.

Moses reviews the story of escape and water journeys (Deuteronomy 32), and as the people finally enter the land of promise under Joshua they cross the Jordan River in a way reminiscent of their departure from Egypt (Joshua 3–5; note: it reverses at ch. 24). The prophet Elijah makes his final journey across water (2 Kings 2), and hints of a similar thing can be detected in the post-exilic (fifth-century) priestly scribe Ezra, who breaks his journey from Babylon-become-Persia at a river; water crossings are retold by Nehemiah, governor of Yehud (Ezra 8, Nehemiah 9). The journey from Babylon back to Yehud is described by the prophet Isaiah in terminology reminiscent of the original liberation from Egypt (see Isaiah 27; 40; 43; 45; 48; 51; 52; 63); and exilic prophet Ezekiel uses water imagery to talk about the new fruitfulness for his community once it resumes faithful cultic wor-

---

[18] For fuller descriptions of all these texts consult Bula Maddison, "Reading the Watery Creation: An Intertextual Story" (M.A. thesis, Graduate Theological Union, 1997).

ship in a new temple (Ezekiel 27–32). The first apocalyptic vision of the prophet and seer Daniel involves water contests, as does the language of the minor prophet Habakkuk (Daniel 7; Habakkuk 3). The Psalms abound in water stories, using its presence in a great variety of ways to construct the relatedness between human beings and God (Psalms 18; 29; 33; 44; 46; 55; 65; 66; 69; 74; 77; 78; 80; 89; 93; 96; 97; 98; 99; 104; 105; 106; 107; 111; 114; 124; 135; 136; 149). The wisdom hero Job uses it as part of the story about himself and God (Job 38–41). The water is a theater—almost a character—for working out the relationship between divine and human.

In the New Testament

The gospels bring the water imagery forward to tell of Jesus, utilizing it variously: Jesus is baptized and commissioned at the water, crosses into the desert before beginning his public ministry (Mark 1; Matthew 3–4; Luke 3–4). He gathers companions at the sea, often teaches there. He crosses the water as part of his ministry, sleeps through a storm as did Jonah, calms waters when awakened; he commands the raging forces of wind and storm, thus claiming his relatedness with God distinctively. And Jesus tells water stories (Mark 4; 5; 6; 8; Matthew 8; 13; 14; 15; 16; Luke 5; 8; John 1; 3; 4). His ultimate adventure is his journey down to the realm of the dead—often watery in tradition—from where he returns with the gift of life to share. Paul uses water imagery to talk about life and death and about God's mighty deeds on behalf of humans, as do other NT writers (e.g., Romans 10:7; 1 Corinthians 10; 1 Pet 3:20–21; Revelation 5; 13). The rite of baptism is constituted by the passage in and out of the waters, signifying death and rebirth.

Once again the point is not to make easy equivalents between one "water story" and another; but we need to see water as more than "the flood," or as "the Sea of Galilee" that wants traversing if territory is to be covered. Water is potentially—for able readers—a matrix rich in significations: it enables the processes of humanization, of sorting the complex relatedness between what we polarize into divine and human beings, stories of searching and gaining wisdom, and of course quests for life abundant.

The Celtic Narrative of Brendan the Navigator

This story, briefly referenced in Chapter 2 of this book, comes into greater visibility in our quest to understand the hero's water journey more fully.[19] Having considered the ancient Near Eastern tradition of water jour-

---

[19] The edition I am working with primarily here is that of John O'Meara and Jonathan M. Wooding, trans. and intro., *[The Voyage of Saint Brendan:]* "The Latin Version," in

neys—to, through, and on the water—where the hero quests for something of great but intangible value, we can look at the Brendan story to suggest its fresh relevance to the story of Jonah.

Brendan is representative of the tradition of monks, those whose whole life is a search for deep and focused relatedness with God, a quest prominent in Christianity; though there are many variants detailing how the journey goes, the end point or pole of relationality with God in Jesus is constant. Concomitant with the union that is achieved/bestowed is holiness of life and wisdom, and as part of the Christian belief system, eternal life. Hence we have here another version of the powerfully-felt drive to find life—immortality or life eternal, existence beyond what is ordinarily experienced. The thirst for monks and those participating in that "archetype" is not simply to attain a life of intimacy with God but to maintain it,[20] and in fact to deepen it, be transformed into it. The quest of Brendan and his companions is expressed, experienced, and embodied as a journey across water, where the living-while-journeying is substantially generative of the goal desired. The journey is both toward something and in companionship with others.

Scholars see affinities between the Brendan tale and various genres: lives of the saints, journeys, sea stories, monster adventures, quests. But recently those familiar with both ancient and contemporary monasticism insist, rightly, that the story is primarily about that way of life: "At the centre of the *Navigatio*'s structure lies the monastic life;" and "[m]onasticism, however, is the subject of the story and such detail is crucial to the interpretation of this unique religious allegory."[21] Though the tale is transparent to other contexts, to disregard its monastic factors is to miss its main referent completely. Biblical allusions and monastic liturgical praxis thread through virtually every page of the story. Thomas O'Loughlin reminds us that the tale was produced by, for, and about people who were trained and accustomed to see and read reality at the several levels we discussed briefly in our Chapter 2 and then more extensively in Chapter 4: the historical, the moral, the spiritual.[22] So though the story may provide data for those interested in travel to strange places or in monster theory, its most persistent

---

W.R.J. Barron and Glyn S. Burgess, gen. eds., *The Voyage of Saint Brendan: Representative Versions of the Legend in English Translation* (Exeter: University of Exeter Press, 2002) 13–64. See also G. O. Simms, *Brendan the Navigator: Exploring the Ancient World* (Dublin: The O'Brien Press, 1989).

[20] O'Meara and Wooding, *Voyage of St. Brendan*, 25.

[21] Ibid. 23, 25.

[22] Thomas O'Loughlin, "Distant Islands: The Topography of Holiness in the *Nauigatio [sic] Sancti Brendani*," in Marion Glasscoe, ed., *The Medieval Mystical Tradition:* vol. 6: *England, Ireland and Wales* (Cambridge: D. S. Brewer, 1999) 4–5.

and grounding reference is Christian monasticism, with its single-hearted quest for God.

Before thinking more about this particular water quest, consider yourself or people you know who are immersed in something the rest of us can readily recognize, such as music or athletics. If our friends are utterly committed to the instrument they play, virtually everything else is oriented in service of it. The point is not simply to deny present alternatives in order to achieve something vaguely remote at some later time; the manner of living—practicing, ushering at concerts, giving lessons, auditioning—builds the relationship with the world of music, whether any one given action can be said to be specifically productive or not. The same thing is true with people who are serious about sports: How they manage their bodies, practice, work out, play, and invest all sorts of resources both reaches out for and already embraces participatively what is beloved and desired.

Less well known and more dubious for many is the God-quest, the utter commitment of all that one is toward achieving a deeper union with God, not simply later but now, while *en route*. Reasons for discomfort around the human life lived with focal energy on God are clear enough: Not all who claim to live such a life are helpful or attractive examples of it. Though many have embarked upon this quest, the endeavor is fragile and not so easily prescribed, codified, or institutionalized. The search for God is oriented somewhat differently from the processes of music and sports, since God is real but intangible—though the material world shouts the presence of God to those alert to it. God can seem remote and not worth the effort, or those who have not matured appropriately in religious and spiritual matters can feel they have outgrown the deity of their childhood, as in fact they ought to have done! Like the story of Gilgamesh, the Brendan story is compatible with the human quest for relatedness with God and its attendant fruits: wisdom, insight, self-knowledge, compassion toward others, reverence for all of life, and so forth. Means and end point are interconvertible. The *Navigatio* makes that equation even more directly, if perhaps with less narrative inventiveness but more liturgical imagination. For many people the journey toward or into God is coterminous with the process of humanization. It is our most important "deed."

So the narrated experience of Brendan's journeying, first around Ireland and later on the seas that lead away from it, is a way of life designed for and capable of bringing him into engagement with God. The story begins and ends in the monastery at Clonfert where Brendan is abbot, and his particular travel is inspired by the story told by a visitor to the place, one Barrind, who narrates his search for the Promised Land of the Saints, where Jesus Christ is the animation, sustenance, and light of all inhabitants. Brendan and a few companions embark on the journey to find the place themselves, if it is the will of God, a sentiment that pervades the story from start to finish. The object of the quest cannot be grabbed untimely but must be sought and received tenaciously and gently. That it takes the group seven years to find a place that was never so far from them is telling; their journey is cyclic, their adventures repetitive and classic. Preparation and process are key. The pilgrims contend against various external opponents: weather, monsters, animals, demons, inhospitable places. But their struggles are also clearly against various internal conditions: The monks are often physically weak; some are tempted to rush inappropriately or lose heart; Brendan's men become fearful; and on occasion a monk gives in to serious temptation, e.g., theft. These are situations to be expected in the lives of monks, even those living prayer, asceticism, solitude, and observance of the Rule at an experienced and mature level. As Brendan journeys, he learns with and from others about the God-quest and is able to be a teacher and guide for his companions and those he meets. Monks who pare down the essentials to a very few and who thus clear the decks of the many, many things that can distract us and obscure the life that is going on within and without commit to deep attentiveness to those processes. More than simply pushing to difficult limits—though it involves that—it is also committing in faith to the pole or matrix of love that is God and letting nothing hinder the journey toward deeper integration. Tellingly, Brendan's story concludes as the journeyers are shown the island they have been seeking. They learn why it has taken seven years: "You could not find it immediately because God wanted to show you his varied secrets in the great ocean."[23] Once he has experienced the gift, Brendan and the monks return to Clonfert, where he dies shortly thereafter, presumably to be folded into the Island in a deeper and more permanent way. The journey being referenced, then, is not so much to an actual geographical place as to an integrative center, which resists polarities and aims to slough off the superfluous for absorption in the One God, or however that center of attraction can be named.[24]

The Brendan narrator ranges along two axes—temporal and spatial—moving through a cycle of seven liturgical years, with feasts and ordinary

---

[23] O'Meara and Wooding, *Voyage of St. Brendan,* 63.

[24] Raimundo Panikkar, *Blessed Simplicity* (New York: Seabury, 1982). Panikkar includes a section in which participants in the seminar he is leading respond to what he has set forth. Respondent Basil Pennington (164–65) notes that monks have to be shaped, in some very profound ways, by the praxis of the monastery where they live but also free enough of its structures to live unpressed by them.

time correctly and continuously celebrated; sites visited repeat, regularly, to be consecrated to the realm of the sacred by a constant dedication to formal worship. And the tensive relatedness between prosaic and sacral time/space is deeply built into both the monastic life and the journey narrative, as though they were simultaneous rather than successive, as indeed they are. It is as though a channel between them allows participants to move easily from one to the others.[25] Cynthia Bourgeault writes, "As Brendan and his monastic 'family' proceed on their journey, observing the wonders of the sea, participating in a regular ascesis of prayer and fasting, as the psalmody rolls around them, linking their actual experienced reality to the great rhythms of liturgical celebration, we begin to get some sense of what sort of an enterprise this is."[26] You may have had some experience of these facets of time—perhaps when someone close to you has died and you live, temporarily, both in your "normal" life but also in the time of saying farewell to a loved one, with all the processes involved both personally and socially in that moment. Bourgeault characterizes this hermeneutic mode as neither strictly "realistic" nor "allegorical" but somewhere in between and other to each of those.[27] Though it can seem a confusing or diffuse way to access meaning, it is actually integrative. Monastic life organizes all that happens on these wild travels. Brendan and his companions begin and end in the monastery, and though they are not there while on the seas, their water-life is structured by all that they have learned and become in the monastery. The boat—and better, the seas—become their monastery. As we all know from one context or another, to focus on one thing while dropping others, to listen receptively to one realm and surrender oneself to it involves both a giving over of oneself and a willingness to receive back, an entrusting of ourselves to a process so that we become players.

Part of this process for monks like Brendan involves an immersion in Scripture: Bible stories open up to include their readers as participants. Christians believe about Scripture that it provides richly to those who engage it whatever is needed for God's self-disclosure with humans. Those attending to the process of relating deeply with God are nourished and built by biblical narratives of others articulating similar experience. Utterly the inverse of "applying messages" to one's life, this process assumes that

---

[25] Cynthia Bourgeault, "The Monastic Archetype in the *Navigatio* of St. Brendan," *Monastic Studies* 14 (1983) 115–17. She refers us to the contemporary work of Panikkar for a useful discussion of the dynamics of liturgy, which will already be familiar to many readers who participate mindfully in the various aspects of the church's liturgical cycle. See also O'Loughlin, "Distant Islands," 6–13 and 16–20, for additional discussion.

[26] Bourgeault, "Monastic Archetype," 119.

[27] Ibid.

the participant is already swimming in the deep and broad sea of experience of God, with a ready-to-hand familiarity with the biblical narratives. The monk, in this case, lives right into the storyline of the Bible, so that its "thick" stories enfold the reader-participant's experience. This quest requires a high participation in the imaginative powers of the human person, as the world in which life is lived becomes populated with all that is redolent and evocative of God.

The clearest Jonah link comes when journeying monks come upon what seems to them a strange island, bereft of sand and grass but affording some wood. Some men manage to land on "the beach" and mark the Paschal Vigil with a Eucharistic celebration, since it is the eve of Easter. Next morning they start a fire to warm themselves and prepare food. But as their cauldron heats up, the "island" begins to roil, thrash, and heave, showing itself not land at all but a large fish. The brothers abandon their preparations and rejoin Brendan in the boat. He explains that God had revealed to him the identity of the "island" previously, hence his choice to stay in the boat: "Where we were was not an island, but a fish—the foremost of all who swim in the ocean. He is always trying to bring his tail to meet his head, but he cannot because of his length. His name is Jasconius."[28] The community accepts Jasconius on its own terms rather than on theirs: a fish, not an island; and in time the animal guides the group helpfully toward the destination they are seeking. Every year of their travels they celebrate the Paschal Vigil liturgy on the back of Jasconius. Without the wider ancient Near Eastern context this episode might seem a mere motif, an animal adventure. But seen contextually as part of the journey toward relatedness with the divine and as disclosive of part of the mystery of that friendship it is much more. The fish, engaged in his own effort at integration, grounds the monks' quest for absorption in God. Six times the "Jasconius Easter" reminds the journeyers that they are in process and not arrived, and yet they have been reassured that their regular encounter with the fish is correct, prescribed, planned for them. Not necessarily tangibly productive in itself, the fish marks for those visiting it that they are where they need to be, doing what is their life to do. For Brendan and his companions the journey toward God is filled with Bible narratives and with every encounter with the physical world that can be experienced. Both environments comprise testing of the human spirit and offer access to the mysteries of God.

---

[28] O'Meara and Wooding, *Voyage of St. Brendan,* 34–35; other translations that mention the episode offer basically the same information, with minor variations (e.g., the age of the trees on the fish's back). The name of the beast derives from the Irish word *Iasc,* fish, according to Barron and Burgess, *Voyage,* 15.

Again we can mine this "fish story" to fill fuller our Jonah reading. Clearly the water journey, once again, is a quest for a relationship with the divine, for holiness, wisdom, and profound simplicity of desire. Since such a project is a life process, a journey with adventures is a wonderful metaphor for or symbol of it. For any journeyer the process is intimately related to the destination. Not all who search will find and be found, but the seeking is constitutive of the finding, at least in some aspects. The adventures of the monk-sailors involve not only challenges from nature but also struggles with their own human topography; wrested from the journey are self-knowledge, patience, courage, compassion. Though these things are not detailed in the Brendan story so clearly as in the Gilgamesh tales, the monastic matrix helps us to know confidently that the quest involves them. And the Irish seas provide excellent analogues for the rigors of self-discipline necessary for a deep spiritual life: not a renunciation of the transcendent nor a minimizing of the immanent.[29] At both levels the challenge is to live deeply, attentively, intensively, wasting nothing and gaining all that can be had. The quest is not simply process; it culminates in some degree of finding what had been sought, even though the seekers know that there is more to be had. Jonah is not a monk, but he is a prophet, an intermediary between God and a human community. The education of Jonah while *en route* needs to suit what it is he needs to learn, not only for himself as an individual but as a servant of others. That is, if Brendan's story advises us well, the Jonah story needs to provide the prophet with what he requires, granted many scholars think he learns nothing!

Brendan's Jasconius shows us that to reduce the fish merely to a positive or negative misses the point. The fish is frightening, especially before the monks come to know him; but once they learn what he has to give them, he has to be primarily helpful, if not quite comfortable, a place to celebrate the return of life (the Paschal liturgy) and to mark progress on the journey. Though Jonah's adventures inside the fish are opaque, to extrapolate from Gilgamesh and Brendan prompts us to see that part of the journey as formative. If he is a wisdom hero, Jonah has little time and comparatively few adventures in which to mature. His short narrative and especially his laconic presence can hardly begin to accomplish what we can see is needed. And yet the relative silence of Jonah's time spent with the fish is able to be approached more seriously, since it is part of the experience and education he needs to have. Those worried by his change of demeanor from inside to outside the fish are instructed by the clear phases through which our other "flood heroes" come. Trust is not learned once and for all.

---

[29] Panikkar, *Blessed Simplicity*, 81.

Finally, we are given by the *Navigatio* a quest that makes its object not quite practically satisfactory. When Brendan and companions reach the island, they leave again, almost at once. Jonah's accomplishments, or the gifts he can be seen to be given, may also be subtly ephemeral and impermanent but at the same time of deep significance to those who reflect deeply on the narrative, as we are striving to do in this book.

Post-biblical Jewish Views

Post-biblical Judaism reads the Jonah story creatively as well. In this section we will investigate how the Jewish midrashic tradition works to gather its readings to expand the biblical tale. That is, we are asking two kinds of "how" questions: How did Jews writing after the biblical period but before modernity proceed? And how did the story take shape in their hands? Since postbiblical commentary elaborates the canonical narrative by adding to rather than changing text, our process of constructing a wider interpretive base from which to interpret biblical narrative is similar to other efforts in this chapter, though they were less ostensibly linked to the Jonah story itself. Our quest here, as you recall, is to enrich the categories through which we approach the Jonah narrative with which we are primarily concerned.

JEWISH MIDRASHIC INTERPRETATION PROCESS

Broadly speaking, midrash is the name for the interpretive processes that characterize virtually all Jewish writing until the modern period.[30] Though it flowered from 400–1200 C.E., it originated before and continued after those centuries.[31] Midrash is most basically a searching out, a questioning and understanding the text; it is also a genre, a set of literature, and a mode of interpretation with clear procedures.[32] The workings of midrash are several: It fills in gaps and surfaces irregularities, resolves them; it responds to questions rising implicitly from certain textual features; it explains points that seem not to have been anticipated originally, showing a

---

[30] Similar to what we discussed in our Chapter 4, Jewish interpretation sees several levels of meaning: *peshat* = literal; *remez* = metaphorical; *derash* = midrash; *sod* = mystery; see Howard Schwartz, *Reimagining the Bible: The Storytelling of the Rabbis* (New York: Oxford University Press, 1998) 37; James L. Kugel, "Two Introductions to Midrash," in Geoffrey H. Hartman and Sanford Burdick, eds., *Midrash and Literature* (New Haven and London: Yale University Press, 1986) 87.

[31] Barry W. Holtz, ed., *Back to the Sources: Reading the Classic Jewish Texts* (New York: Summit Books, 1984) ch. 3, specifically 177–87.

[32] Ibid. 84–90, and ch. 3 in general, where explanation is interspersed with examples.

text ever-relevant; midrash allows fresh experience to find a footing in tradition; it shows God's prescience. It is also useful to recognize what midrash does not attempt, evinces no interest in: It neither contextualizes historically nor aims to alter or explain the text process.[33] It does not enter from large sections of text but from small segments: a letter, a word, a verse. Its goal or purpose, then, is to show how texts can be seen to be in endless dialogue, whether contentious or collaborative, with each other. It is the constant process of pondering that elicits questions, which themselves engender searches, investigations that evoke apt recognition, which leads to insight;[34] things can be pushed farther than they appear to stand. Texts are springboards for imagination, opportunities to relive and reimagine them in our own lives—or perhaps ourselves in their lives. Kugel writes, almost counterintuitively, that the Bible is not so much about our lives as we are about its life: ". . . [B]iblical time becomes 'other,' a world wholly apart from ours, and yet one that is constantly intersecting our own via the [midrashic] strategies just seen."[35] Texts are most definitely not simply pretexts to distill morals and messages.[36]

Certain assumptions underlie the midrashic process. Howard Schwartz explains it in this way: God dictated the Torah to Moses by day and explained it to him by night, meaning that all was revealed to Moses at Sinai but it took and takes longer to approach the myriad levels and layers of possible meaning. Scripture's divine words have an existence independent of their immediate textual circumstances and the ostensible intention of the writer; all is included as part of God's divine plan.[37] Any word or verse is as linked to its most distant fellow as to the one adjacent.

Jewish Midrashic Reading of Jonah

Jewish interpreters have thus by probing the spare biblical narrative drawn further detail from it in a wonderful way. Gathered here is some of the classic midrash, offered in story order. After considering a modern midrashic piece, we will examine the use of the Jonah narrative in the Day of Atonement liturgy. All of this widening will help us approach biblical Jonah more creatively.

Since Jonah's personal origins are left somewhat obscure, tradition fills in, offering two contexts for the prophet's identity. Jonah is said to be the

[33] Kugel, "Two Introductions," 77–79.
[34] Schwartz, *Reimagining,* 16–19.
[35] Kugel, "Two Introductions," 89.
[36] Schwartz, *Reimagining,* 10.
[37] Kugel, "Two Introductions," 79.

young child raised from the dead: either by Elijah in 1 Kings 17, where the prophet was staying with a Sidonian widow and her son during the drought declared against Ahab and Jezebel; or alternatively, he was the son of the woman of Shunem brought back to life by the prophet Elisha (2 Kings 4). In the first instance the suggestion is that the woman's exclamation to Elijah— "Now I know that you are a man of God, and that the word of God in your mouth is truth" (1 Kgs 17:24)—gives substance to Jonah's patronymic, "son of Amittai," that is, of truthfulness. But whichever prophet brought him back from the dead, the journey is Jonah's first on that rarely-taken path.[38]

A second "prequel" to the biblical stories comes as Jonah becomes the anonymous prophet assigned by his "father" Elisha to anoint Jehu as king (1 Kgs 19:15-16; 2 Kgs 8:13–9:10). The prophet Jonah was also sent, in midrashic material, to proclaim destruction to the city of Jerusalem; but it did not occur, a non-event that led to Jonah's reputation of being a false prophet. And so when assigned to proclaim a similar thing to Nineveh, Jonah was disinclined to accept the task, saying, "I know of a certainty that the heathen will do penance, the threatened punishment will not be executed, and among the heathen, too, I shall gain the reputation of being a false prophet."[39] Elsewhere he anticipates that once the nations repent, God's anger will turn against Israel.[40] Thus is Jonah's initial biblical choice of flight from his God-given assignment made comprehensible. To avoid God's particular ability to commission prophecy Jonah left the land of Israel and fled to the sea, out of reach of God's missioning grip. The midrash indicates that the boat Jonah boarded had already been two days out of port; its return seemed to him a sign that his journey was blessed; in his joy and

---

[38] See Louis Ginzberg, *Legends of the Jews,* trans. Henrietta Szold and Paul Radin, vol. 2: *Bible Times and Characters from Moses in the Wilderness to Esther; Indexes* (Philadelphia: The Jewish Publication Society of America, 2003). This represents a fresh edition of an earlier work by the same author, title, and publisher (but published in 1946 and 1954); in the older edition the Jonah information is collected in vol. IV, *Bible Times and Characters from Joshua to Esther,* and the notes gathered in a separate volume (VI). Since the older edition is a bit more detailed, I will leave both sets of references in the next few notes. What Ginzberg has collected can be tracked to other places as well, information he thoughtfully furnishes. The information noted here comes in 1946: IV, 347 and 352. For a very different reading experience consult Yvonne K. Sherwood, *A Biblical Text and Its Afterlives: The Survival of Jonah in Western Culture* (Cambridge: Cambridge University Press, 2000).

[39] Ginzberg 1954: IV, 247; 2003: VI, 1031.

[40] The source is eighth-century *Pirkê Rabbi Eliezer,* a pseudepigraphic work attributed to a much earlier figure. See Gerald Friedlander, translation and annotations, *Pirkê de Rabbi Eliezer (The Chapters of Rabbi Eliezer the Great) according to the Text of the Manuscript belonging to Abraham Epstein of Vienna* (4th ed. New York: Sepher-Hermon Press, 1981) 65–66.

gratitude he paid his fare upon boarding (fortuitously for the owners!) rather than upon disembarking, as was more customary: four thousand gold denarii! But the storm overtook the boat soon enough, though other ships in its immediate vicinity were not afflicted but sailed peaceably by the one in which Jonah slept.[41] Once his responsibility for the storm has been ascertained, the sailors face the question of how to dispose of his provocative presence. As the biblical story narrates, they are scrupulous about not endangering him and try various remedies to improve their perilous condition. But finally, according to one reader[42] the sailors dangle Jonah overboard up to his knees, and when the storm abates, draw him back up. But when its violence resumes, they plunge him in the sea up to first his navel and then his neck, with the same response by the storm and by themselves. Once it becomes clear that the weather will not improve substantially while the prophet is on board, the sailors finally abandon their passenger to the sea.

Once Jonah is overboard, commentators move to the matter of the fish, in great and creative detail. There are numerous stories about it. First, its existence. According to Rabbi Eliezer the fish was created in primordial times. As Jonah entered its mouth, it was as though he walked into a synagogue. The fish's eyes were like windows, admitting light and extending a view for the passenger; and a pearl, suspended within the beast, also provided illumination. In this midrash the fish tells Jonah that its time for living is about to expire and that both of them are to be devoured by Leviathan. But Jonah promises to save them both. Urging his host to bring him alongside the mighty Leviathan, Jonah threatens to leash its tongue and give its body to the other inhabitants of the sea. When it hears his words and sees the mark of Jonah's circumcision, Leviathan flees, saving Jonah's fish and the prophet himself. The fish-host now tours Jonah around the depths of the sea, from which he prays his biblical prayer (Jonah 2). When Jonah reaches the very foundations of the Jerusalem Temple, a place from which all prayer uttered will be granted, he asks for release, which is at once given. His former sailor-companions, still watching out for him, witness these deeds and give the thanks we hear from them at the end of Jonah 1.[43] Another collection of *midrashim,* dealing with the gender discrepancy between Jonah 2:1-2 and 11, tells that Jonah is first swallowed by a male fish and makes his way comfortably inside it. No distress and no prayer to God issues forth. So God appoints a second fish, a female pregnant with 365,000 small fry. Approaching,

---

[41] Ginzberg provides this piece of information as well, 1954: IV, 248.

[42] The story of the sailors and Jonah is in Friedlander, *Pirkê de Rabbi Eliezer,* 69, and Ginzberg 2003: VI, 1031–32.

[43] Friedlander, *Pirkê de Rabbi Eliezer,* 69–71.

she challenges the male fish to disgorge its passenger, else she'll swallow them both. The male fish hesitates, not sure if she is speaking the truth or not, and finally consults Leviathan, who testifies that he just overheard God instruct the female. So the transfer is made, and Jonah, much more crowded and less comfortable, at once prays to God for release, which is granted.[44]

As commentators arrive at the scene in Nineveh there is an unusual story about the Ninevite citizens, stressing the depth of their conversion. Distinct from most Jewish commentary, which is either uninterested in or a bit cynical about the Assyrian change of heart, the midrash says conversion was so powerful that a strange contention broke out. One man who had acquired a field found treasure in it and tried to hand it over to the seller, who demurred, saying title was clearly the new owner's. When neither man felt comfortable to take the money they appealed to a judge, who was able to find out the identity of the one who buried the treasure and hence give it to his heirs, much to the relief and joy of both later owners! When God saw such a conversion, God changed the divine mind as well.[45]

Jonah's distress, starting at the end of ch. 3 and extending into ch. 4, is made additionally comprehensible. Besides the usual reasons rehearsed, the Midrash Jonah informs us that while he was in the pregnant fish the prophet's clothes and some of his skin were burned off by the heat of her body. Consequently, the suffering of his tender flesh, occasioned by the sun and wind—and by countless flies, mosquitoes, and fleas—was irksome to him.[46] But here is where once again our flood stories are helpful: The commentators suggest that Jonah suffered so greatly while experiencing the abyss, and presumably from his other trials as well, that compensatorily he was excused from death and allowed to enter paradise with his wife, who had done good deeds beyond her obligations.[47] So Jonah's links with immortality are at least three: when a child, from within the fish, and at the end of his life.[48]

---

[44] The *Midrash Jonah* can be found in August Wünsche, *Aus Israels Lehrhallen* (Hildesheim: Georg Olms, 1967) 2:39–56. They have been translated into English by James Limburg in *Jonah* (Louisville: Westminster John Knox, 1993) 110–14. Some portions are included in Ginzberg 1954: IV, 249–50, and in 2003: VI, 1033. See also Uriel Simon, *The JPS Bible Commentary: Jonah* (Philadelphia: The Jewish Publication Society of America, 1999) for more information on Jewish commentary.

[45] Ginzberg, 2003: II, 1034–35; Limburg, *Jonah,* 111–12.

[46] Ginzberg, 2003: II, 1035; Limburg, *Jonah,* 112.

[47] Ginzberg, 1954: IV, 253.

[48] For even more rabbinic commentary on Jonah, with almost unbelievably rich and insightful notes, consult the brief work on Jonah edited by Rabbi Meir Zlotowitz, trans. and comm. *Yonah/Jonah: A New Translation with a Commentary Anthologized from Talmudic, Midrashic and Rabbinic Sources* (New York: Mesorah Publications, Ltd., 1988) 77–144,

A short contemporary piece by Joel Rosenberg moves in this same midrashic mode. I select it for those reasons, because it asks questions and because it brings us to the topic of repentance and the Jewish Day of Atonement. Rosenberg asks five questions and replies to them as the process of his rumination on Jonah. First, *how was Jonah called to his mission?* Reviewing how other prophets were called, Rosenberg imagines for us how a presence that seems innocuous though importunate—"just a moment of your time, if you please"—can be admitted to our attention before we realize how inconvenient and life-changing those moments will be: "Go to Nineveh!" A second question: *What was Jonah thinking as he turned and ran*—which Rosenberg cautions us is not the same as asking why he fled. In this commentator's richly imaginative piece Jonah flees to avoid being looked at, hopes to avoid admitting to his own deafness, aims to pretend he was on his way to Jaffa and Tarshish in any case. That is, Jonah's mind is filled with denial of all that is happening. A third query: *What do we make of the fact that everyone in the Jonah narrative is so nice?* What space opens up if we have to notice that we aren't able to claim a spot on the rock of moral righteousness from which to look down on the others? Our commentator asks: "But what if the world—just to be perverse—mended its ways overnight and left us scurrying to catch up?" This step takes us to question four: *Did Jonah repent, since there does not seem much evidence of it once he is at Nineveh?* For Rosenberg, Jonah's feelings unblock while he is in the fish. He sounds repentant! So where is the evidence of it, and why does it seem to fade like dying matchlight? *Finally, what is a prophet—or what is it that we learn, watching the prophet we have in our scope?* Rosenberg suggests that Jonah's and Israel's destinies are shown intertwined. Jonah must learn what Israel must say every year at the liturgy of Yom Kippur: "Deal with us justly and kindly—we have no deeds."[49] Repentance is in gear and moving, but far from complete. And so let us, finally, look at that process before leaving this chapter.

THE DAY OF ATONEMENT LITURGY

In certain key ways like Christian liturgy the Jewish festival cycle shows the profound relatedness of ordinary time and space with their

---

concluding with several pages (145–56) of identification of Jewish sources for ready tracking by those who want more. Even after having worked on Jonah for two years, I was stunned at what I found in these compact pages!

49 "Jonah and the Nakedness of Deeds," *Tikkun* 2.4 (1987) 36–38.

deeper levels. The Jewish year is a round of commemorations and celebrations of events and seasons in which Jews recall the past and make it tangibly part of their ordinary lives. Where I teach this is made vivid each year in the fall as school begins. The school calendar names the important days of the various religious traditions of the member schools, but the actual days off are Christian. So Jewish faculty and students have to balance the prosaic rush of the start of an academic year with festal events, since three major festivals typically come in the first weeks of school. There is not much allowance at a semester's start for the need to prepare and celebrate these major occasions as many Jews like to do. Consequently a *sukkah* (booth) may appear on the porch of the administration building, reminding all of us, among other things, that the sacral and secular are basically the same time/space, for all that we usually live in one of them or the other.

On the Jewish Day of Atonement, Jonah is read in its entirety at the afternoon service after the Torah reading, since "The story of Jonah epitomizes the power of repentance, and serves to reassure the worshipers that God's arm is extended to receive them."[50] Baruch Levine shows how Jonah can assist with the pedagogic, therapeutic, psychological, and moral realms in our lives, which, of course, are also utterly intertwined, for all that we may try to hold them separate. God is the helper in this process. Levine also notes, as has Rosenberg, that denial of the need for change and repentance or transformation is a powerful block to it, since all genuine repentance calls for healthy self-knowledge and our most realistically generous appraisal of others.

Repentance, we learn, is primordially rooted, one of the seven things God created first, since it would be needed for the effective functioning of all else that is. Repentance is attached to God's ever-patient mercy and is coded into the universe for our participation. The process is dialogical: God extends mercy and we are drawn toward it; we cultivate an appropriate sense of the many ways in which we fall short, fail, sin, and reflect that if justice were to be served, we might expect little. But we simultaneously long for closeness to God, who is proffering gifts to us as we do so. Repentance requires also a sense of remorse for the past and an intention or desire to do better in the future.[51] The Day of Atonement is not the only occasion for these processes, but it is designed to host them, offers an occasion when

---

[50] Baruch A. Levine, "The Place of Jonah in the History of Biblical Ideas," in Stephen L. Cook and S. C. Winter, eds., *On the Way to Nineveh: Studies in Honor of George M. Landes* (Atlanta: Scholars, 1999) 201–17.

[51] For an extended reflection on these matters see "Overview: Jonah, Repentance, and Yom Kippur," in Zlotowitz, *Yonah/Jonah*, xix–lxxv, specifically xxxviii–lxiii.

repentance must be sought and evil rooted up, however else we may also attend to those things.[52]

Judaism sees three reasons why the book of Jonah is read on Yom Kippur: It teaches that sincere repentance can overcome a harsh decree; it shows an example of repentance in the Ninevite behavior; and the wonder of Jonah's deliverance in the fish shows the pointlessness of fleeing God. And we learn from it two attitudes: awe and flight at our own shortcomings, and optimistic anticipation of God's eagerness for our repentance.[53] First, let us suppose that God is teaching Jonah basically about his denials of relatedness, all of them, which are so richly commented upon by our many sources. We can see there is at least one in every chapter: when he refuses his prophetic commission, when he comes so close to death, when he is angered at God's mercy to the Ninevites, and when he is outraged at the loss of "his" plant. The teasing out of the various possible motives comprising all these aspects of the prophet is valuable, though not sufficient. It becomes obviously inadequate to ask about Jonah's state at simply one of these moments. Whatever we may need to say from our brief narrative, the journey into God's mercy is a life process in which no one moment, however profound or dramatic, is likely to be definitive.

So if repentance is a dance in which the failings and frustrations of our human experience circle the patient and attractive mercy of God, Jonah is doing well! If denial is the block and silence its guard, then Jonah is flailing toward relatedness, granted he does not sound particularly integrated as he complains at the good that happens to others! The dance takes time; the only bad move is to sit down. With a patient and creative partner—pedagogue and mentor—all is possible. Our story stops, or seems to do so, in a question. Who needs to respond to the questions God has posed? As Jonah goes silent, again we understand that the insight needed is our own.

Conclusions

We have dealt in this chapter with several plausible "Jonah enactments," a word not quite the same as interpretation. It is not that enactments do not interpret; they do. But the participants throw themselves into the narratives more tangibly. I sketched the case that Jonah reenacts one of its an-

---

[52] See R. Nosson Scherman, "Overview: Jonah, Repentance, and Yom Kippur," in Zlotowitz, *Yonah/Jonah*, xxi, lxiv–lxxx.

[53] R. Avie R. Gold, "Insights and Prayers," in *Yom Kippur: Its Significance, Laws and Prayers: A Presentation Anthologized from Talmudic and Traditional Sources*, gen. ed. R. Nosson Scherman and R. Meir Zlotowitz (Brooklyn, NY: Mesorah Publications, 1989) 85, 78.

cient forebears, the Gilgamesh epic—the oldest written story in the human community, so far as I know. The Irish monks reenact the Jonah story as they traverse perilous but necessary waters. The Bible brims with water motifs that, without insisting that we see Jonah in them, allows that possibility. The Jewish midrashic tradition renders old tales ever-fresh by moving them forward into later lives and by demanding of them significance to problems not earlier faced. And liturgy, converging around Scripture, invites current readers to deep and present participation in classic recitals. The pervasive and persistent "backdrop" of water helps us make the connections among the many water passages to survival and more meaningful life.

The "provable link" between this chapter's texts and biblical Jonah is tenuous. Our challenge is to triangulate the biblical story, the selected "intertexts," and the experience of the reader, and reach for a resonance. It is, arguably, an exercise in imagination, meant to stretch our interpretive framework beyond where it had been. Since the fit between Jonah and Gilgamesh or Brendan, the overall resemblance between our focal narrative and the scattered factors of it visible across the pages of the Bible, and even the coherence of many of the Jewish readings is much more tensive, we are in different interpretive terrain than before. We have to work harder, to swim into the materials with our senses alert and see what will happen.

The gain, however, is a sharper focus, a more vivid sense of the stakes involved. My wager that Jonah is cousin to the ancient Gilgamesh story, to Brendan's *Navigatio*, to its midrashic development, and to many biblical water motifs has prompted me to see more intensely the significance of journey through the water, where the outcome is nearly death. Our forebears struggled to find themselves related with the realm of the divine—hoping for one thing, perhaps, and learning to settle for another. We may come to pray with the centuries-old Jewish liturgy: Our deeds are few, we have no deeds. Part of straining forward is failing, and part of failing is regret, fear, anger; how have others negotiated these waters? The stakes are high: life, death, life eternal. How to use our time well, such as it is? How to give ourselves fully to the project of choice so that it can shape us deeply and yet emerge strengthened when it lets us down, as likely it will in some way? How to order our days and what fills them to align and resonate with the most generous hopes of God for us? These are deep matters to learn, and our ancient wisdom tales can help us, if we allow them to do so.

CHAPTER SEVEN

Jonah's Journeys: Fruitful Flailings

We arrive now at the reading that has accumulated or distilled for me. It emerges from my questions—not only the ones with which I started but also all those that have arisen since. To stay engaged with one's questions is crucial. This reading also comes from all our conversations with the twenty-five hundred years of interpreters whose company we have kept on our journey. The point of consulting others is to be genuinely shaped by what they have said, whether we agree or not. So though this is now *my* reading, it comes from the jostling stimulus of many insights.

The search, as you recall, is for meaning and for transformation. The meaning quest involves an awareness of sense and reference but also of deep truthfulness and existential significance. To interpret is to make meaning with a work of art, to find meaning from it, not abstractly but in the contexts of our readerly situation. Such meaning need not be narrow, private, idiosyncratic, or solipsistic; but it must be answerable to the life I live, the things of which I can speak with some integrity. If my meaning quest coincides with the questions and reflections of others, which I hope is the case, it will not be because it is mine but because others can inhabit it in some useful way. In this sense meaning must be shared while simultaneously customized. The event of meaning is richly collaborative. As any of us read and interpret we construct meaning, gain perspective and insight, change, and are transformed. Interpretation is a deeply spiritual act when done carefully. When it is Scripture we are engaging, the gifts given are all the more life-giving and life-sustaining. Transformation is a fruit of engaging deeply God's words uttered within our lives.

Procedure

Reading well-written mysteries is one of my favorite ways of relaxing, and I have long wanted to write one. As part of the preparation of this book I decided to accomplish my goal, using the biblical Jonah story as a plot. I sharpened my pencils, bought a special notebook for the working out of my story, and repaired to my favorite coffee shop so as to have an auspicious start. And only then did I realize that I was unsure what the book of Jonah was about! That is, I was not sure which of the many paths through the story was the one for me to take, which architectonic I would use. Writing the Jonah mystery was an exercise in interpretation I had not anticipated before I began. My choice of main place to explore, that from which I would construct my mystery, was the relationship between the characters Jonah and God. That is, for me the biblical story—and hence my mystery—is most deeply about how those two relate to each other, though for both characters that tie includes others as well. If you were writing a Jonah mystery, you might choose another base.

So for this chapter's integrative task I start at the same point: The basic grounding for my reading is the exploration of what happens between deity and prophet. In brief, that network will investigate Jonah's basic desires to flee, to avoid, to resist, to blame, to project, to act out. It will explore "his" fears that there is not enough for all, that dealing with God and others somehow involves a zero-sum game. My reading will probe the "Jonah" fear of failure and of criticism, which themselves arise from as well as generate anger and resentment, jealousy and pettiness. This nexus of issues brings us into contact with the realm of violence, not so much in the way we may usually think about it, but in the sense of disrespectful coercion of another. The concept of violence in this case rests on the insight and writings of Mohandas Gandhi, who sees it most fundamentally as the refusal to will good for another.[1] The other pole of the relationship to study is the character God, who here will be seen basically as a respectful mentor, a loving friend who wills the good, most deeply, for Jonah and the various others in the story. Jonah needs to learn from God how to love and be loved creatively as God does. When I read the narrative from that point of view I enter the relationship and construct it from my perspective, though as has been stressed repeatedly, with attention fixed carefully on the three worlds of relevance: that behind, within and before the text; as alert to the past as seems apt, I am nonetheless reading for the urgent present.

A second procedural point is to name my grounding methodology. As we have worked on the many readings that fill this book there has been no small amount of discussion about methodology. Every chapter raises the question in some aspect. So the topic has not been neglected. But our ap-

---

[1] For a fresh entry into the works of this genius see Michael N. Nagler, *Is There No Other Way? The Search for a Nonviolent Future* (Berkeley, CA: Berkeley Hills Books, 2001).

proach has been primarily descriptive of others' moves. I have learned a great deal from the many companions we have had on this journey. But when I interpret, my basic mode is adapted from the thinker and theorist Mikhail Bakhtin. Since I have written three books already detailing how his thought can be useful for the interpretation of biblical narrative, I will not repeat it here but refer you to those places.[2] Third, following the succinct example of Joel Rosenberg, I will proceed by posing and tracking a series of short questions about the biblical story. I found his provocative questions and his insightful responses to them to be a wonderful way to read.[3]

Pivot Assumptions about the Narrative

Since we will shortly be adjourning to the end of the biblical book to work at the meaning quest, let me list here several assumptions operative, in addition to the fundamental one set forth above: that the story is driven by the God-and-Jonah relationship. First, that relationship works not simply "personally" but also "professionally": God is one who sends prophets, and prophets are ones who are sent. Second, Jonah "owes" God, in that God can ask him to do a difficult mission and Jonah is not exactly in a position to refuse, though he would like to; it is ultimately not feasible in their particular relationship. Third, the sailors and Ninevites are not so central to the story as they might seem; they assist God with Jonah, Jonah with God rather than being a main focus here. This point does not denigrate them because they are Gentiles or wicked in some (other) way; they are simply minor characters in this story on the basis of my particular sense of its construction. Fourth, crucial is Jonah's overwhelming "chagrin" or anger toward the end of the story—not just once but pervasively; something about the outcome bothers him dreadfully, but not in isolation from his other reactions. Fifth, God stops to assist, as is part of God's and Jonah's relationship; God spends some gentle but pointed care to help Jonah "keep moving."

Sixth, God's patience in dealing with the several creatures is to be noted; no straggler is too unimportant to deal with. Whatever it takes, God is attentive. Seventh, the inconclusivity of the ending is important; and as we learn in certain wisdom genres (e.g., parables), our charge is to fill in. The

---

[2] For a general discussion of Bakhtin see Barbara Green, *Mikhail Bakhtin and Biblical Scholarship: An Introduction* (Atlanta: Society of Biblical Literature, 2000); a more complex and diffuse study may be found in my *How Are the Mighty Fallen? A Dialogical Study of Saul in 1 Samuel* (Sheffield: Sheffield Academic Press, 2003); the most useful place to consult is my other book in this INTERFACES series, *King Saul's Asking* (Collegeville: Liturgical Press, 2003) ch. 1.

[3] Joel Rosenberg, "Jonah and the Nakedness of Deeds," *Tikkun* 2.4 (1987) 36–38.

genre forces our participation in a particular way. Eighth, God's question of 4:11 is highly pertinent: In asking it, God makes available to Jonah and to us some subjectivity. We become privileged to be admitted to that intimacy—which only happens once in the story. We learn various things of God throughout, but none is so revealing as this moment. We glimpse here something of God's inner workings. Ninth, the moment is, I think, analogous to what we learn in the book of Job, though it is all more succinct here. There is divine care for all that is, though we can hardly imagine the quality of God's concern for others, given our desire for divine attention for ourselves. Tenth, God hints at intense and concerned familiarity with those who are existentially confused in Nineveh; the inability to tell right hand from left is no small disability—and with paws, all the more, since there are not only east- and west- but north- and south-paws. And God will help. God's concern is Jonah's discomfort as God deals with "them" as well as with "him/me." To be explored is how the others are part of and have a share in God's concerns, how Jonah can be learning about the story—and he must, since he and God have that sort of ongoing and not-to-be-jettisoned relationship.

Questions to Prompt Reading: Going Backward

Jonah 4

HOW DOES GOD INSTRUCT JONAH IN THE BOOK'S LAST UTTERANCE (JONAH 4:10-11)?

The whole narrative screeches to a halt when God speaks to Jonah in their last scene. God's self-disclosure is stunning, silencing—not in the sense of wiping Jonah out ignominiously—but in providing perspective that is existentially fresh. That is, though we may be able to take the sentence in stride and abstractly, God, like a good teacher, chooses a key moment when the prophet is able to accept some re-creatively useful information; or perhaps Jonah is simply unguarded at the moment and fails to shut out the word God expends. Since the character Jonah does not reply, "my" readerly Jonah receives the information and moves to ponder it, which is to say, I will do it with him, as you are invited to do as well.

What did God say that was so fresh and galvanizing? God begins with an observation with which Jonah can agree, since it correlates with the experience the prophet is having. God says, "'You are concerned about the bush, for which you did not labor and which you did not grow; it came up in a night and perished in a night . . . .'" God offers Jonah a summary of what Jonah has done: He has felt concern for a plant that owed him nothing, that it might make claim on his feelings, that he would "spare" it. In fact, we as readers know that God is the one who appointed the plant and then the worm that devoured it; God's labor, such as it was, is pertinent. God does not tell Jonah that the deity is the prophet's benefactor in the matter of the plant, nor, of course, that God also had a hand in its destruction. That information is for us. The plant works for God, not for Jonah. So God's first point to Jonah is to re-describe, though incompletely, the situation that pertains among creator, prophet, and plant. God's point, I suggest, is that there is no obligation on either side between Jonah and the plant: It does not owe him, or he it. *Owing is not the basis for what is happening.*

God moves on to prompt further insight from Jonah, now with a question. Think about me, God says. What concern, what "sparing" should I feel—and do I feel—when in fact there *is* some effort expended on both sides? Nineveh is a big place, God says, implying plentiful creative energy from God; and there are a lot of people who struggle to tell their right hand from their left, animals as well. God here stresses the moral and spiritual ignorance, or lack of direction, of the human and animal citizenry, though we and Jonah have just seen them do quite well. God's implication seems to be that God has invested in Ninevites and they in God, at least latterly. The analogy turns both on quantity (one small and brief plant compared to a large and populous city) and on quality (nothing owed between Jonah and the plant compared with what God and the Ninevites have built into their bond to date). We can bring to bear, I think, the biblical sense that God is not bound with Gentiles as with Jews, and the Ninevites are not involved with God as explicitly as are Jonah's own people. Still, God seems to say: There is *something* here, at least recently. I sent a prophet to assist them and they responded, even with no specific guarantee. God seems to ask: If you can recognize how you felt, can you understand how I might and actually do feel?

The verb in question is not the usual word for "to pity, have mercy, or feel compassion." The other places this present verb "to spare a thought for" (*ḥus*) occurs can help us see something usefully nuanced.[4] Implied in its oc-

---

[4] The verb comes up about twenty times (Francis Brown, with S. R. Driver and C. A. Briggs, *The New Brown-Driver-Briggs-Gesenius Hebrew and English Lexicon with an Appendix Containing the Biblical Aramaic* [Peabody, MA: Hendrickson, 1979] 299): in Deuteronomy (7:16; 13:8; 19:13, 21) and in Ezekiel (5:11; 7:4, 9; 8:18; 9:5, 10; 16:5, and 20:17 [those latter two a bit different], 24:14) typically use it for what is *not* to happen: Israel is not to spare indigenous inhabitants of the land who might be a temptation; and God is generally loathe to spare Israel, who has sinned egregiously. Texts in Isaiah (13:18) and Jeremiah (13:14) are similar. When Joel 2:17, Neh 13:22, and Ps 72:13 use the verb, the desperate plea is that though sparing seems unlikely, it is sought nonetheless. In 1 Sam 24:11 David claims, somewhat disingenuously, to have spared Saul by "only" cutting his garment when he might

currences is an unevenness of position, where a superior might or might not "spare" an inferior; there is not adequate grounds for either to think primarily in terms of anything deserved or owed. So "spare," with its nuance of condescension, is a better English word than "have pity," which operates differently. God reads Jonah as willing that the plant had been "spared," though neither owes the other. God does not critique Jonah for that feeling but moves to say that it pertains all the more when more is involved, quantitatively and qualitatively. God reads Jonah to the prophet himself and offers a reading of Self for Jonah, a glimpse the prophet would otherwise not have had. And we are offered something additionally, since God does not deflate Jonah by saying that it is thanks to God that the plant was known to the prophet at all. So, to sum up, *God says to Jonah, think about how you feel on the basis of a tiny relationship and I, here, on the basis of somewhat more.* Inferred by me is a crucial third-level point: *God's hint to Jonah that with all the deity and prophet have expended with each other, the "sparing" is all the more germane.* Jonah has survived—been spared—from a great deal: a disobedient journey, a storm, a fish, a risky ministry, a big disappointment, the sun, wind, a worm, anger. God is saying to Jonah: note how it works: for you and a bit of shrubbery, for these near-strangers and me, and now for you and me! For the Jonah I am reading, this triple analogy offers new "perspective." Let us back up and see what has preceded it.

WHY IS JONAH ANGRY (4:5-9)?

This is not an easy question, but let's look carefully at each place. Granting for the moment that Jonah is already in distress (4:1), we have seen him leave the city after a verbal exchange with God (4:2-4). He goes east of Nineveh, builds a shelter, sits under its shade while awaiting something. God appoints a plant of some sort to grow up over Jonah to be a shade for his head to save him from something bad; and, the storyteller relates, Jonah was very happy with the plant. But God next appoints a worm which attacked the plant and devastated it, and then a fierce east wind. With the rising of the hot sun, the unshaded and wind-whipped prophet has some sort of reaction,[5] "swooned" or "was faint." First the narrator tells us

---

have done worse. The oddest use is in Gen 45:20, where Pharaoh directs Joseph to tell Jacob not to spare a thought for the family possessions when they move to Egypt, since plenty will be available locally.

[5] See Jack M. Sasson, *Jonah. A New Translation with Introduction, Commentary and Interpretations* (New York: Doubleday, 1990) 302–06 for a discussion of what the verb is and how it can best be approached. I will assume that it signifies some physical reaction brought on by Jonah's situation: swooned works well enough.

that Jonah wished for death, and then we hear him say it directly: Better to die than to live. It is not clear to whom he is speaking, perhaps to himself. But God overhears him and inquires: "Is it right for you to be angry about the bush?" (4:9). God diagnoses the reaction as rising specifically from the plant's destruction, not simply a result of hot wind and sun. And God asks if Jonah's anger over the plant is a good thing, to which Jonah retorts that it is—enough to die for, sufficient for death. It seems a strong reaction. Let's deal with both question and answer.

First, God's question: We need to recall that we know more clearly than does Jonah the source of the plant. And we have just seen that the topic God broaches is entitlement and expectations of those in relationship. Though it is important to see how the story roots the anger—in the destruction of the plant—the anger itself is also crucial. That is, there are two related but distinct things: the anger itself and its ostensible cause. God's question addresses both: Is the anger productive and is it justified? Is the plant's loss a sufficient context for Jonah's feeling? We can say no, since it was an anonymous gift given him—the point God makes as the conversation moves ahead a lap. You had no investment in the plant and it owed you nothing, God said as follow-up. But does Jonah understand that the plant was appointed by God? I think not. Plants come and go in the experience of all of us; why would Jonah assume a special creation? Why would we, unless we had been told so by the narrator? A key reminder lurks here: *We may know far less than we think we do about how things work in God's world and will do well to watch carefully and creatively.* Though we have information that Jonah does not know, we must allow him his "shorter" angle of vision. If we allow our story to participate here in the ancient Near Eastern *topos* of the search for the plant that brings life, even if the shadow seems faint, the question of the suitability of the anger takes a different path. This plant is a serious thing to have briefly and then lose, its origin aside. *To lose the plant is to face death's inevitability.*

A second question rises from the anger. Is Jonah's anger a good thing? Does he do well with it? God's succinct question again needs a bit of fluffing out. Anger has its positive place as an energy, as an apt reaction to something that is seriously wrong. Anger is often an authentic response we do best to recognize, acknowledge, channel, and transform. But anger can also be destructive, out of control, misbegotten, and wasted. Jonah is angry because he lost something that had made him happy—fair cause for anger. This almost innocuous verb *smḥ*/be happy (4:6) is also part of Jonah's "getting perspective," ours as well.

Now for Jonah's response to God's question—right to be angry: Jonah claims yes, in spades. But his assertion, coming as a repeat (see 3:3), seems to me a point made rather than a rational answer tendered. That is, given what has happened, Jonah *has* to say he is justified; to reply in the negative—"I guess not, LORD"—would reroute the story significantly. Jonah's anger is such that he is unlikely to concede a point or take a way out that he is offered, even if it is aimed to be friendly and helpful. Be slow to decide quickly whether God wants a yes or a no to this question! *Reach again for the analogy: if you, Jonah, can rejoice in a plant you barely knew, what about my pleasure with Ninevites, my being pleased with you?* Does anger at destruction work by the same analogy?

This, I think, is actually the key moment for insight, ours (or mine) with Jonah: *God has said this is not primarily about being owed or entitled but about mutual investment in a relationship.* This is not simply about anger or happiness but offers a moment to see which feeling arises from what situations. Nor can it be reduced to myself vs. the others, especially in relation to God, since God seems to mix us all together, at least in this story. Here is the moment for "Jonah" to take a fresh look at God, which will involve "his" asking how "he" is at the center of the universe. Am I (to re-route the pronouns more honestly) simply the source of my own gratification and frustration, and is it simply my own deeds and needs that are appraised in terms of God's actions? Is there not more? Take another look! *What is to die for and what to live for? What causes anger and what brings joy?* The moment calls on Jonah to recalibrate if he can, to get a fresh perspective if he is able to do so.

WHAT IS JONAH EXPECTING (3:10–4:4)?

As we just saw, the discussion between prophet and deity takes place as Jonah sits outside the city of Nineveh awaiting something. He is there at least overnight, as we learn from the shade plant that arrives one day and goes the next. His job of preaching and prophesying seems accomplished, and so he might have left Nineveh for Israel; but such is not his choice. The narrative indicates that he anticipates seeing something about the city, though of course in Hebrew as in English the word "see" can stand in for non-visual insight of some sort. The dominant and probable view among scholars is that Jonah is waiting for the destruction or non-destruction of the city. It is likely that within the forty-day framework announced he might have some stretch of time to fill; hence the booth for shelter. The precise question is *what, of various possibilities, is Jonah anticipating, and with what desires?*

It is worth recalling that, though the narrator has told us in 3:10 that God has had a change of heart in view of Ninevite repentance, we do not hear that communicated to Jonah. So it is most accurate to say that so far as Jonah is concerned, God has not destroyed the city *yet*. It continues possible, since some days remain. We have noted various commentators with their all-too-accurate observations about foxhole piety and the limits of group repentance, and so forth. That the Ninevites responded at once does not mean they can be expected to stay the course. Perhaps we do not need commentators to tell us that! So Jonah may be read as waiting out the period God specified to see what happens within it; early repentance does not preclude later lapses.

We can next ask what Jonah wants, and again we have other readers to help us factor the possibilities. And here, I think, Jonah has a clear choice. Anger can pop up in its unruly way on any occasion. But the question of ultimate Ninevite fate is another matter. *Does Jonah will the city to be destroyed for its evil or saved for its conversion?* Many scholars think he wants it destroyed, and for good reasons. Jonah may have something against the Ninevites themselves, though we cannot automatically presume to know what it would have been; it will depend on the supposed date of setting and production of the book. And we can anticipate the Jew/Gentile situation, where scholars make Jonah anticipate some sort of equation in which if one group were to benefit, the other cannot fail to lose in some way—a conviction all too clearly shared by many, as we know from history and experience. Finally, we can review the many queries about Jonah's sense of his own professional position as a prophet: how he will seem and be if one thing happens with the city or if another does.

And yet, the crucial question for me in this reading is still—all those excellent points notwithstanding— *what does Jonah truly and deeply want for the city of Nineveh?* Since I have already expressed preference for Jerome, you may not be surprised to hear me say that the Jonah I am reading is *not able to will* destruction for the Ninevites. He wishes he could, since the Jonah of this moment is angry and becomes more so before the book concludes. *But to be angry at something is not at all the same as wishing it destroyed.* All of Jonah's reasons for feeling thwarted remain valid: Perhaps the Ninevites have been or will be cruel to Israel; relations between Jews and Gentiles in regard to God's favor will have many bad days for Jewish people; and which of us likes to feel that others disrespect us or that we may not be quite what we would hope to appear in their eyes? But not even all those explanations require that Jonah want the city destroyed. *In fact, the very "crunch" between those arguments is troublesome and adequate reason for his anger: reasons to wish the city's destruction, posed against the realization that Nineveh's denizens are fellow-creatures.* It would have been simpler and less conflictual for our prophet if he could be clear one way or the other. *But to see the shortcomings (and longcomings!) of this city and still not be able to wish it vaporized: that is angering!* Let us work that seam.

The basic interpretation pattern I appreciated in Jerome was his allowing all the characters to do well. I find that I do best if people expect me to do so, and I find that others work pretty much the same when my attitudes are involved in their lives. As I scrutinize my list of "Ninevites," which is not short—people who have done or will do injustices to me, those who call on God in some way to place me at a disadvantage, those who view me as doing my job or my self inadequately or who I think might be doing that—a residual anger always surfaces. These are perennials in human living, and my guess is that you can with no trouble make such a list yourself. Anger at them? Various wishes and words about them? Yes, frequently. Am I secretly (or perhaps openly) sorry when they have good fortune? Beyond a doubt. But do I want them to suffer evil and be destroyed in some way? No, I don't. So I am going to accord Jonah the same status. Feelings and basic desires of the will are not the same thing. In fact, now the question can be posed: *Is this insight—the urgency to sort feelings from desires and to disentangle one feeling from another—arguably what God and Jonah discuss at the story's end?*

Preliminarily, let me again draw on my experience and invite you to do the same with your own. When I am angry about something, especially if I am conflicted about it, and most especially if I have not pinned down even partially what is bothering me, it is very easy to misdirect the negativity onto something that is not at fault. I could offer examples here, but you can furnish them yourself. Even so simple a thing as driving behind slowpokes when one is running late or following leisurely sightseers when there is no such pressure allows me to register a big difference in my anxiety-driven blame-assigning reactions. Reading Scripture in the way we have been doing is about insight and self-knowledge on the hopeful journey of transformation, so it is important that you are moving along with Jonah and me on your actual life-track here. In the midst of all this *Sturm und Drang,* Jonah becomes unaccountably angry when a shrub arrives without his expecting it and departs without his wishing it. A little thing, really, except we may recognize the power of the symbol. Jonah built a booth for shade, but the unlooked-for plant came to make it better. And then the unwanted worm removed the plant and Jonah is back at square one. Bad weather along the Tigris River has to be expected—hot sun and fierce winds. But the plant was a gratuity. And so Jonah is so angry he wants to die. After all he has been through! Is he really that angry about the loss of the plant? And this is the very point God raises in conversation: *All this anger about something to which you had virtually no relationship?* It is a great question. In my reading God is prompting Jonah to locate more precisely the core of his frustration, more carefully to probe his desire. *It is about relatedness, God hints. You had little relatedness to this plant; I have more to this city, and I have a lot with you.* What, Jonah, are you deeply related with? Who shares a powerful bond with you? What delights you? Who takes delight in you? What does Jonah want for Nineveh and for himself? How does Jonah appraise this network with God as benefactor or opponent? Destruction is too simple.

What Can We Make of Jonah's Outburst (4:1-3)?

The narrator again starts us off. We, though not the prophet, have learned that God has had a change of mind. And the narrator tells us that "it" (an impersonal verb) was very displeasing to Jonah, with anger resulting. *The question here is: What was it that made him mad and what seemed bad?* If you indulge me a bit and assume that Jonah does not know that God has relented from the original threat against the city, then we have to say that what angers Jonah has to be what he saw: the Ninevite repentance described at such comparative length in 3:5-9. Jonah is angry at the effectiveness of his own words in the lives of his opponents. And he blames God. Let us see if that tangled snarl can fit with what he blurts out.

His outburst is a prayer—no small thing! This is not a picket sign, or a petition, not even a journal entry. Jonah prays to God about what he has just experienced and his reaction to it. And his prayer is of the "I told you so" genre, again perhaps familiar to you from relationships with people you care about, God included. This type of utterance is self-justifying in its way, makes the speaker to have known all along, even to have announced that something would occur. Whether this is literally so or not is somewhat irrelevant, though of course it is far more gratifying if one *has* made a big public announcement, not believed by others at the time, but that now looks both shrewd and correct. What matters is how he feels now, given his Nineveh experience; the earlier moment is a separate matter, to be taken up shortly. This prayerful outburst can be understood to involve God, the Ninevites, or Jonah's own sense of himself—and most likely the interrelationship among all of those. *The point of frustration is specifically how those players, especially prophet and deity but not excluding the objects of prophetic proclamation, are tied together.* The story turns on relationships.

My Jonah here is continuing to act out his frustrations; and though his words signify, we need not take them absolutely literally. He bemoans God's propensities: what God abounds in—graciousness, mercy, steadfast love; what God is short on—anger; where it all leads—readiness to relent from punishing (4:2). This is not secret information about God; commentators thoughtfully total the number of places these things are said in the Bible.[6] That Jonah claims he already knew it does not distinguish him so very much. Surprising is the tone. Ordinarily these are characteristics to give thanks for, but here they have made Jonah angry, the narrator says, and Jonah seems to imply as well. But though well known as divine qualities, these features are not entitlements. God is prone to these behaviors, but known for some others as well. These are live options for God, and Jonah seems to know there was danger of God's selecting them. Once again we have distinct paths to follow: how Jonah feels and why.

The feeling is undeniably strong. When Jonah concludes his prayer by asking to die (4:3), we need to take it seriously. Out of proportion it may seem. But we have just seen him repeat the same request twice more (4:8, 9) and we know he has had earlier brushes with death that we will examine shortly: in ch. 3, where he threatens destruction of a city he stands within; in ch. 2 when he begs for release from the fish; and in ch. 1 when he and others are at risk from a storm. Recalling that in Jewish tradition Jonah was revived from death by at least one prophet and later exempted from that fate on the basis of his deeds, and that in ancient Near Eastern tradition he resembles one character who survived the flood and another who struggles plantlessly for immortality, we have to listen when he begs for death. The story of Jonah as we have it here is neither Noah's flood adventure nor anyone's tree of life story. And yet those melodies are playing in the background audibly enough that we register them and can make sense of Jonah's feelings, borrowed, so to speak, from some of his literary colleagues. *Jonah is struggling over whether to die or live.*

If recognizing the subtextual nature of the plant helps us with Jonah's reaction, there is more. Given that the divine characteristics named are really not so bad, the question may be how they are distributed. Since our commentators have rehearsed that point well, let me position it just a bit differently. The Jonah I know best need not label his categories "Jew" and "Gentile" in order to recognize that they involve the question of himself and the others. *The question here, and the nub of anger, may well be the question of whether there is enough for all, and—related—how will "it" be distributed: fairly or not, and by what criteria?* It is easy to scoff at Jonah here, unless we catch a flash from the mirror and once again own who is looking back at us. This question of amounts and fairness (quantity and quality) of God's gifts is highly bothersome to many, perhaps most of God's acquain-

---

[6] Sasson, *Jonah*, 239–68.

tances and even some friends. The point is not so much whether we apportion by race, gender, class, religion, morality, or some other more idiosyncratic measuring rod; *the very sense that God's graciousness is limited and that we may lose out as others gain is the dynamic to recognize.* Whether Jonah—or any of us—is justified to fear this is, again, perhaps not quite the point. The story suggests: *Take a look at it, listen to God talk about it when asking questions about plants, pagans, prophets. Scripture poses to us the things we most need to examine, and here is one of them.*

But that Jonah calls for death does not mean he actually *wills* it, only that he may *feel* like it—again two separable elements that may or may not overlap. Death is one of the stages on which our dramatic Jonah treads when his feelings are profound. To call for it is serious, but safe. When Jonah asks the God who has rescued him so far to allow him to die, I think Jonah can count on the very qualities he has just named; he cannot assume them as his right, but he can trust that they will be there for him. *Jonah trusts God to deal graciously with him at the very moment of railing at the deity for doing the same for others; once again, part of his frustration is his conflictedness: He has to rely for his own life on the very qualities he has just complained about when they assisted others.* And on the topic of others: Must Jonah be read as resenting that God has been gracious to and sparing of the others? It is one of the possibilities. But the Jonah I am reading is being instructed and mentored not so much about them as about his sense of himself. It is all about relatedness, God has said to him. *How to learn to be bound closely and to anticipate that we are to care and act urgently for those with whom we are related intimately? How to widen the circle, quantity, and quality?* So once again we can say of Jonah's anger: is it productive—a good thing used well? This moment is, of course, not unrelated to Jonah's role as God's prophet to others. But it is about something more basic than that: Jonah's creatureliness as it relates him to the creator and to his many fellows. Here Jonah is challenged to think afresh about the ways of God with creatures—all of them, himself included. The point established by starting at the end of the book for this reading is that, most basically, the story works the way in which God and Jonah relate. *God has drawn Jonah's attention to that very thing, has opened the divine heart to show Jonah how the very theological reputation Jonah can cite actually works, not only with Gentiles but with Jonah himself.* Now, since it is confusing to read backwards, though it has served us well, let's take what we learned by reading the last page of the story back to the front of the tale and work forwards with the questions indicated above.

Questions to Prompt Reading: Going Forward

Jonah 1

WHY DOES GOD START THIS PROJECT (1:1-2)?

God sends word to a man we know from elsewhere (I am following the Jewish readings here) was God's prophet, in a way not so very unusual in the Bible: Go and cry out against a city, for I have seen something that troubles me. We can certainly make the link between what God says and sees and the nature of the mission, except now I, at least, suspect that God has seen something else that needs attention; Jonah must do this Nineveh job, since Jonah has something urgent to learn. If you grant with me that this story is *primarily* (though not exclusively) about the relationship between deity and prophet, let's keep our eye on that aspect. *Jonah may think this is about the others, but he will find that it is about himself as well. He imagines that he is the physician, only to discover in time that he is also the patient.* When we are reading Scripture, God has us in mind as well, for we, too, have some perspective to gain if we read skillfully.

HOW DOES JONAH RESPOND (1:3)?

Jonah acts out his feelings rather than communicating them directly. Jonah does not pray here, he simply decamps. Again, scholars have provided many reasons for Jonah's flight; those all work well, and I would hesitate to choose among them, see no need to do so. Motivation is braided, almost always. Jonah acts rather than talks. But this counter is not so unusual a move as some claim; prophets resist God steadily, Jeremiah, Elijah, and Moses being notable examples. Prophets neither are nor are expected to be automatons; God often seems to enjoy dialogue. Perhaps it is disappointing here for God when Jonah goes off silent. The issue, again, is not whether Jonah thinks he can really escape God; he doubtless knows he cannot. But to huff off makes a dramatic statement, and the narrator indulges him. Jonah chooses a sea voyage, no reason why not.

HOW DOES GOD RESPOND (1:4-17)?

God runs after Jonah, here as later, in wind and weather. Though it is possible to see divine anger here, to resent the deity's heedless endangering of many in the pursuit of one—remember, one of our issues to query is the zero-sum game—it need not be read so. The God I am reading is deeply concerned, eager to teach. The storm hurts no one (again, recall the midrashic insight: only the one boat, briefly imperiled). Jonah sleeps for grief, or for depression rising from an inadequate facing and factoring of his own reactions. Flight from God, even if not meant seriously, takes energy; anger projected onto God invites denial, another enervating activity. The sailors are left to face their fears and to utter their prayers, absent their passenger's doing the same. But when they bring him on deck, Jonah readily admits what he has done, at least to his human companions. Though—or since—we miss Jonah's own phrasing of the specific circumstances of his flight (1:10: he is in denial) and must rely on a narrative summary, we are prompted to think about it creatively. We hear Jonah claim to be a God-fearer, which we know is the case. God and Jonah have at least a professional relationship, and as we will see shortly, a personal one as well. What Jonah has done is of urgent interest to us, though all the sailors really need is to separate from him, and so they do. What we learn of God's graciousness and readiness to relent of plans is that though the sailors do end up throwing some of their livelihood overboard before the prophet follows it, they end up praying to Jonah's God themselves, having their prayer (1:14) heard; and in fact as we see the last of them these Gentiles are worshiping the one true God. Though I want to avoid saying that suffering is inevitably good for us—or that it is good for others when it happens to them—my reading here is that the crew gain, not lose, from the storm. To find this God is worth disposing of some stuff—in fact, may be just the exercise needed. God here is concerned primarily for Jonah, but incidentally for others; it is not so much a matter of preferences as of focus. Jonah is the most needy one in this scene. But no words pass between deity and prophet; they mime their communication. Why not? God is neither passive nor permissive; neither do I sense capriciousness or cruelty. God is involved, engaged, intent.

Jonah 2

WHAT HAPPENS IN THE FISH (2:1-9)?

Jonah's fish experience is one of the most important parts of the narrative, not simply his going in and coming out, but his transformation while within. Though Jonah was not digested, however we may wish to explain that phenomenon so beloved of scholars, he was transformed. Visual art often suggests that Jonah turned around while inside the fish, came out differently than he went in. His words may not be quite what all wish him to have said, but we may get more than we anticipate. First, Jonah now prays to God and comments that he did so. His prayer is richly biblical, as many have noted. Jonah knows his psalter well and so is no novice at prayer. Here is where we can see that he and God are, in fact, old friends. You may suspect him of just mouthing the words, but I don't think so. The words of the psalms are active and intrusive, making their way in from the lips of those who say them. Don't say the psalms unless you want to mean them; they may well take over your prayer life.

I want here not to worry about the timing: when Jonah prayed and was rescued, if the order is backwards. Virtually all biblical prayer says thank you as part of the request, as though that were good manners, or more deeply a matter of conviction. That Jonah thanks God for the rescue while he is still within the fish is a testimony to the relationship shared between deity and prophet. Jonah says God answered, whether "simply" by deed or by words, too. God and Jonah may be like an old married couple or a pair of long-ranging friends who are so familiar and intimate with each other's mind and heart that they can anticipate shared conversation and take either part. Somewhat after the manner of Theodore of Mopsuestia, I will fill in a bit here, so we can hear both voices as they harmonize.

To Jonah's "I cried, you heard," God rejoins: "Finally you spoke and I was glad; I had missed you" (2:2). As Jonah accuses, "You cast me . . . your waves and billows . . . . " God smiles: "You bought a boat ticket, chose a water experience!" (2:3). As Jonah wails, "You'll miss me in the temple, though I'll miss you as well," God replies: "Not so fast! We'll meet there again" (2:4). Jonah relates the terrors of his struggle with the primeval waters (2:5-6), and as we recall the great floods that so engage the ancient Near Eastern heroes like Gilgamesh we hear as well the ancient motif of the gods' jealousy of the human beings enacted in the Mesopotamian tales. Only Enki of all the gods was willing to help the flood hero. But our Jonah says that his God, also, brought him back from the pit, rescued him at the very gate of death. "As my life was ebbing, it was you I reached out to," and God says: "I was sitting by my phone in the temple, so relieved when you finally called" (2:7). God deals respectfully with Jonah, throughout, not forcing a way in without some sort of invitational cue. This story is all about relatedness, and that is what we see in this fish transaction. It is also about the others, whom Jonah mentions as he nears his conclusion: "Some are not very loyal—idols and such—but you can count on me!" to which God smiles and nods: "I do count on you, Jonah; and you can rely on me. Deliverance is my gift" (2:8-9). This is some fish.

As you may recall, some find Jonah guilty of foxhole piety. That does not worry me overly, since such piety is better than impiety. Better foxhole piety than foxhole despair. I am far from prescribing such a fish for myself or for you, but it may happen. If it does, the challenge is to get what you can, to reach for what you need. Anticipate help in terms of the relationship with God that you have, and try to have a relationship in terms of which to anticipate. If you do not have such a friendship with God, acquire one. A foxhole may be a step, a phase, a prompt. But actually I don't think that is what Jonah is to be suspected of. Others wonder if his change of heart is sincere, since it seems to have worn off by the end of the story. But I don't see it that way. We do not acquire wisdom in so simple and straightforward a way. Human experience and our capacities to gain perspective from it are not like capital in some bank, accruing interest steadily. The journey is more like the stock market: dramatically changeable, dizzily circuitous, irrationally tumultuous—much more interesting!

How Does God Respond (2:10)?

This moment is quite straightforward. God and the fish—not without the prophet's active assistance—have collaboratively completed the conversion needed so far, and so God commands the fish, which allows the prophet to disembark. Nothing bad has happened, only good—granted, it has involved the sort of suffering that is inevitable in significant relationships. We can see that Jonah has had some moments to fret and fear, and God has worried and grieved as well. Both have also rejoiced and reconciled. Three days is enough for this great journey. A work of art by Albert Herbert shows this moment well: The attractively svelte fish obligingly and patiently opens its mouth, and Jonah can proceed, though he is in no great rush to do so. The question he seems to be pondering is ours as well: What now? He is being instructed, or addressed, by a figure that Wendy Beckett calls a little goose girl,[7] but which I can (also) see is God. On we move.

Jonah 3

How Do God and Jonah Re-commence the "Nineveh Project" (3:1-3)?

God repeats close to the same directions as before to Jonah, except that we all learn that the specific word will be delivered when the prophet is at the city site. Since we do not, here or ever, listen to God's direct discourse in this matter we are freed to construe the language proclaimed there as a divine utterance, co-shaped among God, prophet, and Ninevites; what is needed will be elicited. This is one of God's specialties: customized communication. As others have observed, God does not allude to past inadequacies or disappointments when reassigning the prophet to the

---

[7] Herbert's work is shown and discussed in Wendy Beckett, with Patricia Wright, contributing consultant, *The Story of Painting* (London, New York, and Stuttgart: Dorling Kindersley, 1994) 721.

job. And, again, Jonah does not reply verbally to his assignment but acts, now obediently. Arriving at the large city, he enters it and makes his proclamation. It is not of interest to me to stop here over the time and space of this urban moment, since you have many others to consult.

HOW DOES JONAH PROPHESY (3:4)?

The narrator, spare and discreet as always, does not say Jonah only spoke once, though that is all we hear. There is no indication that the proclamation is delivered grudgingly, though we may suppose that, if we wish. Jonah utters a prophecy that, in this story, is his own utterance rather than God's; by that I mean that elsewhere God can arrive at a scene and deliver verbatim speech for prophets to recite. We do not have that here, so it is my choice to understand that God has left it up to Jonah to decide what is needed, or else their communication proceeds out of our hearing. In either case the choice is an excellent one, since it makes utterly clear the basic scandal of human intermediation of God's word: How does any of us—prophet or bystanders—know whether what the prophet says is what God intends? This problem, stretching at least from Moses to our own day, will not be solved here. *The non-solution is precisely the problem. We cannot check credentials of every sentence that arrives with a "thus says the LORD" tag; in fact, Jonah does not inscribe such a marker on his sentence.* We are about to hear that the Ninevites have no hesitation crediting his word; and we ourselves have been privy to enough of the discussion to have confidence, I think, in Jonah's capacity to say what is needed. I only raise the point to remind us that there are no guarantees here, no non-slippage certificate. Intermediation is a delicate matter always, the more when God and humans are involved!

The sentence itself—"Forty more days and Nineveh 'overturns'"—I have already discussed above (pp. 95–100). Like much human language, it is delightfully ambivalent. And we have various ears through which to hear it. The Jonah I am constructing here selects it to be bracing, compelling. But my Jonah has not quite fully understood the possibilities of his own word choice: Who can have understood the mystery of how overturnings take place? And so Jonah says more than he knows but precisely what he needs to have proclaimed.

HOW DO THE PLAYERS RESPOND TO THE PREACHING (3:5-10)?

The Ninevites are gold-medal winners at positive response. As though they had already worked out a disaster plan, they fall to: belief in Jonah's

God, proclamation of a fast, a quick change into sackcloth. This story, which features overturnings, shows it well here. The king is only a step behind. When the sentence reaches the royal ears he also rises at once to replace his royal garb with sackcloth and his lofty throne with ashes. His words reinforce all that he and the citizens have already commenced: no nutrients, only mourning garb; all shall beseech God while turning from their—our?—evil and violence. And all this the king concludes on the basis that God *may* hear and relent, change the divine mind, turn from fierce anger, so that the Ninevites survive. The wholesomeness of this response precludes more comment. It is important but not the goal of the story. Whatever questions we may have about God and the Ninevites become less important than what happens next. The story is not primarily about the Ninevites. Like the sailors, they have done well, very well. The gain is theirs.

And God's response to the Ninevites' response to Jonah's response to God's word: God takes note of what the citizens of the city did, presumably all of it: fasting, sackcloth, ashes, outcry, turning back, or toward. And God changes God's mind, as the king had hoped enough to mention when making provision for the city. The ponderous scholarly discussion about this move of God's seems to me to be misplaced. The Hebrew Bible narrative is studded with instances where God moves from "plan *alef*" to "plan *bet*" and through the letters to "plan *tav*" and back through again, as many times as are required! Jewish theological commentary is somewhat flexible about this divine characteristic. Christian theology is often uneasy lest such change seem to threaten the divine perfection. But the story I am reading does not feature a God who worries about consistency of reputation, any more than Jonah should be worrying about how people will credit his word if it appears or not to come to pass. *The key thing is relatedness. If the creator loves all the creatures and longs for their company, then if and when they approach, God is happy to unbend from past pronouncements. In fact, God winks, I was there first!* Even some Christian commentators suggest God was intending it all the while! *In this story where things work best when actants do well, God does well too.*

READING IN CIRCLES: ARRIVING BACK AT JONAH 4

God has designed for Jonah a ministry the prophet needed to undertake. God's survey turned up the evil in Nineveh, but not simply that. The prophet and the pagans share a need for God's gentle instruction, each distinctively. Jonah, assigned, acts out his resistant reaction not once but a number of times. But God persists, pursues, not in angry determination but in anxious love. While God woos Jonah, others benefit as well. There are plenty of God's gifts to go around. Care for one creature can splash over onto others. Lavish love. Jonah is a prophet for the sailors and the Ninevites, but they offer him insight into God's ways as well, if he can accept it. And Jonah is no stranger to God, as we learn when he is nestled in what Jerome calls God's paunch.[8] Jonah cries to God, who responds. Jonah emerges changed from his experience. But conversion is never really complete; there are always more possibilities to explore. So Jonah, re-commissioned, preaches effectively, successfully; but he is not satisfied. As is now his integrity, he speaks up his feelings about God's qualities that seem troublesome instead of comforting. And God, attentive and patient, helps him push for additional insight.

Wrapping Up

God works with what Jonah has proffered, which is indeed what God had given him. Three things emerge to learn, at least for me. First, conflictual is confusing and wasteful. Sort things properly: feelings from desires; origins of anger from its trajectories; anger from joy; entitlement from gratuity; how the others might diminish me from how I might shortchange them.

Second, focus on the real question, which is how are we all related. The plant, God suggests, can show you something important. Even a tiny thing can give pleasure, or grief. The bush made you happy, though you knew it briefly and it was not your doing. No obligations or entitlements on either side. Raise you one: Myself and the people of this city, a minimal sort of relationship, though not no bond. And yet it was important to me that when they turned, I meet them at least halfway. So what about us, Jonah, you and me: Such a long-term investment on both of our parts, so much between us. What about my joy in you, Jonah? And if you are happy in a plant, what is your joy in Ninevites, and in me? Am I not to care all the more about you—more than a plant, more than about Ninevites, though caring for them is instructive to see? There is plenty for all: some for the plant, more for the Ninevites, lots for you. Let's have less thought about who owes and how much, about who is entitled and how extensively. The plant and the Ninevites, prophetic as they are, show us that, or can do, if we look at them.

And third, take a new look if you can. Who is God? Who are the others? Who am I? And for this you need to leave these pages, which have taken us nearly as far as we can get together.

---

[8] R. H. Bowers, *The Legend of Jonah* (The Hague: Martinus Nijhoff, 1971) 25.

Provisional Conclusions

All that remains now is quick review of how we have proceeded in this study. Since the last chapter offered a comprehensive and synthetic interpretation of the narrative, there is no need to repeat particulars of content. The point here is to be sure we have gotten all we can from the interpretive process. It is urgent that sophisticated readers of Scripture understand how we manage our task: appropriating meaning. Medieval Dominican Meister Eckhart maintains that "mystical consciousness [is] fundamentally hermeneutical; that is . . . achieved in the act of hearing, interpreting, and preaching the Bible."[1] Our conclusions are named "provisional" simply to reinforce the point that it is the best we can do, for now.

Throughout the study we made questions a particular tool. Many are italicized so that you can pick them wout easily. The questions helped us probe the many points in the story that became meaning-full and rich for us. Though we may not have dealt with every question raised, we have considered a good many of them. Questions have been a productive way to proceed, as they have opened us to many possibilities.

A second major choice made early and sustained was to work conscious of several interpretive realms. You recall that we had two main frameworks: one that simply called attention to Scripture's past and our present, another that helped us distinguish whether we were, at any given moment, examining the several "pasts" behind the narrative, perennial language dynamics within it, or our own existential concerns as we stand before it. We saw consistently that, helpful though such divisions were to provide us with accurate information about our moves, we never escaped our own interests and issues as readers. Those can and must be enriched and addressed in many ways, but they are never well disregarded in a

---

[1] Bernard McGinn, *The Mystical Thought of Meister Eckhart: The Man from Whom God Hid Nothing* (New York: Herder & Herder/Crossroad, 2001) 24–25.

meaning quest such as we have been working on. Part of "answerable" reading for serious interpreters is to know what we are doing!

Finally, let me remind you that, though these interpretive strategies are transferable outside of religious studies, they are particularly at home when believers engage Scripture. As Wilfred Cantwell Smith gives us occasion to learn, "to Scripture" is a praxis of many peoples throughout time and space on this earth: That is, to affirm that some narratives are so helpful to us on our journey of humanization/divinization that our ancestors have specially marked them for us, and we ratify that choice when we read fruitfully. Scripture is no odd quirk of Christians and Jews; it is a classic of the human condition. To participate in such "Scripturing" company is a privilege as well as an urgent necessity.

And so we investigated many pasts: the long history of interpretation or reception, which sought to organize both what others have said about the story and why they were so prompted; the plausibly pertinent circumstances of the book's writers and first readers in post-exilic Judah; the particular analogical ways in which certain ancients mined the language of the narrative for significance deeper than seemed apparent; a possible ancient Near Eastern forebear of our story that offered us insight as to its concerns and motifs. We also looked at literary features of the text, appreciating the rich readings generated by those as interested in language detail as were the ancients but concerned to show why and how they are provocative in themselves. We investigated the work of some who sought to enact the text: as a journey narrative, as liturgy. The heritage we found is rich and diverse and would be the more if we could get at it in other ways. You have missed, I hope, the women readers of Jonah in our quest, which has turned up primarily male interpreters. Believe it or not, there are other things we might have taken up, and what we have dealt with might be arranged in other ways. What is important is to draw from the many eras and ways in which the Bible has been studied as we engage it now. Of course, on any given occasion certain modes of study—even one in particular—might be best; but in general to aim to be inclusive is healthy, granted also demanding!

Not every era has been so concerned about methodology as is our own. I am sometimes bemused when I am asked if I really think the methodology I name and claim as relevant has been useful; occasionally the hint is dropped that my readings would be the same without utilization and discussion of theory. The question may be apt in terms of some particular reading effort, but in general how we approach makes all the difference. I observe my reading to change substantially as I shift my pivotal assumptions, try new interpretive strategies, pose new questions. Surely our present reading would have been radically different without twenty-five hundred years worth of reading companions and the modes espoused here. The exact relationship between one set of information or procedure and another cannot always be clearly labeled; insight does not work formulaically, nor of course is it completely serendipitous.

In general, the more we can see and name the relationship between how we read and what we see, the better. It is all the more important, in these days when one hears the frequent suggestion that we replace the Bible with something more contemporary, that we are able to know and show the value of reading Scripture well: content, process, outcomes. I also recognize and am glad to claim that the reading I offered in our Chapter 7 emerged neither independent of those factors nor in isolation from existential questions that I work at continuously. My point is that reading answerably demands collaboration—as rich as is manageable—and it proceeds best when we are as honest as possible about what we are after. I have maintained that the goal of such answerable interpretation is meaning and transformation. I have found myself deeply engaged with Jonah's story; I feel I know it and him well and that it and its character dynamics have helped me know myself, God, and others more respectfully. Whether such learning has changed me radically is more than I can demonstrate, which does not mean it is not happening.

Without dismissing any of our other work, I would like to review once more the gain from Chapters 3, 4, and 6: the investigation into a likely moment of the book's production, the insight generated by those whose thirst for God prompted analogical reading, the way in which the story seemed to grow when refracted through verbal enactments. The point here is to underline ways in which these particular sets of participants in the Jonah Journey contributed to the reading with which this book culminated.

The ancients who read allegorically, typologically, and midrashically have only recently become interesting to me, I regret to say. Their moves once seemed artificial and valueless, or worse: forced into silly patterns of similarity, reductively narrowed to similarities between Hebrew Bible characters and Jesus, irresponsibly filled out to make sense of points irrelevant to the biblical text. What I learned while studying this pre-critical work with Jonah is that their grounding assumptions make all the difference. In virtually every case—granted distinctively—it is a confidence in God's capacity to speak fully and fruitfully with human beings that prompted analogical inventiveness with the text. Conceding their assumptions about creator and creatures, creation and communication, I can let go of my quibbles about their procedures and concentrate on broader issues these readers raised. Though I see the need to antidote their virtual disregard for history and their blindness to their own ideology, I appreciate their persistent instinct to reach for relevance to their own lives when reading of past events. What they offer us, besides the various riches of particular insights, is the conviction that our present situation orders our understanding of the past. If that present includes a thirst for God, a confidence in God's facility to communicate with us, and a sense of compunction about our various shortcomings in relation to others, then that is what we will read. The challenge is to work out in contemporary terms the bases on which the grounding analogy works. We can also see better than could these ancestors how our own frame of reference can also limit our vision and blind us to what needs healing.

The chapter in which we worked to invent—in the classic sense of that word, which includes "find"—the plausible origins of the story as we have it was valuable in another way. There was nothing immediately analogical about that investigation, which concluded that Jonah was produced by and for those in post-exilic Yehud who found themselves responsible to be animators of their communal traditions. We hypothesized those leaders as still deeply affected by the devastation wrought by the Babylonian defeat and exile of God's people, as residually insecure about their collective guilt before God and about the deity's possible responses to their various changes of heart. The Jonah figure became, in that re-constructive reading, a flawed prophet whose various crises are odd enough to be noteworthy but not so ludicrous as to be scorned. Actually, we can see that this reading, too, aims to uncover analogical resonance between narrative and readers, ways in which recognition opens insight. The Jonah of such an interpretation wrestles with its sense of God's mercy and anger, with the implications of his own diminishing role, with the uncomfortable sense that opponents may be part of our best learning. We, reading, are reminded that we know comparatively little, not only about the ways of God, but even about the ways of the sixth century B.C.E. Into such a vacuum, unless we are careful, we will—unthinking and naïve—presume our own frame of reference exclusively. To uncover or discover the concerns of another generation is salutary. Historians have the challenge to do their work with minute care to process and fact. The past of biblical studies is a vast tell of dogmatic misreadings. And yet, to the degree that we proceed in ignorance of the original referentiality of the text we risk falling into major error about its reference. The challenge is to reconstruct skillfully, provisionally, humbly.

To read our Jonah story in light of a narrative older, longer, and far more complex than itself was a liberating and imaginative move, a sort of wager that such a move was not illegitimate. The point was not to force a relationship but to see if one emerged. To focus on a few scenes near the end of the Gilgamesh story threw light on the conclusion of the biblical work: The perilous journey over the waters, both abetted and thwarted by the divine players in the quest, and especially the hero's engagement with the powerful plant helped me, at least, to cue more significantly to Jonah's anger. Water tales are not lacking in the Bible, and to watch an extra-biblical water story work starkly was instructive for reading Jonah. The prophetic ministry does not lose importance but gains it: The prophet is all the more credible if he, like his hearers, must struggle with some basic question as well as deliver an ultimatum that seems clear. If we take seriously the anthropological challenges of intermediation between the divine and the human realms—however we may wish also to organize their close relatedness—utter transparency may not be the feature. That a prophet experiences richly the range of human adventures with God and fellow-creatures can only strengthen his credibility. If the prophet is wounded as well as healing, nothing suffers. The intensive mode of the enactments—our awareness of those who throw themselves into participation on literal journeys and in liturgy—remind us of the power of this narrative. Reading the older story raises for our consideration the experience mediated: the gradual and painful stages of humanization, the uncertain quest for divinization, the joy and grief of intimate relationship, the temptations and taming of violence, dreaded questions about the willingness of the cosmic realm of the divine to assist us.

Notice that in each case, and surely in "our" Chapter 7, much devolves on the reader! The challenge presented to all of us is to become skilled readers: good questioners, clear about frameworks, steeped in historical matters, sensitive about literary depths. But additionally, we do best to be thirsty readers, knowing at least partially what is life-giving for us as we read. So the challenge and adventure of "Scripturing" is to gain perspective: to see what we deeply desire, to move toward it, to remain awake and intentional as we journey, to share the fruits of what we gain with others. Journey well! We are in great company!

BIBLIOGRAPHY

Ackerman, James S. "Satire and Symbolism in the Song of Jonah." In Baruch Halpern and Jon D. Levenson, eds., *Traditions in Transformation: Turning Points in Biblical Faith*. Winona Lake, IN: Eisenbrauns, 1981, 213–46.

Adam, A.K.M. "The Sign of Jonah: A Fish-Eye View," *Semeia* 51 (1990) 177–91.

Alexander, T. Desmond. "Jonah and Genre," *Tyndale Bulletin* 36 (1985) 35–59.

Band, Arnold J. "Swallowing Jonah: The Eclipse of Parody," *Prooftexts* 10 (1990) 177–95.

Barron, W R.J., and Glyn S. Burgess, gen. eds. *The Voyage of Saint Brendan: Representative Versions of the Legend in English Translation*. Exeter: University of Exeter Press, 2002.

Batto, Bernard F. *Slaying the Dragon: Mythmaking in the Biblical Tradition*. Louisville: Westminster John Knox, 1992.

Beckett, Wendy. *The Gaze of Love: Meditations on Art and Spiritual Transformation*. New York: HarperCollins, 1993.

Beckett, Wendy, with Patricia Wright, contributing consultant. *The Story of Painting*. London, New York, and Stuttgart: Dorling Kindersley, 1994.

Ben Zvi, Ehud. "Inclusion in and Exclusion from Israel as Conveyed by the Use of the Term 'Israel' in Post-Monarchic Biblical Texts," in Steven W. Holloway and Lowell K. Handy, eds., *The Pitcher Is Broken: Memorial Essays for Gösta W. Alström*. Sheffield: Sheffield Academic Press, 1995, 95–149.

_____. "Looking at the Primary (Hi)Story and the Prophetic Books as Literary/Theological Units within the Frame of the Early Second Temple: Some Considerations," *Scandinavian Journal of the Old Testament* 12 (1998) 26–43.

_____. "What's New in Yehud? Some Considerations," in Rainer Albertz and Bob Becking, eds., *Yahwism after the Exile: Perspectives on Israelite Religion in the Persian Era*. Assen: Van Gorcum, 2003, 32–48.

_____. *Signs of Jonah: Reading and Rereading in Ancient Yehud*. Sheffield: Sheffield Academic Press, 2003.

_____. "Introduction: Writings, Speeches, and the Prophetic Books—Setting an Agenda," in *Writings and Speech in Israelite and Ancient Near Eastern Prophecy*. Atlanta: Society of Biblical Literature, 2000, 1–29.

Berlin, Adele. "A Rejoinder to John A. Miles, Jr., with Some Observations on the Nature of Prophecy," *Jewish Quarterly Review* 66 (1975–76) 227–35.

Borgen, Peder. "Philo of Alexandria as Exegete," in Alan J. Hauser and Duane F. Watson, eds., *A History of Biblical Interpretation. Volume 1: The Ancient Period*. Grand Rapids: Eerdmans, 2003, 114–43.

Bourgeault, Cynthia. "The Monastic Archetype in the *Navigatio of St. Brendan*," *Monastic Studies* 14 (1983) 109–22.

Bowers, R. H. *The Legend of Jonah*. The Hague: Martinus Nijhoff, 1971.

Brenner, Athalya. "Jonah's Poem out of and within its Context," in Philip R. Davies and David J. A. Clines, eds., *Among the Prophets: Language, Image and Structure in the Prophetic Writings*. Sheffield: Sheffield Academic Press, 1993, 183–92.

Bridges, Herb, and Terry C. Boodman. *Gone With the Wind: The Definitive Illustrated History of the Book, the Movie, and the Legend*. New York: Simon & Schuster/Fireside, 1989.

Brown, Dennis. "Jerome and the Vulgate," in Alan J. Hauser and Duane F. Watson, eds., *A History of Biblical Interpretation. Volume 1: The Ancient Period*. Grand Rapids: Eerdmans, 2003, 355–79.

Brown, Francis, with S. R. Driver and C. A. Briggs. *The New Brown-Driver-Briggs-Gesenius Hebrew and English Lexicon with an Appendix Containing the Biblical Aramaic*. Peabody, MA: Hendrickson, 1979.

Brown, Robert E. *Jonathan Edwards and the Bible*. Bloomington, IN: Indiana University Press, 2002.

Burton-Christie, Douglas. *The Word in the Desert: Scripture and the Quest for Holiness in Early Christian Monasticism*. New York and Oxford: Oxford University Press, 1993.

Chase, Steven. *Contemplation and Compassion: The Victorine Tradition*. Maryknoll, NY: Orbis, 2003.

Cherry, Conrad. "Symbols of Spiritual Truth: Jonathan Edwards as Biblical Interpreter," *Interpretation* 39 (1985) 263–71.

Clark, Mary, trans. and intro. *Augustine of Hippo: Selected Writings*. Ramsey, NJ: Paulist, 1984.

Clifford, Richard J. *Creation Accounts in the Ancient Near East and in the Bible*. Washington, DC: The Catholic Biblical Association of America, 1994.

Craig, Kenneth M., Jr. *A Poetics of Jonah: Art in the Service of Ideology*. Columbia, SC: University of South Carolina Press, 1993.

_____. "Jonah in Recent Research," *Currents in Research: Biblical Studies* 7 (1999) 97–118.

Dalley, Stephanie. *Myths from Mesopotamia: Creation, the Flood, Gilgamesh and Others*. Oxford and New York: Oxford University Press, 1989.

Dawson, David. "Plato's Soul and the Body of the Text in Philo and Origen," in Jon Whitman, ed. and introductory essay, *Interpretation and Allegory: Antiquity to the Modern Period*. Leiden and Boston: Brill, 2000, 89–107.

Elata-Alster, Gerda, and Rachel Salmon. "The Deconstruction of Genre in the Book of Jonah: Towards a Theological Discourse," *Journal of Literature and Theology* 3 (1989) 40–60.

Friedlander, Gerald, translation and annotations. *Pirkê de Rabbi Eliezer (The Chapters of Rabbi Eliezer the Great) according to the Text of the Manuscript belonging to Abraham Epstein of Vienna.* 4th ed. New York: Sepher-Hermon Press, 1981.

George, Andrew R. *The Babylonian Gilgamesh Epic: Introduction, Critical Edition and Cuneiform Texts.* 2 vols. Oxford: Oxford University Press, 2003.

_____. *The Epic of Gilgamesh: The Babylonian Epic Poem and Other Texts in Akkadian and Sumerian.* London: Penguin Books, 1999.

Ginzberg, Louis. *The Legends of the Jews.* Vol. IV: *Bible Times and Characters from Joshua to Esther.* Vol. VI: *Notes to Vols. III–IV.* Philadelphia: The Jewish Publication Society of America, 1954 and 1946.

_____. *Legends of the Jews,* trans. Henrietta Szold and Paul Radin. Vol. II: *Bible Times and Characters from Moses in the Wilderness to Esther; Indexes.* Philadelphia: The Jewish Publication Society of America, 2003.

Gitay, Yehoshua. "Jonah: The Prophecy of Antirhetoric," in Astrid B. Beck, et al., eds., *Fortunate the Eyes That See: Essays in Honor of David Noel Freedman in Celebration of his Seventieth Birthday.* Grand Rapids: Eerdmans, 1995, 197–206.

Gold, R. Avie. "Insights and Prayers," in R. Nosson Scherman and R. Meir Zlotowitz, gen. eds., *Yom Kippur: Its Significance, Laws and Prayers: A Presentation Anthologized from Talmudic and Traditional Sources.* Brooklyn, NY: Mesorah Publications, 1989, 41–96.

Green, Barbara. *Mikhail Bakhtin and Biblical Scholarship: An Introduction.* Atlanta: Society of Biblical Literature, 2000.

_____. *How Are the Mighty Fallen? A Dialogical Study of Saul in 1 Samuel.* Sheffield: Sheffield Academic Press, 2003.

_____. *King Saul's Asking.* Collegeville: Liturgical Press, 2003.

_____. "The Old Testament in Christian Spirituality," in Arthur Holder, ed., *The Blackwell Companion to Christian Spirituality.* Oxford: Basil Blackwell, 2005, 37–54.

Harris, Wendell V. *Dictionary of Concepts in Literary Criticism and Theory.* Westport, CT: Greenwood, 1992.

Hauser, Alan J., and Duane F. Watson. "Introduction and Overview," in Hauser and Watson, eds., *A History of Biblical Interpretation. Volume 1: The Ancient Period.* Grand Rapids: Eerdmans, 2003, 1–54.

Hegedus, Timothy. "Jerome's Commentary on Jonah: Translation with Introduction and Critical Notes." M.A. Thesis, Wilfrid Laurier University, 1991.

Herring, George. *What Was the Oxford Movement?* London and New York: Continuum, 2002.

Hill, Robert C., trans. "Commentary on the Prophet Jonah," in *Theodore of Mopsuestia: Commentary on the Twelve Prophets.* Washington, DC: Catholic University of America Press, 2004, 185–205.

Holbert, John C. "'Deliverance Belongs to Yahweh!': Satire in the Book of Jonah," *Journal for the Study of the Old Testament* 21 (1981) 59–81.

Holtz, Barry W., ed. *Back to the Sources: Reading the Classic Jewish Texts.* New York: Summit Books, 1984.

Kavanaugh, Kieran, O.C.D., intro. and trans. *Teresa of Avila: The Interior Castle.* New York: Paulist, 1979.

Kovacs, Maureen G., trans and intro. *The Epic of Gilgamesh.* Stanford, CA: Stanford University Press, 1989.

Kugel, James L. "Two Introductions to Midrash," in Geoffrey H. Hartman and Sanford Burdick, eds. *Midrash and Literature.* New Haven and London: Yale University Press, 1986, 77–103.

Lacocque, André, and Pierre-Emmanuel Lacocque, foreword by Mircea Eliade. *Jonah: A Psycho-Religious Approach to the Prophet.* Columbia, SC: University of South Carolina Press, 1990.

Levine, Baruch. "The Place of Jonah in the History of Biblical Ideas," in Stephen L. Cook and S. C. Winter, eds., *On the Way to Nineveh: Studies in Honor of George M. Landes.* Atlanta: Scholars, 1999, 201–17.

Limburg, James. *Jonah.* Louisville: Westminster John Knox, 1993.

Maddison, Bula. "Reading the Watery Creation: An Intertextual Story." M.A. Thesis, Graduate Theological Union, 1997.

Magonet, Jonathan. *Form and Meaning: Studies in Literary Technique in the Book of Jonah.* Sheffield: Almond Press, 1983.

Marcus, David. *From Balaam to Jonah: Anti-prophetic Satire in the Hebrew Bible.* Atlanta: Scholars, 1995.

Marsden, George M. *Jonathan Edwards: A Life.* New Haven and London: Yale University Press, 2003.

McGinn, Bernard. *The Mystical Thought of Meister Eckhart: The Man from Whom God Hid Nothing.* New York: Herder & Herder/Crossroad, 2001.

McGinn, Bernard, and Patricia Ferris McGinn. *Early Christian Mystics: The Divine Vision of the Spiritual Masters.* New York: Crossroad, 2003.

Miles, John A., Jr. "Laughing at the Bible: Jonah as Parody," *Jewish Quarterly Review* 65 (1974–75) 168–81.

Murphy, Catherine M. *John the Baptist: Prophet of Purity for a New Age.* Collegeville: Liturgical Press, 2003.

Nagler, Michael N. *Is There No Other Way? The Search for a Nonviolent Future.* Berkeley, CA: Berkeley Hills Books, 2001.

Nichols, Aidan, O.P. *Discovering Aquinas: An Introduction to His Life, Work, and Influence.* Grand Rapids and Cambridge: Eerdmans, 2003.

O'Loughlin, Thomas. "Distant Islands: The Topography of Holiness in the *Nauigatio [sic] Sancti Brendani*," in Marion Glasscoe, ed., *The Medieval Mystical Tradition: Vol. 6: England, Ireland and Wales.* Cambridge: D.S. Brewer, 1999, 1–20.

O'Meara, John, and Jonathan M. Wooding, trans. and intro. *The Voyage of Saint Brendan:* "The Latin Version," in W.R.J. Barron and Glyn S. Burgess, gen. eds., *The Voyage of Saint Brendan: Representative Versions of the Legend in English Translation.* Exeter: University of Exeter Press 2002, 13–64.

Oswald, Hilton C., ed. *Luther's Works. Vol. 19: Lectures on the Minor Prophets: II: Jonah, Habakkuk.* Trans. Charles D. Froehlich (1525) and Martin H. Bertram (1526). St. Louis: Concordia Publishing House, 1982.

Panikkar, Raimundo. *Blessed Simplicity.* New York: Seabury, 1982.

Pusey, Edward B. *The Minor Prophets: A Commentary.* Grand Rapids: Baker Books, 1950.

Ramsey, Boniface, trans. and annotations. *John Cassian: The Conferences.* New York and Mahwah, NJ: Paulist, 1997.

_____. *John Cassian: The Institutes.* New York and Mahwah, NJ: Paulist, 2000.

Rosenberg, Joel. "Jonah and the Nakedness of Deeds," *Tikkun* 2.4 (1987) 36–38.

Sasson, Jack M. *Jonah: A New Translation with Introduction, Commentary and Interpretations.* New York: Doubleday, 1990.

Schaff, Philip, ed. *Nicene and Post-Nicene Fathers, 1st ser.* Vol. 1: *The Confessions and Letters of Augustin* [sic], *with a Sketch of His Life and Work;* Vol. 2: *Augustin: City of God, Christian Doctrine;* Vol. 3: *Augustin: On the Holy Trinity, Doctrinal Treatises, Moral Treatises;* Vol. 8: *Expositions on the Book of Psalms.* Peabody, MA: Hendrickson, 1994.

Scherman, R. Nosson. "Overview: Jonah, Repentance, and Yom Kippur," in R. Meir Zlotowitz, trans. and comm., *Yonah/Jonah: A New Translation with a Commentary Anthologized from Talmudic, Midrashic and Rabbinic Sources.* New York: Mesorah Publications, 1988, xix–lxxv.

Schneiders, Sandra M. "The Study of Christian Spirituality: Contours and Dynamics of a Discipline," *Journal of the Society for the Study of Christian Spirituality* 6.1 (1998) 1, 3–12.

_____. "Biblical Spirituality," *Interpretation* 56 (2002) 133–42.

_____. "Approaches to the Study of Christian Spirituality," in Arthur Holder, ed., *The Blackwell Companion to Christian Spirituality.* Oxford: Basil Blackwell, 2005, 15–33.

Schwartz, Howard. *Reimagining the Bible: The Storytelling of the Rabbis.* New York: Oxford University Press, 1998.

Sherwood, Yvonne K. *A Biblical Text and Its Afterlives: The Survival of Jonah in Western Culture.* Cambridge: Cambridge University Press, 2000.

Simms, G. O. *Brendan the Navigator: Exploring the Ancient World.* Dublin: The O'Brien Press, 1989.

Simon, Uriel. *The JPS Bible Commentary: Jonah.* Philadelphia: Jewish Publication Society, 1999.

Smalley, Beryl. *The Study of the Bible in the Middle Ages.* 3rd ed. Oxford: Basil Blackwell, 1983.

Stein, S. J., ed. *Jonathan Edwards: Notes on Scripture.* New Haven: Yale University Press, 1998.

Sternberg, Meir. *The Poetics of Biblical Narrative: Ideological Literature and the Drama of Reading.* Bloomington: Indiana University Press, 1985.

Stewart, Columba, O.S.B. *Cassian the Monk.* New York and Oxford: Oxford University Press, 1998.

Taylor, J. H., Jr., trans. and annotation. *St. Augustine: The Literal Meaning of Genesis.* New York and Ramsey, NJ: Newman Press, 1982.

Trible, Phyllis. *Rhetorical Criticism: Context, Method, and the Book of Jonah.* Minneapolis: Fortress, 1994.

_____. "The Book of Jonah: Introduction, Commentary, and Reflections," *The New Interpreter's Bible.* Nashville: Abingdon, 1996, 7:463–529.

Valkenberg, W.G.B.M. *Words of the Living God: Place and Function of Holy Scripture in the Theology of St. Thomas Aquinas.* Leuven: Peeters, 2000.

Weisheipl, J.A., O.P. *Friar Thomas D'Aquino: His Life, Thought, and Work.* New York: Doubleday, 1974.

Whitman, Jon, ed. *Interpretation and Allegory: Antiquity to the Modern Period.* Leiden, Boston, and Cologne: Brill, 2000.

Wills, Garry. *Lincoln at Gettysburg: The Words that Remade America.* New York: Simon & Schuster, 1992.

Winter, S. C. "A Fifth-Century Christian Commentary on Jonah," in Stephen L. Cook and S. C. Winter, eds., *On the Way to Nineveh: Studies in Honor of George M. Landes.* Atlanta: Scholars, 1999, 238–56.

Wünsche, August. *Aus Israels Lehrhallen.* Vol. 2. Hildesheim: Georg Olms, 1967.

Young, Frances. "Alexandrian and Antiochene Exegesis," in Alan J. Hauser and Duane F. Watson, eds., *A History of Biblical Interpretation. Volume 1: The Ancient Period.* Grand Rapids: Eerdmans, 2003, 334–54.

Zlotowitz, R. Meir, trans. and comm. *Yonah/Jonah: A New Translation with a Commentary Anthologized from Talmudic, Midrashic and Rabbinic Sources.* New York: Mesorah Publications, 1988.

INDEX OF TOPICS

Ahab, 127
Alexandria, 54, 65–67, 69, 70, 73
allegory/allegorical/allegorize, xix,
    16–17, 20–21, 23–24, 29, 54, 58,
    61–65, 67–70, 79, 90–91, 119, 122,
    156
anagogical/heavenly, 20–21, 68, 131,
    138
analogy/analogical, xvii, 16, 26, 34,
    36, 43, 52–54, 57, 60, 62, 64, 65,
    68, 71, 74–79, 81, 96, 106, 115,
    119, 124, 137–38, 141, 155–57
ancient Near East, 4, 9, 11, 28, 40, 53,
    55, 58–59, 63, 72, 75–6, 79, 85–86,
    108–09, 116, 118–19, 123, 140,
    145, 149, 155
anger, xviii, 19, 21, 31–32, 45, 47–48,
    50, 56, 59, 74, 80, 110, 113, 133,
    135–36, 139–47, 149, 152, 157
animals, xvii, 9, 18, 31, 57–58, 60, 73,
    86, 121, 123, 138
Antioch, 3, 19, 54, 66–70, 72–73, 75
Antiquity/ancient times/ancient inter-
    preters, xix, 10, 15, 19–20, 28, 34,
    48–49, 55, 64, 75–77, 79, 105–06,
    132–33, 155
Assyria, 10, 31–32, 47–48, 57, 105,
    108, 129
author/authoring, 11, 20, 23, 28, 30,
    40, 43, 58, 63, 66, 70, 73, 76, 78,
    80, 87–93, 95, 99, 101–02, 104

Babylon, 2, 41, 48, 98, 108–09, 117

character/characterization, xvii, 2, 11,
    16, 19, 37, 39–40, 44–46, 55, 57,
    59, 63, 68, 74, 83–84, 87, 95,
    98–99, 135–37, 143, 145, 156
Christian, xiv, xvii, xix, 1, 3–4, 11–13,
    16–17, 20, 28–29, 54, 58, 60–63,
    65–66, 68, 70, 72, 74–75, 78,
    80–81, 104–05, 152, 155

Day of Atonement/Yom Kippur, 108,
    126, 130–32
death, xviii, 2, 16, 21, 43, 55, 57–58,
    60, 75, 79, 101, 110, 114, 118, 121,
    122, 133, 140, 143, 145–46, 149

Elijah, xvi, 58, 60, 94, 116, 127, 147
Elisha, 127
Enkidu, 110, 114–15
exile/pre-exile/post-exile, 38–43,
    45–49, 83, 155, 157

fish/whale, xv, xvii, xviii, 9, 11, 18, 21,
    25, 30–31, 47, 51, 55–57, 59–61,
    71–72, 75, 78, 99, 100, 107, 116,
    123–24, 128–30, 139, 145, 148–50
flood, 72, 108–14, 116, 118, 124, 129,
    145, 149

genre, iv, 11, 19, 24, 37, 43, 49, 67,
    88–93, 103–05, 119, 125, 136–37,
    144

Gentile, xv, 16, 21, 31, 40, 56, 61, 66, 71, 75, 100, 105, 136, 138, 142, 145–46, 148
Gilgamesh, 109–16, 120, 133, 149, 157

hermeneutics, xvi, 12–13, 29, 38, 55, 65, 73–75, 78, 122, 154
historical, 4–10, 15–17, 20, 23, 27–28, 30–37, 39, 41, 43, 45, 48–50, 52–53, 55, 58, 63–64, 67, 69, 73–74, 77, 79, 81–82, 89–91, 101–02, 104, 119, 126, 156

ideology, 85, 103, 156
immortality/eternal life, 108–10, 113, 115, 119, 129, 133, 140, 145
intertextual/intertextuality, 11, 16, 51, 59, 62–63, 79, 94, 105, 133
irony/ironic, 91–95

Jasconius, 123–24
Jeroboam, 44, 48
Jerusalem, 2–3, 21, 41–43, 46–49, 52, 71, 94, 127–28
Jesus/Christ, xix, 2–3, 12–13, 15–16, 18, 21–22, 24–25, 29, 31, 56, 58, 60–62, 67–71, 74–75, 78, 108, 118–20, 156
Jew/Jews/Jewish, xiv– xvii, xix 1–, 3, 8, 11–12, 15–16, 18–19, 21, 23, 31, 40, 48–50, 54, 56, 60–63, 65, 67–68, 70–71, 75, 80, 100, 103–05, 108, 125–26, 129–33, 138, 142, 145, 147, 152, 155
Jezebel, xvi, 127
John the Baptist, xvi
Judah/Yehud, 2, 37–41, 43, 46, 49–50, 53–54, 117, 155, 157

lectio divina, 22
Leviathan, 128–29
literal, 17–18, 20–23, 58–60, 65–68, 71, 73, 75, 82, 144, 158

literary, xix, 6, 9–10, 15, 33, 35–36, 43, 50, 52–53, 63, 70, 73, 81–82, 84–86, 88–95, 100–02, 104, 106, 145, 158
liturgical/liturgy, xv, 60, 119, 122–24, 130, 133, 155, 158
lots, 21, 25, 31, 61

meaning, xi, xiii–xiv, xix, 1, 3–4, 8, 10, 13–14, 19–20, 22–24, 29, 32, 34, 39, 48, 50–54, 58, 60, 63–65, 67–69, 73, 75–78, 80–82, 85–86, 91, 95–102, 108, 126, 134, 154, 156
medieval/Middle Ages, xv, 20, 22, 119
mercy/graciousness, 18, 24–25, 40, 46, 48, 56–57, 72, 105, 131, 138, 148, 157
methodology, xvi, 12, 32, 36, 40–41, 103–04, 135, 155
Midrash/midrashic, 62–63, 69, 91, 105, 125–30, 133, 147, 156
modernity/modern, 4–5, 22–23, 27, 29, 32, 36, 50, 53, 64, 69, 73, 77, 79, 103, 105–06, 125
monastic, 19–21, 23, 119–24, 133
moral/tropological, 20–22, 58, 61–62, 65, 67–70, 93, 110, 146
Moses, 48, 60, 108, 147

narrator/narrative, xiii–xiv, 1–2, 4–5, 8, 10–11, 13–15, 19–20, 34–35, 38–39, 51, 53–54, 58–60, 67, 69, 72, 79, 80, 82–85, 87–91, 93–94, 96, 99–100, 102, 104–05, 116, 122, 136–38, 140–41, 144–45, 147–48, 151–52, 154–55, 157
Nineveh/Ninevite, xv, xvii, xviii, 9–11, 18, 25–26, 31, 39–40, 46–48, 56–58, 60–62, 71–73, 83–84, 87, 95, 97–98, 104–05, 108, 115–16, 127, 129–30, 132, 136–39, 141–44, 147, 150, 152–53

overturn/*hpk,* 11, 27, 42, 47, 87, 95–99, 151–52

parody, 92–95

Persia, 2, 41, 46, 49, 52–53, 94

perspective/insight/self-knowledge, 13–14, 19, 24, 27, 34–35, 40, 46, 48, 51, 55, 58, 74–75, 77–80, 82, 102–03, 105, 108, 120, 124, 126, 131–32, 134–35, 137–38, 140–41, 143, 146–47, 150, 152, 155–58

plant/bush/ivy/gourd, xviii, 31, 46, 59, 84, 114, 132, 137–41, 143–46, 153, 158

Plato, 17, 65

postmodernity/postmodern, 5, 27, 33, 50, 62, 73, 103, 105

pre-critical/pre-modern, 4, 15, 20, 27, 39, 101, 156

prophet/prophecy/prophesy, xv–xix, 2, 8–11, 20–22, 25–26, 30, 31, 37, 39, 40–42, 44–47, 51, 56–58, 61, 64, 69–72, 83, 85, 87, 89–90, 92–95, 97–99, 105, 112, 116, 124, 127, 129–30, 132, 135–39, 141–44, 146–58

questions, xiii– xix, 1, 4–15, 20, 24, 26–28, 32–37, 45–47, 49, 50–56, 59, 62–63, 67, 82–83, 85–87, 89–94, 96, 104, 107, 109, 111, 113, 125, 130, 132, 134–46, 150, 152–58

Rabbis/Rabbinic, xvii, 3, 8, 105, 128–30

reader/readerly/reading, xvi.xix, 2, 4–6, 8–12, 14–17, 19, 23–24, 26, 30–39, 41, 43, 44–55, 58, 60–65, 67–70, 73–81, 85–108, 117, 122, 128, 133–39, 142–48, 153–58

reception, 6–7, 9, 15, 36–37, 52, 155

Reformation, 23, 27

Renaissance, 23, 27

repent/repentance/change of heart/mind, xv, xviii, 8–10, 18, 20, 31–32, 42, 44–46, 48, 56–57, 61–62, 71–72, 80, 98, 104, 129–32, 141–42, 144, 150, 152–53, 157

rhetorics/rhetorical, 85–87

sailors, xvii, 25, 29–30, 40, 56–59, 62, 71–72, 83–84, 86–87, 99, 124, 128, 136, 148, 152–53

satire, 90–95

self-knowledge/perspective, xiv, 46, 48–49, 74, 77, 80, 108, 124, 126, 131, 143

spiritual/spirituality, xvi, 4, 12–13, 17, 20, 22–23, 32, 54, 58, 65–68, 70, 73, 119–20, 124, 138

temple, 2–3, 41–42, 47, 72, 112, 118, 128, 149

theology/theological, 17, 22–23, 32, 39, 43, 45, 47, 73, 103–04, 152

Torah/Tanakh/Hebrew Bible/Hebrew Scriptures, xvi, 2–3, 13, 15–17, 20, 24, 26, 34, 43, 45, 65, 75, 92, 97–98, 132, 152, 156

transformation/ humanization/ divinization, 8, 13, 134, 140, 143, 148, 155, 158

type/typology/typological, xix, 16, 29, 32, 54, 58, 62–63, 68, 70–72, 79, 82, 156

Urshanabi, 111, 114–15

Utanapishtim, 109, 111–16

violence, 11, 112, 135, 152, 158

worlds: behind, within, before text, 5, 8, 11, 34–36, 58, 135, 154

INDEX OF BIBLE CITATIONS

Genesis
1	117
1–3	105
3	17
4	60
6–9	117
19	97
29	117
31	117
42:20	139

Exodus
1	117
13–15	117
17	117
20	117
27	117

Numbers
33	117

Deuteronomy
7:16	138
13:18	138
19:13, 21	138
21:18	84
26	47
32	117

Joshua
3–5	117
24	117

1 Samuel
24:11	138

1 Kings
general	89
17	58, 127
19	94, 127

2 Kings
general	37, 48, 89
2–4	117
8–9	127
14	44

Ezra
8	117

Nehemiah
9	117
13:22	138

Proverbs
22:20-21	66

Psalms
general	6, 148–49
15	21
18	118
29	118
33	118
44	118
46	118

55	118	*Jeremiah*	
65	118	general	22
66	118	13:4	138
69	118	16:14-15	84
72	66, 138	20	94
74	118		
77	118	*Ezekiel*	
78	118	5:11	138
80	118	7:4	138
87	21	8:18	138
89	118	9:5, 10	138
98	118	16:5	138
99	118	20:17	138
103	60	24:14	138
104	118	27–32	118
105	118		
106	118	*Daniel*	
107	118	7	118
111	118		
124	118	*Jonah*	
130	118	1	xvii, 9, 18, 20–21, 25,
135	118		29–31, 45, 56–57, 59,
136	118		71, 83–84, 86–87, 99,
149	118		128, 132, 147–48
		2	xvii, 9, 11, 18, 21, 25,
Job			30–31, 47, 56, 58–59,
general	137		61, 71–72, 75, 83,
38-41	137		86–87, 94, 107,
			128–29, 132, 148–50
Tobit		3	xviii, 9–10, 18, 25–26,
14:13-14	58		31, 39, 45, 47, 56, 59,
			83–84, 86–87, 96,
			98–99, 129, 132,
Isaiah			140–48, 150–52
general	89	4	xviii, 8, 10–11, 18, 20,
7	22		25–26, 31, 39, 45–47,
13:18	138		56, 59, 83–84, 86–87,
27	117		104, 129, 132, 136–46
40	117		
43	117		
45	117	*Nahum*	
48	117	general	71
51	117		
52	117	*Habakkuk*	
63	117	3	118

Joel
2:17   138

Matthew
general   16
1:5-26   61
3–4   119
8   119
13–16   118
12:38–42   16
26:39   61
27:45   61

Mark
general   16
1   119
4–8   118
15:33   61
16:4   16

Luke
general   16
3–4   118
5   118
8   118
11:29–32   16
15   62
22:45   56
23:44-45   61
23:46   21

John
1   118
3   118
4   118

Romans
10:7   118

1 Corinthians
2:7-8   66
9:9-10   66
10:1–4   66, 118

Galatians
4:22-26   66

Ephesians
5:32   66

Colossians
2:17   66

Hebrews
8:5   66
10:1   66

1 Peter
3:20–21   118

Revelation
5   118
13   118

INDEX OF AUTHORS

Ackerman, 92–94, 104
Adam, 100–04
Alexander, 88–91
Andrew of St. Victor, 21–22
Antony of Egypt, 20
Augustine of Hippo, 16–18, 31, 58

Bakhtin, 96, 136
Band, 92–94
Barron, 119, 123
Batto, 109
Beckett, 13–14, 74, 150
Ben Zvi, 34, 36–52, 54, 94, 98,
    101–02, 106
Berlin, 92–93
Boodman, 35
Borgen, 65
Bourgeault, 122
Bowers, 15, 21, 153
Brendan the Navigator 19, 108–10,
    118–25, 133
Brenner, 92–94
Bridges, 35
Brown, 27–28, 59, 65
Brown-Driver-Briggs, 97, 138
Burgess, 119, 123
Burton-Christie, 20

Calvin, 28, 57
Cassian, 19–20
Chase, 22

Cherry, 29
Clark, 16
Clifford, 109
Craig, 82–86

Dalley, 109–10
Dawson, 65

Eckhart, 154
Edwards, 27–29, 32
Elata-Alster, 103–05

Friedlander, 127–28

George, 109–15
Ginzberg, 127–29
Gitay, 92, 94
Gold, 132
Green, 15, 96, 136

Harris, 90
Hauser, 59, 63, 66
Hegedus, 55–64
Herring, 29
Hill, 70–72
Holbert, 92–94
Holtz, 125
Hugh of St. Cher 21, 23

Jerome, St. 18, 22, 54–66, 68, 71,
    73–75, 78, 80, 142–43

Kavanaugh, 26
Kovacs, 109
Kugel, 125–26

Lacocque, 64
Levine, 131
Limburg, 129
Luther, 24–25, 27, 64

Maddison, 117
Magonet, 86, 91
Marcus, 92–94
Marsden, 27
McGinn, B., 19, 66, 154
McGinn, B., 19, 66
Miles, 92, 94,
Murphy, xvi

Nagler, 135
Nichols, 23

O'Loughlin, 119, 122
O'Meara, 118–19, 121, 123
Origen, 54, 65–70, 73, 75
Oswald, 24–25

Panikkar, 26, 121–24
Pennington 121
Philo 54, 65
Pusey, 29–32, 36

Ramsey, 19
Rosenberg, 130–31, 136

Salmon, 103–05
Sasson, 84, 89, 91, 97, 139, 145

Schaff, 18
Scherman, 132
Schneiders, 12–13
Schwartz, 125–26
Sherwood, 15, 127
Simms, 119
Simon, 129
Smalley, 22
Smith 155
Stein, 29
Sternberg, 85, 87
Stewart, 19

Taylor, 18
Teresa of Avila 25–27
Theodore of Mopsuestia 54, 68–73, 149
Thomas Aquinas 23
Trible, 85–88

Valkenberg, 23
Vergil 59

Watson, 59, 63, 66
Weisheipl, 23
Whitman, 63–65, 79
Wills, 7
Winter, 69, 72
Wooding, 118–19, 123
Wright, 150
Wünsche, 129

Young, 66–70, 73

Zlotowitz, 129, 131–32